The Unplanned Revolution

Observations on the Processes of Socio-economic Change in Pakistan

T0351952

The Unplanned Revolution

Observations on the Processes of
Socio-economic Change in Pakistan

ARIF HASAN

OXFORD
UNIVERSITY PRESS

OXFORD
UNIVERSITY PRESS

Oxford University Press is a department of the University of Oxford.
It furthers the University's objective of excellence in research, scholarship,
and education by publishing worldwide. Oxford is a registered trade mark of
Oxford University Press in the UK and in certain other countries

Published in Pakistan by
Oxford University Press
No. 38, Sector 15, Korangi Industrial Area,
PO Box 8214, Karachi-74900, Pakistan

ISBN 978-0-19-906590-5

Second Impression 2021

Typeset in Minion Pro
Printed on 68gsm Offset Paper

Printed by Mas Printers, Karachi

Contents

Preface

This book, including the introduction, consists of extracts from various papers prepared by me for national and international seminars, workshops and conferences; field notes prepared for a number of consultancies for government agencies, national and international NGOs and international organisations; articles for the media; and extracts from my personal diaries, covering a period of more than twenty-five years. I have chosen only those parts of my writings for this book that try to capture social change that has been taking place in Pakistan, the actors and factors behind it, the trends it is setting in motion and some of its causes. Many of these observations were made in the 1980s and 1990s. Conditions have changed considerably in Pakistan since then. Therefore, I have added postscripts to a number of chapters to update information and to identify new trends that have emerged or are in the process of emerging.

Abbreviations

ABK	Anjuman Behbood-e-Khawateen
ACCP	Action Committee for Civic Problems
ACHR	Asian Coalition for Housing Rights
ADBP	Agricultural Development Bank, Pakistan
ADB	Asian Development Bank
AFB	Anjuman Falah-o-Bahbood
AKDN	Aga Khan Development Network
AKCS	Aga Khan Cultural Services
AKES	Aga Khan Education Services
AKRSP	Aga Khan Rural Support Programme
AIOU	Allama Iqbal Open University
APC	All Party Conference
ASB	Anjuman Samaji Behbood
BACIP	Building and Construction Improvement Programme
BIAD	Balochistan Integrated Area Development
BIF	Baloch Ittehad Foundation
BOT	Build-Operate-Transfer
CAA	Civil Aviation Authority
CBR	Central Board of Revenue
CIDA	Canadian International Development Agency
DC	Deputy Commissioner
DC	District Council
DHA	Defence Housing Authority
EPI	Expanded Programme for Immunization
EPZ	Export Promotion Zone
FWO	Frontier Works Organisation
GoS	Government of Sindh
IFIs	International Funding Institutions
IIED	Institute for Environment and Development
ISD	informal subdivision
IT	Information Technology
IRC	Indus Resource Centre
KCR	Karachi Circular Railway
KCS	Khajji Cooperative Society

KDA	Karachi Development Authority
KESC	Karachi Electric Supply Corporation
KKH	Karakoram Highway
KMC	Karachi Metropolitan Corporation
KPT	Karachi Port Trust
KWSB	Karachi Water and Sewerage Board
LHV	Lady Health Visitor
LNWA	Lyari Nadi Welfare Association
LPG	liquefied petroleum gas
MNA	Member National Assembly
MPA	Member Provincial Assembly
MQM	Muttahida Quami Movement
MSS	Mahigeer Samaji Sangat
NGORC	NGO Resource Centre
NHA	National Highway Authority
NWFP	North-West Frontier Province
OCT	Orangi Charitable Trust
OPP	Orangi Pilot Project
PEN	Poverty Eradication Network
PHED	Public Health Engineering Department
PFF	Pakistan Fisher Folk Forum
PILER	Pakistan Institute of Labour Education and Research
PPP	Pakistan Peoples Party
RDD	Rural Development Department
RHC	Rural Health Centre
RTI	Research & Training Institute
SAIS	School of Advanced International Studies
SCF	Save the Children Fund
SHI	Secure Housing Initiative
SITE	Sindh Industrial and Trading Estate
TEB	Traffic Engineering Bureau
TRDP	Tharparkar Rural Development Project
UC	Union Councils
URC	Urban Resource Centre
VEC	Village Education Committee
WAPDA	Water and Power Development Authority
WTO	World Trade Organization

Pakistan: Geographical Divisions

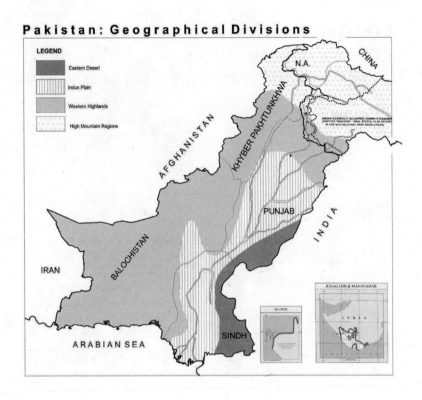

Pakistan: Political Divisions

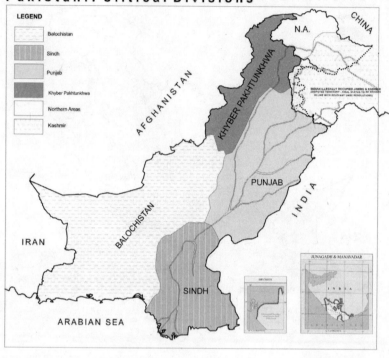

Introduction
The Process of Socio-Economic Change in Pakistan

Social and economic change in Pakistan, as in the rest of Asia, has been so enormous that it can be termed revolutionary. However, this change has not been institutionalized or even politicized. One of the major reasons for this is that politics in Pakistan for the most part has been all about bringing politics back and freeing it from the domination of the civil-military bureaucracy.

Socio-economic changes have been different at different locations in the country depending on accessibility, social structure, clan and tribal affiliations and a host of macro and micro factors. However, some changes have affected Pakistani society universally. Broadly speaking, these are migration from India in 1947, the introduction of green revolution technologies, urbanization and migration to the Middle East, Islamization of the Zia era, globalization and structural adjustment, and more recently the Musharraf government's devolution plan.

Much of what I am going to say in this introduction regarding socio-economic changes in Pakistan is based on my earlier work, my association with the Orangi Pilot Project (OPP) and the Urban Resource Centre (URC) in Karachi and their replications in other parts of Pakistan, my teaching at public sector universities since 1979, research consultancies, and diaries of my travels in Pakistan since 1968.

THE PROCESS OF CHANGE

Migration from India was a turning point in the history of Pakistan because of the processes it set in motion. The demographic change that occurred as a result of migration was staggering. According to the 1951 Census, 48 per cent of the urban population of Pakistan had originated in India and migrated since August 1947.[1] The census further shows that a large number of towns in the Punjab had a population increase of anything between 90 to 192 per cent in the intercensal period between 1941 and 1951. The two major cities of Sindh also increased by over 150 per cent in the intercensal period. However, many of the smaller towns in Sindh and almost all towns in the North-West Frontier Province (NWFP) registered a large population decline since the migrating Hindus and Sikhs were not replaced by Muslim migrants from India.[2]

This migration from India had a major impact on the sociology, economics and politics of Pakistan. Traditionally caste and professions were interlinked in pre-partition India and Pakistan. Neighbourhoods, whether urban or rural, were built around caste or clan and each caste or clan had its community organization in the form of a council of elders or *punchayats*. The link between caste and profession was quickly shed by the migrants and the neighbourhoods in which they settled, for the most part, no longer remained clan or caste based. As a result, their community organizations became ineffective and died over time. A fiercely upwardly mobile, go-getting culture (which my friend Talat Aslam refers to as *challo*) replaced a society in which social and economic mobility was difficult if not impossible. Local elders in the Punjab and Sindh feel that the culture of 'no values' that emerged as a result of migration was transferred to the local population as well and came to dominate Pakistan's economy.[3] It also created a division between the indigenous population and the locals which was further strengthened where the locals and the migrants spoke different languages such as in Sindh and the Saraiki belt in the Punjab.

The other change that took place due to the migration was that from a multi-religious, multi-cultural society, Pakistan became a uni-religious society attempting to become a uni-cultural one as well. This uni-culturalism has been resisted by the smaller provinces and is one of the reasons for the break up of Pakistan in 1971. However, the migrant population has universally supported this trend until recently.

The physical impact of the migration on the cities of Punjab and Sindh was considerable. The inner cities, where most of the richer Hindus and Sikhs use to reside, were taken over by poor refugee families. Their densities increased within a few months due to the subdivisions of large homes and the occupation of open areas for make-shift residential accommodation. Religious and community buildings were also occupied and turned into residential accommodation. The refugee migration was the beginning of the environmental degradation of a number of old cities and the destruction of their cultural heritage both in physical and social terms.[4] It was the beginning of the creation of slums in the urban areas of Pakistan. The comparative tolerance of squatter colonies in Pakistan, as compared to other Asian countries, is the direct result of the migration from India and the support given to refugee reception camps and informal settlements by the government and various social welfare and religious organizations. However, the impact of migration on the politics and sociology of Pakistan has never been seriously studied although its repercussions are often discussed and explored.

Introduction of Green Revolution Technologies

The building of perennial irrigation systems and land colonization by the British had already weakened the feudal system in the rural areas of central Punjab. However, the introduction of green revolution technologies in the 1950s and 60s by the Ayub government brought about fundamental changes in the relations of production in the agricultural sector all over Pakistan.

Before partition the feudal order and its institutions in almost all areas of Pakistan organized and financed agricultural production, supported the government in developing and maintaining agricultural infrastructure through a system of *baigar*, helped the district administration in maintaining law and order and administering *shamlaat* lands,[5] created conditions conducive to the collection of revenue, and guaranteed to the establishment the results that it required in the political arena. It was able to do this through well-established clan and tribal affiliations, a barter subsistence economy for the vast majority of the population, its control at the local level for deciding personal and property disputes, and a subservient artisan class (referred to as *kammis*), which was denied all social and economic mobility, and was along with the feudal culture which reflected these relationships, the back bone of the system. The green revolution technologies changed all this.

The new crops introduced by the green revolution required hybrid seeds, fertilizer and pesticides. For optimum profits, mechanization was required. As a result, seed, pesticide and fertilizer agencies sprang up in the rural areas and *mandi* towns and dealers for tractor, diesel engine and tube-well spare parts made their appearance along with mechanics for operating and maintaining the mechanized systems. Since the imported spare parts were expensive, urban based entrepreneurs established lathe machines to manufacture them in the small market towns and a huge light engineering industry and services sector developed as a result.

The new technologies were capital intensive and required loans for agricultural production. The government established banks in the rural areas for this purpose. However, these loans could only be accessed by politically powerful landlords. The smaller producers, who comprise the majority of farmers,[6] came to depend on middlemen who purchase their produce at a fraction of its value in exchange for funding their outlay on seed, fertilizer, pesticide, tractor hire and the expense of surviving in the period between sowing and harvesting the crop. The vast majority of small producers are in perpetual debt to these middlemen, the majority of whom are urban based.[7] Similar changes have taken place in the fisheries sector where almost all coastal fishing communities are now involved in commercial fishing. They are heavily in debt to middlemen who often receive funds from fisheries related large scale industries and lend them to fishermen for mechanising their boats, purchasing nylon nets and ice (for preserving fish) and for financing their deep sea fishing trips.[8]

Changes in the marketing of agricultural produce also occurred. In the 1970s, the Suzuki and Toyota pick-ups made their appearance. Very quickly they replaced the camel, donkey and bullock cart as means of transporting agricultural produce from the farms to the market towns. As a result, the distance between the market towns increased and the transporters emerged as a powerful interest group. Soon they established their links with the middlemen and together with the middlemen they have come to dominate the financing of agricultural produce and its marketing.

These changes transformed social relations based on barter to cash relations. As a result, they freed the kammis from servitude and because the kammis had marketable skills they have improved their social and economic standing. They have also migrated to the cities and to the Middle East in large numbers and have sent money back to their villages. They have acquired urban values and lifestyles and are in the process of educating their children.[9] In the three local body elections in the Zia era, they and the rural entrepreneurs emerged as councillors and they increasingly defeated their feudal opponents in the election process. As local body representatives their interests were in the provision of piped water supply, electricity, roads and girls' education. Major changes also occurred in land tenure and ownership patterns. Tenant-cultivated farms and acreage declined considerably between 1960 and 1990.[10] My colleagues and I felt at that time that these entrepreneurs and artisans would come to dominate the politics of Pakistan but for reasons discussed later, this did not happen.

As a result of this process, it can be safely said that the feudal system in Pakistan does not finance or organize agricultural production, maintain agricultural infrastructure, help the establishment in maintaining law and order or in administering *shamlaat* lands. Nor does it decide personal and property matters of the rural population except in small islands of retrogression. Yet the feudal system is a major pillar of the Pakistan establishment even though its institutions have become ineffective. Why this is so will be discussed later in the Introduction.

Urbanization

Urbanization has had a major impact on social change in Pakistan. The country's urban population has increased by 37 million since Independence or from 17.8 to 32.5 per cent of the total population.[11] Researchers feel that this is under estimated.[12]

The causes for urbanization have been documented in some detail by various researchers. Migration from India was a major factor in the 40s and 50s.[13] The eradication of malaria and small pox in the mid-50s resulted in an increase in Pakistan's population and was one of the reasons for an increase in rural-urban migration.[14] The green revolution technologies were a push factor to the urban areas and industrialization during the Ayub era was a major pull factor.[15]

However, the state could not cater to the needs of the rural migrants. It could not provide housing as a result of which *katchi abadis* and informal settlements, created out of the subdivision of agricultural land, were developed[16]. The informal developers who created them by bribing government officials have emerged as a powerful interest group in the urban development drama. The state could not provide employment either, and as a result an informal employment sector also developed. This sector had evolved by the 1990s to support formal sector industry, especially light engineering, garments, leather, carpets and packaging enterprises.[17] A services sector catering to the needs of lower income communities and settlements also evolved in the shape of hawkers and manufacturers of second grade consumer items. Similarly, the state could not provide effective and affordable transport services to the working class population so it disinvested in them and has been replaced by a private sector that has evolved through a system of informal high interest loans.[18] Since all of the private sector service providers and entrepreneurs function through bribing government officials and the police, they have set up organizations to present their claims and guard their gains. No urban development plan can be implemented effectively without the involvement and consent of these organizations. Over the years their scale of operations and power have increased as a result of increasing government failure to cater to the needs of the poorer sections of the urban population. Similarly, as a result of ineffective and corrupt city management, other interest groups such as shopkeepers, *mandi* operators, traders' associations have also developed and are constantly engaged in negotiating with government agencies and officials.

At present the majority of Pakistan's urban dwellers live in *katchi abadis* and informal settlements.[19] They have organized to protect themselves against eviction and to lobby for regularization and infrastructure. Where de-jure and/or de-facto security of tenure exists they invest in physical infrastructure and support local entrepreneurs in building and running schools and health clinics[20]. In a period of 15 to 20 years, these settlements changed from purely working class neighbourhoods to settlements where an increasing number of young people acquire education to become white-collar workers, professionals and entrepreneurs. However, environmental conditions, social services and employment generation do not keep pace with social change and aspirations of the younger generation. This is a cause of frustration, anger and a desire to migrate to other countries. The younger generation of the lower-middle class, which is fiercely upwardly mobile, also has similar problems and desires entertainment and recreational activities which for the most part are non-existent for them.[21] The demand for these activities is increasing as the second generation of city dwellers has now come of age and unlike their parents (who were pioneers), they feel that they have a claim on the city and its institutions.

All the larger cities of Pakistan are physically and socially divided between informal settlements and planned areas. There is very little public space that is shared between the rich and the poor. The politics of the Zia era also led the elite to ghettoize themselves and to develop recreational and entertainment facilities exclusively for themselves in their own areas. This too is discussed later in the paper.

Between 1981 and 1998, urban literacy has increased, especially female literacy. In the age group of 10 to 24 male and female literacy has increased to over 70 per cent. Similarly, the married population has declined and in the age group of 15 and 25 years there has been a marked decrease in the number of married women.[22] Literacy and late marriage are interlinked and as such the fertility rate has also declined with 91 per cent of married urban women having knowledge of modern contraception.[23] The use of television has also increased and along with literacy and a change in marriage patterns is a major cause of a change in social attitudes. However, similar changes have not taken place in the rural areas and as a result there is an increasing difference in the social indicators of urban and rural Pakistan.[24] What this means for the future is important and needs to be discussed.

Another change which will have long term repercussions on family life and society as a whole is the emergence of educated professional women. For example, the majority of students at the University of Karachi are women. In the disciplines of medicine, planning and architecture, they constitute an overwhelming majority to the extent that there is some talk of having a quota for men in these disciplines.[25]

As in the rural areas, urban informal sector operators, local contractors and tradesmen won the local body elections in the Zia era from the low and lower middle income urban settlements. Many of them, especially in the smaller towns had strong rural links and a culture of interaction between rural and urban local body representatives was developing. As will be discussed later, globalization and the Musharraf government's devolution plan put an end to this process.

Migration to the Gulf and remittance of money from there is seen by many community elders as having destroyed social cohesion and the joint family system. Jealousy between family members and a change of lifestyle among the beneficiary nuclear families within the clan structure are held responsible for this. Migration and the remittance economy are also held responsible for the decline of interest in agricultural production and in 'working together'. It is also held responsible for the non-acceptance of village and community organizations as arbitrators in matters related to property and personal law.[26]

The Politics of the Zia Era and its Repercussions

The Zia era has had a major effect on determining social attitudes in Pakistan. This effect is likely to continue for the foreseeable future. Soon after coming to power the Zia government began a process of consolidating the hold of the religious establishment on the Pakistan state and society. Afternoon prayers in all government offices were encouraged and space for them was created. This was adopted by non-government organizations as well including international hotel chains. A system of *Nazim-e-Sala'at* was introduced for all neighbourhoods. They roamed the neighbourhoods at dawn informing people that it was prayer time and that they should come to the mosque. People who did not come to the mosque were contacted and requested to attend prayers. *Zakat* and *ushr* were introduced. The *Shia fiqh* opposed *zakat* and were exempted from it. Because of these actions of the Zia government people soon knew who was a Sunni, Shia, Bohri, Aga Khani, Zikri and Qadiani, something that was unknown before. *Hadood* and blasphemy laws were introduced and became weapons for the persecution of women and minorities.

The Zia government also banned political and extra curricular activities at public sector schools, colleges and universities. Politics, sports, music and entertainment vanished almost overnight. Debates and quiz programmes on television and radio were permitted but their topics had to conform to the government's Islamic agenda. Again, private sector educational institutions also followed the systems introduced at the public sector institutions, more out of fear than conviction.

At the high school level the teaching of world history and world geography was discontinued. As a result, students are now taught only the History and Geography of Pakistan in a subject called Pakistan Studies and they are also taught a version of Islamiat which was revised during the Zia era and is still taught. An evaluation of the curriculum of these subjects along with that of Urdu and English[27] identifies that it was insensitive to the religious diversity of Pakistan, that it incited the students to militancy and violence and encouraged bigotry and discrimination towards fellow citizens (especially women and religious minorities) and towards other nations. It also glorified war and the use of force. It is still in force.

In addition to the above, *maddrasah* education was encouraged and *maddrasah* certificates were declared equivalent to normal university degrees. As a result, *maddrasah* graduates could be recruited as functionaries in state institutions. Budgets for cultural activity were drastically curtailed and important institutions like the PIA Arts Academy, NAFDEC and Lok Virsa became ineffective. Patronage to the *urs* of *sufi* saints and folk heroes (in vogue since pre-British times) was withdrawn and banning music at these festivals was attempted. A new media policy was introduced. The appearance of a large number of prominent writers and thinkers on television and radio was banned and so was the poetry and songs of progressive poets and musicians. Classical music and dance were also banned and folk music and dance were discouraged. Dancing women could not be shown on the screen and nor could alcohol drinking. Minimum distances between men and women on the screen were specified and covering the head made compulsory for women comperes and newscasters.

These enactments of the Zia era were supported by the religious establishment who became the custodians of public morality. In lower and lower-middle income neighbourhoods they were able to impose their will. As a result, recreation and entertainment disappeared from the public sphere. Schools of music and dance which were common before the Zia era, closed down. Theatre performances in the larger cities vanished or could only be held for the elite and upper middle classes in the cultural centres of foreign missions such as the Goethe Institute and the Pak American Cultural Center. The new culture created enormous problems for working women (since working was discouraged by the neighbourhood mosques), especially in poor and lower middle income areas, and they disappeared as waitresses, chamber maids in hotels and as entertainers, professions in which they were employed in Karachi, Lahore and Rawalpindi. The *hijab*, which used to appear sporadically in urban areas, became universal in the lower, lower-middle and middle income settlements of the country.

Pakistan's elite and upper middle classes are 'westernized'. They could not relate to the changes that were taking place around them, especially in the educational institutions where their children studied. Consequently, elite families stopped sending their children to public sector universities and colleges. They also stopped participating in public life and visiting museums, zoos and parks. They created their own world separate from the rest of Pakistan and de-politicized themselves. As a result, both rural and urban culture suffered and there was a serious decline in standards of education and in the maintenance and growth of public sector real estate and recreational facilities.[28] The students I teach today at public sector universities are totally different from the ones I taught in the early eighties. Then they were a mixed lot with a sizeable number from the elite areas of Karachi and many were the products of English medium schools and colleges. They were interested and involved in politics. Today there are no students from the elite areas and almost none from English medium schools and for the most part they are de-politicized. They are all the product of the Zia era and find it difficult to shed what they have been taught in spite of their understanding that there is a conflict between what they have been taught and the reality around them. The observations of teachers at other public sector institutions with whom I have discussed this phenomenon are no different.

Political parties in the Zia era could not hand out patronage since there was no politics except the politics of trying to bring back democracy. State institutions had also come under the influence of the religious establishment. Consequently, people turned to their ethnic and clan relationships, wherever they could, for support. Power lay with the religious establishment and as a result a close link between the religious establishment and clan leadership developed, strengthening the religious establishment further.

With the complete control of the religious establishment on power in Pakistan, the politics of the Zia era finally institutionalized corruption and nepotism which already existed in Pakistani society. This destroyed government institutions (especially the judiciary and development related organizations) and governments that have followed Zia have not attempted to reverse this culture but have promoted it for their benefit.

The Zia era coincided with the period of urban consolidation in Pakistan. For this consolidation effective state organizations that could cater to the needs of a young population living increasingly in a cosmopolitan world were required as an alternative to the system of patronage by clan and religion based groups. There was a need for dialogue and for promoting the creativity of a population that was freeing itself from feudal influences. However, this did not happen. The political populism of the Bhutto era was replaced by a religious populism and a negation of the rich diversity of Pakistan society leading to its fragmentation and to suspicion and conflict between its different religious and ethnic groups.

The Zia era and the Afghan War were also responsible for the introduction of drugs and guns in Pakistani society and politics. The drug mafia became a powerful lobby and invested in real estate (formal and informal) and transport. In many areas of rural and urban Pakistan, it was able to co-opt the local administration and the police. A number of press reports have highlighted this nexus between the mafia and law enforcement agencies. Another result of the emergence of the mafia is that a very large number of young Pakistanis have become drug addicts.

This has become a serious social and economic issue and has affected the lives of large sections of society.[29]

The end of Zia did not end the Zia era. Recently, the Nazim of Karachi has banned music in public sector schools and colleges. No one has protested. At a show organized by the Department of Visual Studies at the Karachi University, students under the influence of religious groups destroyed pieces of art, sculpture and equipment. No action was taken against them. Students playing music in their studios while working have been told that music is not permissible and they have obeyed.

The extent to which the Zia era changed the mindset of the people of Pakistan can be judged from the case of the urinals. Urinals were removed from all public toilets in Pakistan in the Zia era since it is against the *Sunnah* to urinate while standing. In the post-Zia era they have made a comeback but they are hardly used any more. Similarly, liberal university teachers feel that conditions are not better from their point of view than in the Zia era. As one of them put it 'the seeds he sowed have yet to produce their full harvest'. However, globalization, satellite television and the emergence of consumerism and corporate culture is changing society and reversing the attitudes developed in the '80s and '90s.

Globalization and Structural Adjustment

Globalization, the WTO regime, structural adjustment and the IT revolution have had a major impact on Pakistani society as well. The requirements of the corporate sector are introducing new players in society and changing attitudes and social relations. The sector requires graduates in various subjects and technicians to service its needs. Formal and informal educational institutions purporting to produce these human resources (except of para-professionals) are increasing and so are their graduates and teachers. The corporate sector also plays at being socially conscious. It funds social sector development and cultural activities. However, most of this support goes to elite organizations and the cultural activities are also located in elite areas from which lower and lower middle groups are excluded. The corporate sector's architecture is now dominating the cities and is in sharp contrast to the sedate international style architecture of government institutions. Its land requirements (bordering on land-hunger) is changing landuse patterns and evicting poor communities. A new interest group with an elite culture (though not with an entirely elite following) is emerging. Corporate farming is also being promoted by the government of Pakistan.[30] If that materializes the corporate sector's role in Pakistan's economy and politics will also increase although it would result in dispossessing millions of Pakistani tenant farmers of their tenancy rights guaranteed to them under law.[31]

With the emergence of satellite television a demand for media professionals and performers has been created in the last decade. Discussion and debate on issues which could not be debated earlier has become possible. There are now over forty Pakistani satellite channels and their number is increasing. Another influential sub culture involving tens of thousands of people and including advertising agencies and their corporate sector clients, is emerging. This sub culture also challenges the legacy of the Zia era although it lacks the confidence to express this challenge clearly.

Structural adjustment has had a negative impact on social development in Pakistan. It has led to the privatization of a large number of profitable state enterprises and to the sacking of thousands of employees. Privatization of water, electricity, the irrigation department and other utilities is on the cards. NGO studies reveal that this will have an adverse effect on the poorer sections of society. As a result of structural adjustment there has been a sharp increase in utility charges and a decrease in poverty related subsidies.[32] Public sector university fees has increased by over 200 per cent in the last five years and a further increase of about 600 per cent has been recommended to make the universities subsidy free. Meanwhile, private universities and schools, unaffordable to the poor, have mushroomed. Thus, it is impossible to achieve the democratization of education envisaged by the social contract in the 1973 Constitution. Higher education for the foreseeable future will only be for those who can afford it and there will be a major difference between the nature of education that is delivered to the rich and that which is delivered to the poor. It is therefore not surprising that poverty and the gap between the rich and the poor have increased dramatically in Pakistan[33] or that Pakistan's HDI ranking has declined.

The WTO regime has adversely affected the informal sector especially in the light engineering industry. The introduction of cheap Chinese goods is leading to the closing of a large number of formal and informal industries related to light engineering, plastic and China clay products, stationary and ball point manufacturing units, building construction products and a whole range of consumer items. This is one of the reasons for the growing unemployment in the informal settlements of Pakistan's urban areas.[34] Another reason is that the skills that the new economic developments require do not exist in poor communities and the means of acquiring them are also non-existent.

To deal with increasing poverty and marginalization of poor communities the government of Pakistan has initiated a number of poverty alleviation programmes and an aggressive NGO sector has emerged to make use of the funds that the programmes have made available. Over the years this NGO sector has moved from being an altruistic one to a professional one. It has acquired corporate sector culture but its activists and mid-level employees belong to the urban lower middle classes or to rural families who have acquired an urban education. This sector is also operated by the elite who have close links with the corporate sector and with the more liberal elements in the Pakistan establishment. However, the NGO sector, except for a few organizations, does not involve itself in politics or challenge government policies. Much of its agenda is determined by the funding it receives from foreign NGOs and governments. The poverty alleviation programmes and much of the NGO sector do not look at poverty and marginalization as an integral part of society as a whole. Their programmes seek to address only micro level poverty related issues and have little or no impact on macro level policies that are creating poverty. As a result they increase the rich-poor divide.[35]

Globalization and structural adjustment has also changed the manner in which the state funds development projects. Most of the infrastructure projects that are being considered today are to be funded on a Build-Operate-Transfer (BOT) basis by international companies. For the companies to be interested the projects have to be large and profits have to be high. The cost of these projects is sometimes more than 200 per cent higher than if they had been built locally with local funds.[36] Looking at the government's urban development plans, it seems that BOT operators, international contractors and finance providers will determine the nature of urban development to the detriment of the poorer sections of society. Their vision and manner of operation has become a part of not only government planning institutions but also of academic and professional institutions.

Globalization and structural adjustment have changed the culture of the Pakistan state. Government has now abdicated its social responsibility and as such its relationship with the people of Pakistan has undergone a change. The corporate sector and international contractors and BOT operators have emerged as a new power group. As a result, the emergence of local entrepreneurs and middlemen as a political power has declined and continues to do so. Political parties do not figure in the new power relations because so far none of them has presented an alternative to the emerging development paradigm or tried to identify the nature of relationship that they can have with it.

The Impact of Devolution

The 2001 Devolution Plan of the Musharraf government has brought about fundamental changes in the structure of local government and its relationship to provincial and federal government structures. The concept of federation as embodied in the Constitution has been weakened by local governments having direct access to funding from the federal government. Also since elections to district *nazims* (mayors) are indirect and can as such be easily manipulated by the establishment, respectable citizens do not stand for elections and so new blood cannot be infused into the system. Traditionally influential families have again become interested in becoming local government representatives because of the increased political and financial powers of the *nazims* and because of the possibility of winning the elections with the support of the establishment. In this respect, the devolution process has not only failed to bring new people or classes as local government representatives but has strengthened the power of the traditionally more powerful groups at the district level. In addition, to stand for election for the post of district, *tehsil*, town or union council *nazim*, one has to be a matriculate. This has debarred a large number of social activists and political workers from being elected and has again strengthened the hold of the more affluent (though not necessarily more influential or popular) sections of society on local government institutions in Pakistan.

Studies, carried out in a few union councils of the Punjab,[37] seem to indicate that clan and caste grouping have increased as a result of the Devolution Plan and that development has become more unequal as *nazims* have invested in areas which voted for them or in areas which were politically powerful and of advantage to them. Is this because unlike before the *nazims* have power to decide on development priorities and in theory at least the bureaucracy is subservient to them? Similarly, community, labour and peasant boards provided for in the

Plan have not materialized. Is this for the same reason? Hopefully the research being carried out will determine the reasons for the problems that the Devolution Plan faces and its social implications.

However, because of the Devolution Plan, 33 per cent of councillors are now women. For the first time in Pakistan's history, they are politically visible as elected representatives and with every passing month they are asserting themselves. This is something that cannot possibly be reversed.

THE SITUATION TODAY

Pakistani society today is in a state of flux. There are divisions of every possible nature in it. There is very little interaction or dialogue between the various groups that represent these divisions and as a result the divisions are consolidating. A major negative fallout of this is that young people are confused and desperately in search of an identity. However, recently satellite television channels have instituted programmes where discussions and debates take place on various issues that were taboo in the media before and which relate to conflicting points of view regarding social and political issues.

With the army takeover in 1999 and with the enactment of the Devolution Plan, the centre has become even more powerful than before. At the same time, because of structural adjustment and an increase in population, the provinces have to share decreasing financial and natural resources. The two things put together have increased the centre-small provinces divide. This expresses itself in Sindh and the NWFP through their opposition to the Kalabagh Dam, and at the national level in the small provinces' objections to the National Finance Commission award formula. An increasing number of educated young people are also supporting the Pakistan Oppressed Nations Movement. The present political system does not have space in it to address these issues or to even accept them as important.

There is also a serious rural-urban divide. The social indicators of the rural areas lag behind those of the urban areas and the gap is increasing. Educated and enterprising persons and artisans from the rural areas are migrating to the urban areas and the rural economy is increasingly controlled by urban based *arthis* and *bayparis*. This process is impoverishing rural society both financially and politically and further marginalizing landless labour which forms the overwhelming majority of the rural population. Much of the bonded labour in the agricultural sector consists of landless labour and one of the major reasons for their being bonded is that they do not have a place to stay as they have no access to land for residential purposes.[38]

A cash economy has emerged in the rural areas and has made feudal institutions ineffective. However, feudals in many areas of Pakistan still hold power which is disproportionate to their economic power or to their performance in the election processes. This is because democracy in Pakistan is manipulated and there is a strong nexus between the army, traditional power groups and the civil administration. The Station House Officer of the local *thana* (who is all powerful) is controlled by the influentials who bully their opponents and the local population through him. Police reform would go a long way to change this state of affairs. However, no such reform is in the offing.[39]

There is also a big town-small town divide. In the large cities (such as Karachi, Lahore, Hyderabad, Multan, Faisalabad, Rawalpindi) literacy is high and there is a rapidly decreasing gap between male and female literacy. Educated women are visible in work places and more recently in politics. Satellite and cable television is common and there are the re-beginnings of entertainment and culture. International fast food chain outlets exist in all middle and lower middle income areas. Families from working class areas also frequent them. Cyber cafes and beauty parlours for women have sprung up both in middle and lower income areas. ISO 9000 requirement for exporting industrially produced items has improved working conditions in formal sector factories. Nuclear families have increased. However, the aspirations of young urban Pakistanis are not met due to unemployment, absence of affordable education, the clash between their desires and their family pressures, bad environmental conditions, the absence of entertainment and recreation, and above all, the existence of corruption, nepotism, police brutality and inequity in society.[40] It is therefore not surprising that 38 per cent of all young Pakistanis wish to migrate abroad[41] and that 80 per cent of all formal sector trained IT graduates have applied for jobs abroad.[42]

The situation in the small towns is worse. Massive environmental degradation has destroyed the cultural built-heritage of these towns. The elite have migrated and as such there is a lack of city ownership, little investment in industry and human resource development, and most planning is unregulated.[43] Social fragmentation has taken place and unlike in the past, neighbourhoods are no longer multi-class. Respect for learning and for teachers has disappeared and religious extremism has replaced traditional tolerance of diversity. Women from small towns have received education and become doctors, teachers, employees in government and the corporate sector, though in the larger cities and not in their own towns. There is large scale unemployment among the educated and since jobs in the small towns are few and badly paid, an increasing number of young persons migrate, with the result that the towns have become politically weak and socially backward.[44]

There is also a rich-poor divide in the urban areas. This is not only a social but also a physical divide and it is increasing as the government over the last decade has not invested in social housing and has no plans to do so in the future. The poor live in unserviced high density settlements increasingly on the outskirts of the city. There is little or no shared public space between them and the richer sections of society. Most of the major investments in recreation and entertainment have been made through the private sector and are unaffordable to lower income groups. The cinema was an exception but due to the anti-cinema policies of the Zia government, which were not changed in the post-Zia period, cinemas have closed down all over Pakistan.

To a great extent the increase in these divisions is due to parallel systems of education in Pakistan. There is the Urdu–English divide, the public sector-*deeni maddrassah* divide, and now after the establishment of private universities and an increase in public sector university fees, the rich-poor divide. The level of public sector education has declined all over Pakistan. There are ghost schools and ghost teachers. There are schools without buildings and there are school buildings without students and teachers. Also the Zia period curriculum remains unchanged. In addition, institutions equipped to provide skills and train para-professionals are not being created by the state or by the private sector. Young people in working class areas constantly point out that without these skills they cannot have access to the job market.[45] The state of education in Pakistan is of major concern to the lower middle and lower income groups as they are obsessed with providing education to their children.

In the past decade, the NGO movement was promoted by International Funding Institutions (IFIs), donors and the Pakistan establishment as an alternative to public sector institutions especially in the field of education, health and community-based infrastructure. Apart from small islands of success, the NGO sector has failed miserably.[46] It does not have the expertise or resources to manage large funds and even where it has been successful, it has failed to reach out to landless and marginalized groups. However, a small number of NGOs working on human rights have mobilized women councillors, the media, and sections of Pakistani society for the repeal of blasphemy laws and the *Hadood* Ordinance; for the enactment of laws against honour killings and violence against women; and for peace with India. Although they have been able to create a fairly vocal network and to win over a number of politicians and state functionaries, they have not been able to bring about a change in the manner in which the state perceives these issues.

As mentioned earlier, the younger generation in the urban areas of Pakistan aspires to become a part of the 'new world'. Though it is extremely religious, there is a conflict within it between what is perceived as traditional values based on Islam and this 'new world' and its institutions and values. Interviews with the urban young suggest that they prefer to decide on marriage partners themselves but cannot disagree openly with their parents; they wish to live as nuclear families but cannot afford to do so; they not only participate in the entertainment that religious groups consider un-Islamic but would be happy to promote it; they question the position of women in Pakistan, blasphemy and *Hadood* laws but in the absence of guidance from religious scholars or those whom they consider to have legitimacy, they cannot decide. In the majority of cases, these two worlds co-exist even if unhappily, within individuals and families. However, because of the better organization of the religious lobby, supported by the Pakistan establishment (which exerts considerable peer pressure) the majority of them cannot publicly express themselves verbally or in terms of behaviour. Subsequently, there is a difference between their private and public beliefs and behaviour patterns. The more thinking individuals constantly talk about reform in Islam but do not know where it is going to come from or the shape it should take. Others have turned to the glorification of Sufism and its values but do not know how these can be used to reform religion or society for that matter.

What will happen to Pakistani society when this generation comes to power in the next ten to fifteen years? And what will the children of this younger generation be like given the fact that it is questioning tradition? These are important questions and need to be considered by social scientists and politicians.

Without a process of dialogue and reconciliation between the divisions in Pakistani society, the problems that this introduction has identified and which this book deals with, cannot be resolved. Nor can the aspirations of the younger generation of Pakistanis be fulfilled peacefully in the near future. These divisions are used and accentuated by the Pakistan establishment (increasingly representing only the armed forces) to stay in power. It is obvious to even the most dull-witted observer of the Pakistan political scene that a democracy manipulated by the establishment and the elite will only weaken the social and political fabric of Pakistan and that free and fair elections and an end to what common Pakistanis call 'group *bandi*' is the only solution. How this can be achieved without turmoil, conflict and possible disintegration of the state is the challenge that we face today.

Sources: Much of this Introduction consists of extracts from the author's paper prepared for a Conference at Johns Hopkins University at the School of Advanced International Studies (SAIS), Washington DC, USA, 8 November 2004

NOTES

1. Arif Hasan: *Urban Change: Scale and Underlying Causes: The Case of Pakistan*; unpublished report, 2002, prepared for the IIED, UK.
2. Towns where populations increased are located in the districts of Bahawalnagar, Rahim Yar Khan, Faisalabad and Toba Tek Singh. Towns where populations decreased are located in the districts of Dera Ghazi Khan, Layyah and Rajanpur. Sindh's urban population between 1941 and 1951 increased from 11.85 per cent of its total population to 29.2 per cent and the NWFP urban population decreased from 18.01 per cent of its total population to 11.3 per cent in the same period.
3. See Section on Punjab 1992 in Chapter 4.
4. Khalid Bajwa, *Development Conditions of Androon Shehr, the Walled City of Lahore*, unpublished Ph.D. thesis, Catholic University of Leuven, 2007.
5. Shamlaat, Ashaish and Gowchar lands (community and grazing lands) on which villages in Pakistan were built have now been encroached upon or sold by powerful landlords and/or traditional community leaders. This is one of the major reasons, along with the end of the caste system, why the rural poor can no longer acquire land for housing.
6. 93.1 per cent of farms in Pakistan are between 5 and 25 acres. (Akbar Zaidi, *Issues in Pakistan's Economy*; Oxford University Press, Karachi, 1999)
7. Author's observation based on conversations with *mandi arthis* and *bayparis*.
8. Chapters 12, 13, 14 and 15 deal with these issues.
9. In 1982–83 Pakistani workers remitted US$2,885.67 million, over 71 per cent of which came from the Middle East. (Akbar Zaidi, *Issues in Pakistan's Economy*: Oxford University Press, Karachi, 1999)
10. They declined between 1960 and 1990 in acreage terms from 39.2 to 16.1 per cent and in the number of farms from 41.7 to 18.7 per cent. (Government of Pakistan: *Pakistan Economy Survey*: Islamabad, 1995)
11. Government of Pakistan, *Population Census Reports*.
12. Reza Ali, *How Urban is Pakistan?*, paper published in Akbar Zaidi's *Continuity and Change*, City Press, Karachi, 2003.

13. Due to Partition, 4.7 million Sikhs and Hindus left Pakistan and 6.5 million Muslims migrated to Pakistan. As such 1.8 million persons were added to Pakistan's population in a few months (Iffat Ara and Arshad Zaman, *Asian Urbanization in the New Millennium: Pakistan Chapter*, paper written for the Asian Urban Information Centre for Kobe, August 2002.

14. Arif Hasan, *Urban Change: Scale and Underlying Causes: The Case of Pakistan*, unpublished report, 2002.

15. Ibid.

16. It is estimated by the author that over 50 per cent of Pakistan's urban population (or 26 million) lives in *katchi abadis* (9 million) or agricultural subdivision settlements (17 million).

17. According to the Karachi Development Plan 2000, 75 per cent of the city's labour force was employed in the informal sector in 1989.

18. Aquila Ismail, *Transport: Urban Resource Centre's Karachi Series*, City Press, Karachi, 2002.

19. Arif Hasan, *Working With Communities*: City Press, Karachi, 2001.

20. In Orangi Town, a huge informal settlement in Karachi, there are over 700 private and/or community schools and over 900 clinics according to surveys carried out by the Orangi Pilot Project. A similar situation exists in the older *katchi abadis* in the city.

21. Chapters 19 and 21 deal with these issues.

22. Government of Pakistan, *Population Census Reports*.

23. Quoted in Akbar Zaidi's book, *Issues in Pakistan's Economy*, Oxford University Press, Karachi, 1999.

24. Government of Pakistan, *Population Census Reports*.

25. According to press reports 68 per cent of the students at Karachi University and 81 per cent of students at the public sector medical colleges in Karachi are women. In the Architecture and Planning Department in the public sector in Karachi, over 90 per cent of the new students are women.

26. See Section on Punjab 1992 in Chapter 4.

27. A.H. Nayyar and Ahmad Salim, *The Subtle Subversion*: SDPI, Islamabad, 2004.

28. Arif Hasan, *The Political Alienation of Pakistan's Elite*, paper published in Akbar Zaidi's *Continuity and Change*, City Press, Karachi, 2003.

29. The role of drug money and its relationship to land and politics is described in Chapter 15. According to the Pakistan Country Report of the UNDCP (September 2002), there are 1.5 million heroin addicts in Pakistan. In 1979, there were none. In addition, there are another 1.5 million chronic addicts that are on drugs other than heroin.

30. According to newspaper reports the government of Pakistan has identified eight million hectares of land for corporate farming.

31. A population of over one million is struggling to maintain its tenant's status at the Okara Military farms in the Punjab.

32. According to a paper prepared by the Pakistan Institute of Labour Education and Research, Karachi, poverty related subsidies in Pakistan decreased from 5.2 billion in 1992 to 284 million in 2002.

33. According to official figures poverty in Pakistan decreased from 46.54 per cent in 1969–70 to 17.32 per cent in 1987–88. It increased from 17.32 in 1987–88 to 33.5 per cent in 1999–2000.

34. The unemployment rate in Pakistan in 1961 was 2.83 per cent. In 1998 it had increased to 19.13 per cent. (Government of Pakistan, *Population Census Reports*)

35. Much of the poverty alleviation programmes deal with water supply, sanitation, solid waste management, primary education and preventive health. These are basic municipal functions and they cannot be dealt with at a national level by NGOs and communities alone without effective municipal and local government institutions manned by appropriately trained professionals. These institutions are non-existent in most of Pakistan and where they do exist the quality of professionals working in them has declined over time due to political interference in their functioning, nepotism, corruption and lack of public accountability.

36. The rehabilitation of the Karachi Circular Railway on BOT basis has been estimated at 15 billion rupees. Retired chief engineers of Pakistan Railways insist that if the Railways carried out the rehabilitation, it would cost less than 5 billion rupees. An investment of 15 billion also means fares that are unaffordable to the majority of the lower income group. Some of these issues are discussed in Chapter 20.

37. Dr Ali Cheema, presentation made at the Akhtar Hameed Khan Memorial Forum, Karachi, 7 October 2004 of an ongoing study related to the Devolution Plan being carried out by the Lahore University of Management Sciences.

38. A. Ercelawn and M. Nauman, *Unfree Labour in South Asia, Economic and Political Weekly*, India, 29 May 2004.

39. The Citizens Police Liaison Committee (CPLC) has proposed comprehensive reforms in the police sector since 1998 and has pointed out that these would bring security and justice to the common citizen. However, police reform was not a part of the Devolution Plan of the Musharraf government in 1999.

40. Chapter 19 and 21 deal with some of these issues.

41. Naseer Nadeem and M. Ashfaq, *Brain Drain: Causes and Implications*; *Dawn Economic and Business Review*, Karachi, 18 October 2004.

42. Hasan Zaidi, *Information Technology in Sindh*, paper written for the IUCN's under publication *The State of Environment and Development in Sindh*, October 2003.

43. Perwaiz Vandal, *The Lesser Cities of the Punjab: Forgotten or Neglected*, paper presented at the Urban and Regional Planning Forum at the NED University, Karachi, June 2004.

44. A fascinating response given by Sultan Barq by email on 3 June 2004 to Anjum Altaf of the SDPI in Islamabad. Anjum Altaf had written to a number of people about their opinion and observations on *What is Happening in Small Towns?*

45. This is according to the investigations of the Orangi Pilot Project and the Urban Resource Centre, Karachi who are running programmes to train para-professionals in architecture, engineering and social work disciplines.

46. One of the most ambitious programmes of the government was the Social Action Programme. It was closed down in May 2002 because of corruption, lack of ownership, financial and human resource constraints of the NGOs and public sector. (*Government Winds Up Social Action Programme*, Daily *Dawn*, 15 May 2002)

PART ONE: THE MOUNTAINS

Three of the greatest mountain ranges in the world, the Karakoram, the Himalayas and the Hindukush, meet to form the northern mountain region of Pakistan. This region has an average altitude of 3,000 metres and contains several peaks of over 6,700 metres altitude. It also contains the largest glaciers in the world outside the polar region. These glaciers feed the Indus River system on which most of Pakistan's agricultural and other human activity depends.

Rainfall varies considerably in the northern mountain region. Where it is substantial or where soil conditions react favourably to the melting snows, there are extensive pine and fir forests and lush pasture lands. For the most part, however, the area is barren, sparsely populated and inaccessible, except for the valleys which are fed by glacial rivers and springs. Agriculture and pastoral activity, on a small scale and at subsistence level, is carried out in these valleys by harnessing the sources of water; fruit trees and orchards are common. In addition, a large variety of deciduous trees such as maple, poplar, birch and willow grow in these valleys.

The northern mountain region consists of the administrative units of the Northern Areas, the Kohistan, Dir, Mansehra, Chitral, Bajaur, and Malakand districts of the NWFP and the major part of Azad Jammu and Kashmir. The area includes the valleys of Chitral, Dir, Swat, Gilgit, Hunza, Baltistan, Murree and Kaghan.

The social and economic changes described in this part of the book deal with the Northern Areas where the Aga Khan Development Network (AKDN) is operative. The same changes are occurring in the other mountain areas as well due to a change from a barter to a cash economy, the demise of the artisanal and caste system, the development of a remittance economy and the introduction of urban values and education. Forests are disappearing, agriculture is being abandoned, educated youth can find no jobs in their native towns and villages and tourism and urbanization is creating severe environmental problems.

This process of change in the Northern Areas is faster and more conflict free than in the other areas of the mountain region because of the inputs of the AKDN. This section of the book describes this change and consists of extracts from field notes written while working on the evaluation of AKDN built environment and education related programmes.

1

Northern Areas: 1986

This was my third visit to the Northern Areas. This time, after three weeks of travelling the length and breath of it, and speaking to hundreds of people from all walks of life and all ages, I think I was able to paint a picture of its transition from feudalism to its present state.

Settlements in the Northern Areas exist only where agriculture can take place. Such locations are few and far between. Thus interaction between different settlements has seldom taken place. Where settlements have been close together, they have often fought each other for control of meagre land and resources. Due to this most of the settlements were fortified and are in locations that are difficult to access.

The Northern Areas consisted of fiefdoms and their society consisted of three classes: the rulers (Mirs, Rajas), their serfs; and the Beyricho. The last named are musicians and blacksmiths and are considered low caste. Their language, Beyrizki, unlike other languages of the Northern Areas, is Indo-European, with similarities to the North Indian Prakrits. As such, it is possible that they were imported into the Northern Areas by the rulers or were wandering gypsies who were enslaved by the Northern Area societies.

The older generation in all the villages visited paint a similar picture of conditions in the Northern Areas when they were children. The ruler was supreme. He taxed the serfs by acquiring a part of their agricultural, fruit and dairy products, administered justice and handed out punishments, recruited people from among the serfs for war, and through *beygar* (which is called *rajaki* here), maintained and developed agricultural infrastructure. He did all this through a bureaucracy that was drawn from his family and courtiers. In addition, he could call upon any one from among his serfs to do *beygar* for him.

Social custom in the Northern Areas dictated that every agricultural family should be self-sufficient. They were to produce their own fruit, grain, dairy products, wool for their clothes and fuel for cooking.

Seeking assistance for these items from another family or borrowing any of these items was considered degrading and even if one did it, it was at night so that people did not get to know about it. This arrangement produced almost no surplus, and whatever surplus there was, was taken away by the rulers or exchanged with wandering Kashmiri merchants for tea (which was a luxury) or cotton textiles. As such, there was no cash economy, no markets and shops (except in Gilgit and those too belonging to Kashmiris) and no connection with the outside world for the vast majority of people. The children of the courtiers, however, did leave the Northern Areas to study in Kashmir and the rulers kept in touch with the court of the Maharaja in Srinagar.

Apart from the Beyricho, there were no artisanal castes in the Northern Areas as in the rest of Pakistan. As such, most families had some member or the other who could work timber and stone for house building and for making certain types of agricultural implements. Where metal work was required the services of the Beyricho were enlisted in exchange for food.

However, the families did do a lot of collective work. If a family wished to build a house or to add to it, neighbours got together to help. In exchange the family provided food to the persons who worked with them. The practice still continues. Taking animals to the mountain grazing lands was also often a collective activity, and of course for land colonization and for the development and maintenance of agricultural infrastructure, large scale collective work was organized by the feudal order. In addition, festivals with collective dancing in which both men and women participated, were also held during harvesting, sowing and marriages. During the festivals polo matches were also played.

Houses were never built on the farm lands. They were built in fortified settlements called *kots*. This was for purposes of security and defence. In addition to houses, the buildings consisted of *langar khanas* and *pir khanas*. All old architecture, including the houses, are of the same design. They are built around a central fireplace and are almost square in shape. There are no internal walls. The division of space is created by varying the floor levels and each space has a specific function and a name. The external walls are of mud bonded-stone-rubble and are windowless. The only opening is in the centre of the roof above the fire place. The roof is supported on the walls and on four timber posts. These are sometimes linked at plinth level by timber members so resist earthquakes. The floor is normally of compacted earth, and in the case of more affluent houses, of timber boards. The roof consists of rough timber rafters covered with the branches of trees. These in turn are covered with *halli*, the skin of the *tall* (birch) tree for water proofing, and finally with *gara* (mud mortar). In the poorer homes, animals were also kept in a special place in the room in winter, to provide warmth.

The older generation reports that there were no roads when they were children, only tracks on which horses could move. As animals could only be afforded by the rich, people walked for days from their villages to their destinations, sleeping at night at *langar khanas*, during their journey.

The picture painted by the older generation no longer holds good. Things have changed and the reasons for change and the milestones of change can both be easily identified. The first major milestone was the war for independence against Dogra rule. The people of the area defeated the Dogra army and police with sticks and stones and joined Pakistan. The Northern Areas became a sensitive area in the Indo–Pakistani Kashmir dispute. The army moved into the area to build jeep tracks, bridges and cantonments. The people provided labour for this activity and in the process acquired building skills and money, as they were paid in cash for their work. The tracks made mobility possible and the interaction between people of different regions in the area increased. Many residents joined the army and this process received a big boost when the Aga Khan in 1960 or 1961, issued a *farman* commanding his followers to join the army. A large number of young men obeyed the *farman* and were stationed in different parts of Pakistan where they came into contact with more 'evolved' societies and came back with new ideas. They also received salaries in cash and this money found its way to the Northern Areas.

In 1964, the building of the Karakoram Highway (KKH) was undertaken and the people of the regions it passed through came into contact with the Chinese and worked on the KKH as paid labour. Rations and items of daily use came to the area for use of the Chinese and Pakistani soldiers building the KKH and these were acquired by the residents. However, the most important aspect of the process of road building was the introduction of new ideas and values and a new way of looking at society.

The KKH was opened in 1972. Tourists started to visit the area and the local population started to engage itself in the developing tourist industry. At about the same time, army men started to return as pensioners to their villages. They had cash and new ideas. They wanted development, schools, toilets, health centres and a better way of life. In all the villages I had visited, it is these army men that are at the forefront of promoting change and development projects. They are the most effective social activists.

The most important change that took place was in 1974 when the Bhutto government abolished the feudal authority. The peasants became free. Mobility, both social and physical became easy. Young men went to Karachi to study and to work. A strong link between Pakistan's largest city and its most mountainous area developed. The educated boys came back to form political parties and pressure groups for development. An interest in the revival of local languages and culture also surfaced. City culture and middle class values and lifestyle found its way into the society.

Along with the abolition of feudal authority, the Northern Areas was divided into three newly formed districts. The Pakistan bureaucracy moved in, creating a large number of jobs for the local population and initiating fairly large building programmes to house the civil administration and develop a social and physical infrastructure. The people worked on these projects and in the process further trained artisans and managers were produced and the cash economy started to consolidate itself.

And finally, the Chinese frontier was opened in 1980 and as a result the tourist industry boomed. A large number of foreigners started to visit the Northern Areas and hotel accommodation, food, trekking, sight-seeing, transport and their other requirements had to be satisfied. All this has resulted in a big change in occupations, attitudes and the physical environment.

The Northern Areas is now a cash economy. There are markets and shops in various settlements. The tradition of self-reliance has ended. People are moving away from agriculture into trade, commerce, service sector jobs, tourism related services, transport and artisanal work. They have discovered that this is far more lucrative than agriculture. An increasing number of young men work in Islamabad and Karachi and send back money. Gilgit now imports large quantities of wheat which is marketed to the villages whereas previously there was almost no wheat sold in the market. Agriculturists are turning to planting orchards and cash crops and middle men from the Punjab and NWFP are providing support to them in those areas which are easily accessible.

The people working in the commercial and services sectors are emerging as the new middle class. They are moving out of their one room houses in the *kots* to houses on farmlands and building homes in the towns. These houses have more than one room built round the traditional one room house. They have latrines, verandahs and bedrooms. They are eating away at the limited agricultural land and transforming the rural landscape.

The establishment of the Aga Khan Rural Support Programme (AKRSP) and other AKDN initiatives have also had a major effect on the area. The emergence of village organizations which operate savings and credit programmes are creating new community level institutions. The programme for the establishment of girl's schools will completely change the society within a decade. People are anxious to get their girls educated since they say that educated boys are not willing to marry uneducated girls and as such they may marry outside if educated girls are not available. Traditionally children were responsible for grazing animals. However, since they now go to school there is no one left to graze animals and so the number of animals has declined and a further fall is expected.

Most of the developments described above are taking place in an ad-hoc manner. As such, they are adversely affecting the built and natural environment. This deterioration is likely to increase considerably in the near future unless steps are taken to plan for it in an environment-friendly manner. This can only be done through the AKRSP Village Organizations or through Village Organizations developed especially for this purpose. Also, a major social revolution would come about once the girls who are going to school today come of age. What the repercussions of this revolution will be is very difficult to predict.

BUILDING A SCHOOL

I visited a number of schools built and financed by the village community themselves. One such school is at Nazimabad. The village consists of 150 houses and most of its population are land owners. Some are businessmen in Gilgit and three in Karachi. Thirty to thirty-five persons are ex-army men and over forty are serving.

A small school functioned since 1950 in the village in a *langar khana*. In 1976, the government constructed a primary school in the village. It soon became insufficient as it had only three classrooms and one teacher.

Motivation for the present school was provided by the chairman of the Regional Education Board. This was followed by a meeting of all the households where it was decided to construct the school. Land was purchased for 25,000 rupees from Ghulam Kadir and his brother Karimuddin. This land was worth much more but the brothers considered it as their contribution towards the school building effort.

A committee of twelve persons was formed for organizing construction. A sketch plan of the school was given to the committee by the Board. It had been prepared by Amir Ali Mulji, a Karachi architect. The village committee then selected master mason Yakook Khan to oversee the school construction. He was helped by ten to twelve other masons during construction. Yakook has twenty years' experience of working as a mason on government projects in Gilgit, Chilas and Skardu with contractors and engineers. He and some of the twelve masons left their work in the towns and came to Nazimabad at the behest of the committee. They worked free of cost. During construction they used water levels, plumb line, string for laying horizontal courses and the three, four, five triangle for laying out right angles. These techniques Yakook learnt while working in the towns of the Northern Areas for army and government projects. He has handed them down to his apprentices.

Six carpenters worked on the roof of the building. They were all from Nazimabad but were working in the towns of the Northern Areas. They also came to Nazimabad at the behest of the Tamirati Committee and no payment was made to them either for the work they did. They had also learnt their skills by working on government and army projects. All the carpenters and masons have now gone back to their jobs in the towns.

Stone was brought from the river by tractors. A tractor was rented from Gulmit at 200 rupees for eight hours. It made four to six trips in a day. The *matoris* broke the stone after it arrived. Each *matori* can break two tractor loads in a day. The *mistries* hammer dressed it. Each *mistri* can make about forty stones per day and two masons working together can put up two tractor loads of masonry. The tractor worked for about 300 days.

Cement was used for the floors and the pointing of stone work. The laying was done in mud mortar. Lime used to be used when there was no road. Now with the KKH, cement is easier to obtain than lime although it is twice the cost.

Timber came from Nagar, about seventy miles away, by truck. It was purchased in tree form from the government. Village people went to Nagar, chopped up the trees, put the timber on the jeeps which carried it to the KKH, and there the villagers loaded it onto trucks bound for Nazimabad. The committee organized this whole effort, including food for the volunteers, who went to Nagar for this mission.

Five thousand rupees were paid to the government for the trees and 20,000˙ rupees were spent on cutting and transporting them. Yet this timber was not enough and people contributed *Sufaida* trees from their farmlands as·well.

The carpenters used the *gunia* or steel right angle, water levels and spirit levels during construction. They also marked out sawing lines on the timber with nails. All these techniques were unknown in the village before the carpenters worked with army and government engineers and contractors.

The school began in 1979 and was completed in 1984. The delay in completion was due to a lack of funds. On further questioning it became obvious there were other reasons. There was no work plan. No quantities for materials required had been worked out. The committee depended on estimates for labour and materials worked out by the artisans and these were always grossly under-estimated. This created bad relations between the artisans and the committee members. The villagers were not given sufficient notice about when the funds were needed.

The ex-army personnel in the village and the *nambardar* were in the forefront of this effort and its result would have been so much better and cheaper if this community work had been supported by professional advice and supervision.

The Nazimabad school project is not unique. There are many such examples all over Pakistan. Training of artisans on new projects using new technologies and tools, has introduced new ways of doing things and new approaches for collective action. These ideas and skills they have taken to their villages. The leadership of the village is now being taken over by those who have been exposed to these new ideas and technologies and to new ways of doing things. This leadership needs professional advise without which its work will always face problems whose solutions will only develop through a long and painful process of trial and error. It is necessary for Pakistan's professional colleges and institutions to establish a link with community projects so as to be able to develop an appropriate curriculum for professional education.

Field notes written while working on an evaluation of the Self Help School Building Programme of the Aga Khan Foundation, September 1986.

2

Northern Areas: 2000

We left Gilgit for Farfu village and arrived there at 10:00 hours after an hour's drive. Ghulam Saeed who accompanied me, collected a number of people. We had a meeting and I enquired about their village.

The village has about 150 houses. It has twelve carpenters and eight to twelve masons. The villagers informed us that twenty years ago there were no skilled artisans in the village and the ones who are working here now were all trained at army and government projects and they have multiplied through the *shagardi* system. There are seven to eight shops and they give items to the residents on credit for a year—from harvest to harvest. All of these, except one, have come into being in the last six to seven years. The entire younger generation, including the girls are studying and some girls are matriculates, they inform us very proudly. Almost all the generation of up to twenty years has at least passed middle school. This too is a recent phenomenon. A number of the residents are working in Karachi and about thirty persons are in the army. So the village is not badly off, more so because they have additional land one and a half hour's walking distance away. There is no road to this land and they get to it and bring produce from it on donkeys which each house owns. As in the rest of the Northern Areas, they do not work on each other's land as labour as it is considered degrading not to be self-sufficient.

There are two saw mills in the village, both established in the last eight years. One of them is owned by Shah Nazir who is also a carpenter and mason. His saw mill is not doing well because the village has imposed a ban on the use of timber from its forest except for the personal use of the village residents. There is a Village Timber Committee that regulates the use of timber and supervises the ban. The villagers agree that this committee is the result of the promotion of village organizations by the AKRSP.

Shah Nazir works as a carpenter or mason for about 200 days a year and this, and not agriculture, is the main source of his income. He says that two to three new houses are constructed in the village each year and there are about ten to fifteen new improvements of between 1,000 to 10,000 rupees.

The residents claim that only 30 per cent of the village purchases firewood at about 50 rupees per maund. The rest collect it from the forest and bring it to the village on donkeys. One man working all day can bring in one donkey-load of timber, which is two maunds. In a year a household of ten persons requires about 100 maunds.

At the meeting concern was also voiced at the conditions of the *Kot*. It is too congested, it is collapsing. People are leaving it to build on their farmlands and as a result the farmlands will disappear. What can be done? The villagers want to know. They want to save both their heritage and their environment. They need professional assistance.

KARIMABAD

Immediately after arriving in Karimabad we visited the restored Baltit Fort. The houses along the pathway to it from the road below have been rehabilitated and the pathway has also been paved in stone. The paving of the pathway should have been rougher or more uneven as one tends to slip on the way back.

Internally, the Fort has been very well restored but the exhibits and the way they are presented could have been much better—and still can be. The lovely cafeteria in the local style just outside the Fort does not function and an ugly concrete construction has been put up on the pathway just before the Fort entrance. But then this is after all the Northern Areas and you cannot get everything right in one go.

After dark I went for a walk from Baltit Inn up to the bazaar. It was slightly chilly and there was a waxing crescent moon in the sky. The Baltit Fort, all flood lit, stood out, guarding the settlements below. This restoration and flood lighting of the Fort has transformed Karimabad. It has given it an identity, a focal point, a link with history, a sense of aesthetics to its residents.

I drop in at the shops along the bazaar, I ask the shopkeepers if their trade has improved as a result of the Fort 'restoration. No, they say, it has not but it will (when conditions in Pakistan are better) as the Fort is now famous throughout the world. The shopkeepers say that because of the Fort' restoration the people have become more environment conscious. So much for those who say that conservation of the built heritage is not development. From my conversation with them I also discover that the Town Management Board, envisaged by Reza Ali and me in 1992, is not just a paper reality but a major actor in deciding how development takes place.

MOORKHUN

On arrival at Moorkhun, we were met by resource person Aman Ali who informed us that the coordinator of the Building and Construction Improvement Programme (BACIP) Karimullah Khan was not available as his sister and then his aunt had died—both within two days. Many of the men of the village had also gone to Passu in connection with the funeral. So we sat down at Aman Ali Shah's house for a chat regarding the village and BACIP. We were joined by Inayatullah who has worked in Saudi Arabia as a driver and has just disinvested in a tractor that he used to hire out.

According to our two informants, one part of the village has forty-two houses and the other seventy-two. All people have land and all of them plant seed potato because it gives them money. Because of planting seed potato they cannot fulfil their wheat requirements and so they have to purchase flour from Gilgit. About twenty houses have a family member in the army and three persons work in Saudi Arabia and two in Kuwait. About twenty to thirty persons trade regularly with China but since the army take over, permission to go to China is difficult to obtain. A number of persons also work as loaders and unloaders at Sost which is nearby, and about twenty-five to thirty persons also have shops there. Sost is where the customs offices and storage facilities are which deal with the Gilgit–China trade. Also, all transport to and from China begins and terminates at Sost. However, all business at Sost lasts only from April to October for nothing happens in winter in this region. Residents of Moorkhun remember the time when Sost did not exist as a transit station for the Pakistan-China trade. At that time people had to seek employment in distant places and since that was difficult, the village was far poorer than it is today.

There is no tourism related work for the residents of Moorkhun since there is no access to their glacier, but now a track is being constructed and this will surely bring tourists to them. There are eight carpenters and three masons in the village and some of the carpenters can also do masonry work. There are no blacksmiths. This work only Beyrichos can do and there are none here. The village has one saw mill.

There is no *kail* or *dayar* trees in this region. The village pasture lands do have juniper trees on them but the village has decided to ban their cutting since these are ancient trees which they wish to protect. A village timber committee supervises this ban. Again, the people claim that the concept of committees came to them in the mid-eighties through the AKRSP. People have planted *sufaida* but it cannot meet the timber and firewood demands because at this height the *sufaida* requires twenty to thirty years to mature.

Kail or *dayar* for construction purposes is acquired from Chilas through a permit by a contractor and he sells it to the saw mill from where people buy it.

The village has pasture lands at Khunjrab about 30 kilometres to the north. Most of the households collect firewood from there and transport it by tractor to the village. Three persons working all day for nine days collect 105 maunds or three tractor loads. About fifteen to twenty houses purchase firewood that comes from Chilas at 150 rupees per maund. They estimate that about 140 maunds of timber per winter is used by an average household in their village. This means 21,000 rupees if you purchase it. People also burn coal that comes from China. It is cheaper than purchasing timber. They also hope to get coal from the Chaporsan *nulla* mines which AKRSP have taken on lease. Everyone in the village agrees that the building of the KKH and the presence of tractors and jeep tracks have made it possible for them to acquire firewood cheaply and with much less labour and effort.

Two to three new houses are built every year in the village and about ten to fifteen small improvements are also made. The entire school going age population goes to school and an average of 2,000 rupees per family per year is spent on children's diseases. The most common disease is winter flu. Aman Ali Shah, our host, is a carpenter by profession. The village has two Village Organizations. The seventy-two house Village Organization has a saving of 11 lakh rupees and the forty-two houses one of 7 lakh rupees. It seems to be a rich village.

GINDAI

We travelled for about six long hours to the rest house in Yasin, half an hour beyond Gindai. During the journey both Nahida (who works as a Social Organizer for BACIP) and Gul Sambar (our driver) spoke a lot regarding their families and their aspirations and longings and of course about BACIP. Gul Sambar also spoke about life in his village when he was a child and how everything had changed since then.

Nahida mentioned that her mother used to say that the people of Yasin and beyond were so poor that they used to give away their daughters to the rich people in Hunza so that they could at least have enough to eat. According to Gul Sambar it is said that they would give away a daughter simply for a box of tea. How true all this is one cannot say because here, like almost everywhere else, I suppose stories related to women and sex are exaggerated.

We spent the night at the Yasin rest house. The Deputy Commissioner (DC) was also there with gun carrying levies. He is investigating a murder. Why he should be doing this and not the police is beyond my understanding and no one at the rest house can explain it.

After breakfast I spoke to the *chawkidar* of the rest house about the cost of living in Yasin and how they acquired all that has now become necessities of life. He said that their lives had been made easy by the Pathan shopkeepers and traders who have settled here. They give everything on credit, both monthly and seasonal, and much cheaper than at Gilgit. Clothes, tea, soap, shoes, batteries, matches and all the '*parchoon*' goods are made available by them. A *shalwar-qameez* suit for instance, they provide for just over a hundred, whereas in the Gilgit bazaar it is difficult to get a suit for less than 400 rupees. In addition, they buy back old shoes, clothes, plastic, metal tins and bones. They also purchase animal skins which no one else does in Yasin. He feels the future of agriculture in Yasin is bleak because the younger generation simply wishes to go away to Karachi or do some sort of trade and business rather than work on the lands. He adds that he does not blame them, for what do you get from agriculture anyway?

We arrived at Gindai and went to the house of Mohammad Faqir, the coordinator. (I think the house was of Mohammad Faqir's brother, who has just had his leg amputated because of cancer). Mohammad Faqir has retired from the army and has received the various monetary retirement benefits so he is comparatively free and rich. Daulat and Sultan Hameed are the male resource persons. Daulat is a stone mason. Almost all his work is in and around Gindai but he has also worked for 'private' parties in Hunza. Saba Parween and Ayisha are the female resource persons. Saba Parween is a teacher. She has done her intermediate from the AIOU and Ayisha has done her matric locally. Very few of Pakistan's academies and so called intelligentsia know how much the Open University has benefited the remote regions of Pakistan, and especially women who cannot go to colleges because of the distances involved and an absence of hostel accommodation. These educated girls were almost non-existent in the Northern Areas which I knew eight years ago. They have come of age and the social culture of this place has already changed and in so short a span of time. During this visit I was constantly talking to women, many of them housewives, in Urdu, simply because they have been to school. The last time I was here in 1992, this was not the case.

We all sit and discuss the village. The village has no fort or cluster. Almost all of its 102 houses are on farmland. I enquire why there is no fort and get two replies. One, that unlike between Hunza and Nagar, there were no enmities between Yasin and other areas and the other, that there was nothing in Yasin so why should anyone attack it.

The village has five to six carpenters, ten to twelve masons and nine to ten shops all of which give materials on credit. According to our hosts, apart from one shop, all the others have come into being within the last ten years. There is one blacksmith but he is not a *dom* or *beyricho*. This is also a radical change because in the past, no agriculturist would have performed the work of an outcaste. This blacksmith has two apprentices working with him who are not *beyricho* either. Three to four new houses are constructed every year and ten to twelve improvements. Sixty to seventy persons from the village are in the army and fifteen young men are studying in Karachi although there is no one from here working abroad like in some other villages. All children, girls and boys, go to school. Everyone agrees that these are big changes and that in another ten years Gindai will have a city culture. Everyone also agrees that the gap between the rich and the poor will increase to an undesirable extent.

Transport of goods to Gindai is the main problem that our friends identify during the meeting. Because of this everything is expensive. For the poorer households there is no other source of income other than their lands, and this is not enough. As a result, about 5 per cent of the population works on the farms of their neighbours although traditionally this was considered degrading. The number of such persons is increasing and as such old values are being demolished. This will make it easier for new values to take route.

It is miserably cold for five months and one cannot survive without firewood. Most families get firewood from the *nulla* which is five to eight hours walking distance away, depending from which part of the *nulla* you gather the firewood. Some people gather and sell it at 120 to

150 rupees per maund and a very minimum of seventy maunds is required to survive the winter. This is a huge expense and cannot be met adequately by agricultural income alone. In addition, the whole of October is spent in collecting timber for the winter and if a daily wage is applied to this activity, it works out to a seasons' income on a two *kanal* farm in Gindai.

In our various discussions during our journey, Gul Sambar gave me some interesting information. In the *nullas* of Singal (there are seven according to him) Gujjars have grazed their goats ever since he can remember. Before they were given this permission against payments in the form of goats, milk, *ghee* and butter. But now the Singal VO takes 25 rupees per goat per season from them. This sum comes to over 150,000 rupees per year and is made a part of the VO's savings. Cash has replaced barter even in dealings with Gujjars! This change is irreversible.

Field notes written while working on an evaluation of the Building and Construction Improvement Programme of the Aga Khan Foundation, November 2000.

3

Northern Areas 2003: Women's Education

In the majority of villages in the Northern Areas, especially in the non-Ismaili areas, middle and high schools for girls are not available and as such they cannot study beyond the primary level. To overcome this handicap, girl students usually do their middle and/or high school privately through tuitions. A trend developed whereby existing primary and/or middle school premises started to be used after school hours for tuition purposes. These coaching centres were supported and built by the AKES from the early 1990s onward. They are run as a partnership between communities and the AKES in areas where regular NGO and/or government middle and high schools for girls do not exist and where there are at least 30 students (including middle and high classes) of which at least 20 are girls. One such coaching centre is in the Shia village of Jafferabad.

JAFFERABAD COACHING CENTRE

Jafferabad has a population of 250 to 300 households. The Aga Khan Education Services, Pakistan (AKES-P) built school has four rooms. In the morning it is a primary school and in the afternoon it is a coaching centre.

Bakhtawar Shah is the chairman of the school management committee and the school founder; Shabbir Hussain is the coaching centre in-charge and was educated at SM Science College, Karachi and has been a government teacher at the high school in Nilt; and Shaikh Muhammad Haneef is the religious leader at the Imambara. They have all worked for establishing this centre.

The coaching centre began in 1998 at the AKES school. The coaching centre was begun because there were no middle and high government schools for girls in 1998. The 'progressive' members of the community realized that because of the absence of women's education they could not compete with Hunza. They were worried as they had been 'left behind'. Also, their women could not speak Urdu and as such could not communicate with doctors regarding their illness. This was a serious problem. They did not know of the world outside their home, they could not understand the news on the radio.

The coaching centre was begun by two female teachers. Both had Karachi links. Tahira Saba was born in Karachi since her parents migrated there. They came back to Jafferabad and she was one of the founders. The other was Mehrab Kiyani who still teaches at the Centre. The nature of her Karachi links could not be defined properly. However, there is consensus that Karachi and these two women have been a major contributor to a change in perceptions regarding women's education.

At present, there are five community teachers and 115 students in classes 6 to 10. The fee is Rs30 per student. The Tanzeem-e-Haideri (a local *Anjuman*) and the PTA manages the matters of the coaching centre. The members give donations and a grant is received from the AKES. Community teachers are paid between Rs1,200 and 2500. The coaching centre also pays Rs7,400 per year to the owner of the land on which the school is built. Three science students for matric have appeared for the first time this year. There were no laboratories for them but the centre's teachers made arrangement with the government high school for use of their laboratories. This was possible because some of the community teachers teach at the government school. Eighteen to twenty girls do their middle school every year from the centre.

The Tanzeem collected Rs125,000 with great difficulty and with great sacrifices on the part of the parents of the students to get the Rs500,000 matching grant from the AKES. They got it but with a fall in interest rates it no longer helps very much. They are looking for alternatives.

The community feels that there are many problems that they face at the centre. The school has no boundary wall and so girls and their parents have a sense of insecurity. The classrooms are not enough and there is no laboratory. There is a need for books. Many students cannot acquire them as they are expensive and this makes a number of girls leave education. A library creates a culture of learning and an environment for other than subject based education. There is no library. In addition, the centre's staff can only give three hours a day to teaching and this is simply not enough. They get tired teaching all day. The community has no complaints regarding the building. They are thankful to the AKES for having provided them with the school.

There were many objections to girls' education when the coaching centre was being set up. Religious leaders objected and pointed out to the villagers that their girls would be corrupted and that it was improper that men would be teaching young girls. However, support was given to the promoters of female education by a few religious leaders such as Shaikh Muhammad Haneef. He says he supports women's education because every Muslim man and woman has to acquire *Ilm*. Also, if the male teachers are respectable there is nothing wrong with women being taught by them. Shaikh Muhammad Haneef says that there are divisions among the imams on this issue but time is on the side of the progressives. Every girl who does her matric and goes beyond it is making the retrogressive elements fade into the background.

GHULMIT COACHING CENTRE

Another interesting coaching centre is at Ghulmit. Gul Nijaat and Mariam who are from Ghulmit teach there. They are sisters. Their father and mother were uneducated and the father got a job at the Wah Factory near Rawalpindi. Both Mariam and Nijaat were born there. Nijaat was in class 7 and Mariam in class 6 when they shifted back to Ghulmit. Before that they used to come to Ghulmit for their holidays. They have four brothers, younger than them, all studying at government schools in the village. At Wah, the social environment in which they grew up was very different from that of Ghulmit. It was freer and more open. There were much less restrictions on women. It was difficult for the sisters to adjust to the conditions that they encountered on their return to their native village. However, they claim that they have adjusted now. Their father wanted them to have an education.

Gul Nijaat studied at the DJ School in Danyore and did her matric in 1996. At Danyore she stayed in her aunt's house. On her return to Ghulmit, she started teaching at the Shah Wali Private Model School where she taught mathematics to class 8. The AKES field staff told her about the scholarships and the method of acquiring them. She got a scholarship and as a result she did her FA from the Islamabad Board. She was helped by teachers of the local government schools who coached her for her FA. Currently, she is doing her BA from the AIOU in Education and Economics. After studying and teaching she works on the family land in the evening. She is married now and her husband is a telephone operator in Gilgit. She wants to continue to teach and her husband supports her both in her desire to study and in her desire for continuing teaching.

Mariam is one year younger than Gul Nijaat. She did her matric in 1997 and taught herself with the help of her elder sister. She studied at home for her FA and is now doing a CT from the AIOU. Her parents wanted to educate both the girls, perhaps because of the Wah environment. People in the family opposed their education perhaps because the younger generation in the extended family is not educated. Mariam teaches in the middle government school in Ghulmit and at the coaching centre in the afternoon.

Both the girls wanted to go out of Ghulmit to study but due to family considerations they were not able to do so which they regret. Both the girls agree that without the coaching centre it would have been difficult for them to receive further education and without the scholarship it would have been impossible.

The coaching centre where the girls teach was begun in 1997 by 'Sir' Talib, a government school teacher. Five teachers teach here of which three are women. Conditions (*halaat*), they say, determine the fee structure. The coaching centre in-charge is Muhammad Issa who did his FA from the SM Science College in Karachi. He is currently doing his BA from the AIOU. For the last two years he has been teaching in the village government school in addition to teaching at the coaching centre since 1999. There are 103 students at the coaching centre and on an average eight of them do their matriculation every year. In addition to fees, money is collected after the harvests to support the coaching centre. Donation is voluntary. The centre acquired a matching grant but due to a cut in interest rates there are big problems.

The Village Education Committee (VEC) looks after teaching quality, manages finances and mobilizes the community to support the education programme for women. There was very strong opposition to the coaching centre since the majority of the village population did not want their girls to be educated and objected strongly to male teachers teaching them. Therefore, male teachers who were acceptable to the parents were chosen. Opposition has slowly declined. Eighty per cent of the graduates of the coaching centre are teaching in the English medium school in Nagar of which three are in Ghulmit. The pro-women's education part of the community says that they are the soldiers (*sipahis*) of change.

THE MINAPIN COACHING CENTRE

Anila Perween is from Minapin village in Nagar. Her father is a land owner with substantial landholdings. Both he and her mother have no education. However, her father's brother received education and finally joined government service. He became a DC and in that capacity he moved around the Northern Areas. She visited her uncle often and so did her brothers. They saw that their uncle's children were being educated and they too wanted to be educated. Their uncle also advised their father to educate his children. Subsequently, she lived with her uncle and did her matric from Skardu in 1996 where her uncle was posted. One of her brothers played a crucial role in encouraging her to get educated.

Anila Perween was the first girl to do her matric from Minapin. At this time a coaching centre was started in a SAP built school and she became a teacher there. She was also the first female teacher in the village. As such, she became a role model and young girls started coming to her for advice and wanted to be like her.

In 1997, the AKES was looking for women to whom they could offer scholarships for further education. Since Anila was the only matriculate, she was the only candidate. A scholarship of Rs200 per month was given to her and she did her FA from the AIOU and took her examination in Gilgit. It is possible that without this scholarship she would not have done her FA. The scholarship gave legitimacy to her desire to study and she did not have to ask her family for money while she was getting the scholarship. This was very important.

Looking back at the establishment of the coaching centre and her decision to teach over there, she says that 75 per cent of Minapin was against the establishment of the Centre and against her teaching. However, now things have changed and the daughters of those who opposed the Centre and her teaching, are studying in the coaching centre. One of the major objections to the Centre was that men would be teaching young girls. To overcome this problem the male school teachers visited the homes of prospective girls students (those who had done their primary and middle school) and assured their parents that their daughters' honour would be safeguarded. It worked, but slowly and over time.

Anila Perween has one older sister who is uneducated. She has three brothers. One is a driver and has done his middle school. The other has done his MA from Karachi and the third his BA and is teaching in

Skardu. Anila Perween was married in 1999 and now she has two kids. Her husband is in Lahore and works at the Civil Aviation Authority (CAA). She is willing to take a teaching job anywhere in the Northern Areas and says that if necessary she will go there alone with her kids. She will manage. The decision will be her own.

She says that for the time being girls will accept the husbands that their parents choose for them. After all she agreed to marry the man her parents chose. But maybe it will not be so in the future.

Anila Perween refused to be photographed. She said that society (*muashara*) did not allow it.

GENERAL FINDINGS

Change in the non-Ismaili areas is coming about through young men who for reasons of acquiring jobs and better incomes, have gone to Karachi for education. These young men have a vision of their villages which is very different from the existing social and economic realities of the areas in which they live. This is a major difference between the Ismaili and non-Ismaili areas. In the case of the former, the AKDN is the major catalyst.

Since education is relatively new in the Northern Areas, there are major differences of levels of education within the same families. One brother and/or sister may be completely uneducated whereas other siblings may have done their Bachelors and even their Masters. The educated and uneducated do different types of jobs and earn very different salaries. Often uneducated sections of the extended family oppose education. These are serious problems and in the coming generation they will divide not only extended families but also nuclear ones.

The values of the cash economy have come to dominate the Northern Areas even where the cash economy has not consolidated itself. People now express the fact that they have little time for community work; they are busy with trade and commerce and so they cannot work on their farmlands; it is no longer easy to get people to donate land for community buildings (even if a job at the building is promised in return), they now demand cash; and they do not wish to live as a community in clusters but wish to build homes on their farmlands.

Education is also seen as creating problems of marriage both for boys and girls. In the eighties families wanted to educate their girls because they were afraid that boys who were getting educated would not marry uneducated girls. Later, it was said that girls should not study beyond matric because then they would become too old to get married. Now it is being said that girls who have done their Bachelors and beyond are fussy about whom to marry and do not listen to their parents on these issues. Many of them remain unmarried or marry outside their village communities. There is also a feeling that less educated men seldom wish to marry highly educated women and that there are not enough educated men. All this points to a major change in social customs and a rejection of traditional values.

It is also often mentioned by community members that women, because of having access to the DJ School system, get a better education than men. Also, they have better jobs opportunities. There is a feeling that they have left the men behind and that something needs to be done for the men as well.

During this visit, as in previous visits, it was noticed that families who get educated and get service sector jobs, do not work on the land. They let out the land on contract or employ labour to manage it. A form of serfdom and/or landless labour class seems to be developing in the Northern Areas. The term *muzaira* was heard to be used twice during this visit to identify people who work on the land of others. How this will affect socio-economic relations remains to be studied.

English medium schools are sprouting all over the Northern Areas. Most of them are private institutions, and communities prefer them since learning English means access to better jobs. However, it is generally agreed that good English teachers are not available. If this is true then the education provided by these schools will be of bad quality as compared to Urdu medium schools. Maybe the solution lies in using English terminology while teaching in Urdu and improving English language classes. In addition, many of these schools are badly designed, with poor thermal insulation and even poorer structures that cannot possibly withstand a medium intensity earthquake. This will be a major disaster for the region. Something needs to be done about it.

Although good classrooms have been created and training programmes have been put in place, teachers complain of a lack of libraries and laboratories. They also feel that newspapers and magazines are necessary so as to broaden the outlook of students and teachers. Without them education remains limited to subjects only and this they feel is no education.

There is also a desire, and it was observed in previous visits to the Northern Areas as well, that students should be taught the history, culture and geography of their region. They should know of their heroes, their folklore, their music, their architecture and languages. Right now they study about people and areas with which they have little or no relationship. It is felt that the Aga Khan Cultural Services, Pakistan (AKCS-P) has a role to play in this regard.

Extracts from author's field notes prepared during the evaluation of the NORAD Funded Education Programme in the Northern Areas of Pakistan, 2003.

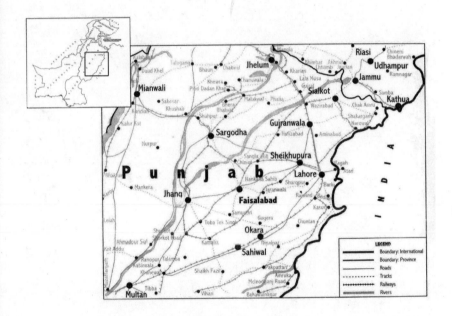

PART TWO: THE INDUS PLAINS AND THE WESTERN HIGHLANDS

The Indus plains in Pakistan lie south of the mountain region and between the Indian frontier in the east, and the western highlands, and extend down to the Indus delta country in the south. This entire region is flat and the soil consists of fine alluvium deposited by the Indus and its tributaries.

The upper plains are watered by the Indus and its five eastern tributaries: the Jhelum, the Chenab, the Ravi, the Sutlej and the Beas. They combine near Multan to form the Panjnad River which joins the Indus at Rajanpur. The upper Indus plains are a vast area and intensive agriculture through canal irrigation is carried out in the *Doabs*, as the areas between the rivers are called. The lower Indus plains consist of the area below the meeting of the Panjnad with the Indus and extend down to the delta where the river used to fan out into the sea before the dams and barrages were built on it. They too are canal irrigated.

Most of the area of the Indus plains has historically been an arid desert. The only natural vegetation of any substantial quantity has been along the rivers. This has consisted of tamarisk and *tali* forests sustained by the yearly flooding of the rivers. Most of these forests, especially in the upper plains, have been cleared in recent times for irrigated agriculture.

The Indus plains contain 77 per cent of Pakistan's population and almost all its major cities and industries. Income per capita and literacy rates are higher here than in the rest of the country, especially in the upper plains, and communications are much better developed. Social and economic change in the plains has been far greater than anywhere else in the country mainly due to urbanization, commercialization of agriculture, industrialization and the 1947 migration from India. One could have said in the mid eighties that in much of the plains, change had consolidated itself and that a new world had been created. However, the neo-liberal development paradigm, globalization and the WTO regime has again created a situation of flux.

The entire region of Pakistan west of the River Indus and south of the mountain region (except for the Peshawar and Charsadda valleys in the NWFP, the Derajat plain in the NWFP and the Punjab, and the plains between the Indus and the Kirthar range in Sindh), form the western highlands of Pakistan. The Potohar plateau, east of the Indus and encompassing the whole of the Rawalpindi division, also forms a part of this region. The western highlands of Pakistan are, by and large, arid, rocky and sparsely populated. As one moves south from the Potohar plateau towards Balochistan, the aridity increases and the major part of Balochistan is a desert. Small communities carry out rainfed agriculture and nomadic pastoral activity.

The chapters in this part of the book deal with the changes that have taken place in the plains and the western highlands. These chapters are derived from the author's personal diaries and from his reports for the 1985 UNICEF Water Mission of which he was a part.

4

Changes in Social Relations

BALOCHISTAN 1985

I had dinner with Deputy Commissioner (DC) Makran and discussed the *Zikris*. According to the DC, Mohammad Murad, the founder of this sect, was from Attock and was known as Attoki. He is buried at Koh-i-Murad in Turbat. Every year on 27th Ramzan the *Zikris* perform *Haj* at his *ziarat*. According to the DC, there is usually a gathering 30,000 to 40,000. Women and children also come. Their *kalma* is different from that of the Musalmans as they also use the name of Mohammad Murad in it. They are against *namaz* and consider *zikar* to be enough. Attoki came to Turbat about two centuries ago and preached a liberal Islam. He was a Punjabi. They exist only in Makran, Karachi and some parts of Kalat. The local *mullahs* want them to be declared non-Muslims. However, the *Zikris* I spoke to at Koh-i-Murad deny that Haj is performed there. They say that this is propaganda against them and that at the Koh they only perform *ziarat*. Also, they say that their *kalma* is not different from other Muslims and that they are not against *namaz*.

The *chawkidar* of the DC, Nayar Khan, is full of praise for the *Zikris*. It seems that he is one. He says that Attoki was the Imam Mehdi. He points out that no one until a few years ago was anti-*Zikri*. He blames the Pathan *maulvis* who have come to dominate the Baloch mosques for the hatred against them. A Japanese professor of cultural anthropology, who also came to dinner at the DC's, says that there is a study on the *Zikris* at his university but it is in Japanese. The professor is Dr T. Matsui of the Kobegakiun University.

Later, I went to Tomb, 80 kilometres from Turbat to see the houses of the Gichkees, with Nayyar Mahmood. We crossed the Kech Kaur and then travelled along it. The whole valley is full of date, mango and guava orchards. Bare hills. Good mud architecture. Base and boundary walls of angular or random masonry set in mud mortar. Later, crossed the

Nahing River. Tomb is 35 kilometres from Maund which in turn is 25 kilometres from Iran.

People at Tomb informed us that petrol is smuggled from Iran in Toyota pick-ups and brought to this region. It costs much less than petrol from Karachi. It sells for 20 rupees per gallon as opposed to 35 rupees which is the price in Karachi. A lot of other items such as matches (made in USSR), plastic utensils and fruit also come from Iran. Relations of our officials with the Irani officials are not too cordial.

Irrigation in the region is with *karez* from the Nahing and Kuch rivers. Both are at present dry and so water in the *karez* is very low. Both rivers are perennial but it has not rained for the last two years. Due to lack of rains the *ghabarbunds* have also failed. According to the farmers, the irrigation systems are no longer looked after since there is no one to organize the maintenance and also because very few people are interested in doing agriculture related manual labour.

A *Zikri maulvi* lives at Kolanch near Pasni. His name is Vaja Dad Karim. He has become an MPA. He is a Syed. According to the people we met, the *maulvis* are agitating against him but the local Baloch population is not bothered as they are not fanatical Muslims.

We had a long talk with Mehrab Khan Gitchki who complained that since all the young men of the area had gone to the Gulf, agriculture had suffered. No labour was available. The result was that the villages were empty and Tomb, which used to send wheat, *jawar* and corn to the coast, now imports all these items. Affluence from the Gulf makes it possible for people to buy these things at a high cost but the poor become poorer. The other problem is that Pathans and Brohis have started to come from the north as labourers. This is resented and at the same time due to shortage of labour, tolerated.

A shopkeeper in Tomb says that twenty five years ago only a few houses were made of mud or were *katcha*. The rest were made of straw and mat. The *katcha* houses are the result of the Gulf affluence. Artisan professions were hereditary but now through the *shagardi* system they are available to everyone. The Luri were the blacksmiths and singers but now they have taken to other professions as well.

On the way back we passed the Miri Fort from where Punnu went to Bhambore to meet his Sassi. It is interesting to note that the legend is as deeply embedded in Balochi folklore as in that of Sindh.

Levy Dost Mohammad

Dost Mohammad has been in the levies for fifteen years. He says that the greatest achievement of the Pakistanis which has benefited the people of the area has been the ending of the *sardari* system by Bhutto.

In the past the *sardars* (according to him) could call upon anyone to work for them without paying them anything. In addition, most productive areas paid a tax to him. In spite of Pakistan law, the *sardar* administered his own justice. The benefits that the end of the *sardaris* would bring was not understood by the poor Balochis before, because they were told that the government was anti-Baloch. Now, however, the poor realize that they made a mistake in supporting the *sardars* but at that time they were so ignorant that they could not have done otherwise. Dost Mohammad feels that now the *sardars* have no future. People feel deeply for the execution of Bhutto and there is a realization that he was their friend. Due to growing contacts with the Baloch in Karachi it is possible that the Pakistan Peoples Party (PPP) will win in Makran if there is an election. The poor are with it and the rich against it. But then, it is possible that Dost Mohammad says all this just to please me because for some reason he has decided that I am pro-PPP.

Dost Mohammad says that he cannot live within the salary he receives. He lives in a shack in Turbat. He cannot build a *katcha* house because he has no savings and for the same reason no one would give him credit. He says that none but those who have relations in Muscat can afford such houses. He complains that he gets no medical assistance when his family falls ill, his child's education is not looked after and he has no fixed working hours. He says the bigger officers get a host of benefits. Things were different before. Education for children was not considered necessary for people of his class. Health issues were God's will. But now he says that even a levy like himself needs education or he cannot get a job. People want doctors and prayers are not sufficient for them. Also, land holdings have become so small that one cannot live off them. 'What is the solution?' I asked him, he replied, 'a good government that is interested in the welfare of the poor'.

Vaja Ghulam Ali, a shopkeeper, feels that all Turbat needs is a road link with Karachi and electricity from the grid system. The rest he says will follow. The electricity will make tube wells possible which will make it possible for dates, melons and other fruits to be grown in abundance. The existing irrigation systems, he feels, are difficult to maintain as well as old fashioned. The road will make the Karachi market accessible. The Makranis will then no longer have to go to Muscat. The other issues are simply health and education. The present government schemes are all useless and only meant for lining the pockets of the *motabirs*, government officials and elected representatives.

The chief minister arrived with his entourage this morning and went straight to the rest house to address a public function. On the way he passed the Turbat College which is not too far from the rest house. The roof of the college was crowded with students, about 600 in number, carrying banners with anti-martial law slogans. While he addressed his meeting the students kept raising slogans like '*girti hoi diwaroon ko ek dhaka aur do*' and '*amriki samraj murdabad*' (death to American Imperialists), the same slogans students raise in Karachi. The students were different from Karachi students though. They seemed younger, angrier, and were unshaven and dressed in dark colours. Their leaders addressed them in Urdu, I wonder why. Levy Dost Mohammad was most amused at this performance. He kept saying 'Jam Sahib is such a big man' and these students disagreed with him. There is no respect for him any more.

Extracts from the author's personal diary, Turbat, 1–4 October 1985.

SINDH 1987

In the barrage lands there is no shortage of drinking water. In most cases people gather water from the canals and smaller water courses. In the majority of villages there is a pond which is used by the animals and by the village population, for drinking purposes, when the canals are closed for about six weeks for yearly cleaning.

The social structure in the villages is related to the system of land tenure. In some villages there is peasant proprietorship, which may be collective clan ownership, or individual ownership, and in other villages there may be a feudal landlord. At the village of Basram Bangla near Mirpurkhas, both these social structures are present. This village has been chosen by the Rural Development Department (RDD) for a hand pump scheme.

Basram Bangla consists of 20 to 25 houses. The community is ethnically homogeneous. They are all Rajputs from Rohtak in India. They own the land they till and the size of proprietorship varies between 12 to 32 acres.

At present, the community collects its water from two shallow wells. One of the wells has a horizontally displaced hand pump on it. This pump was installed about five years ago by the community..Mohammad Iqbal, a local of the village, installed the pump without any assistance from a *mistri*. The pump worked perfectly for five years and only needed to have its washers replaced every three to four months. This was done by Mohammad Iqbal without any difficulty. After a few repairs Mohammad Iqbal started to keep spare washers in stock so as to save him visits to Mirpurkhas.

Recently the pump stopped supplying water. On investigation it was discovered that the horizontal underground pipe had rusted. The villagers have got together to replace this and the pump is functioning again, but with less efficiency than before. Mohammad Iqbal was responsible for getting this work executed. As a result, he is now considered an expert by the community and they have decided to pay him for his skills whenever they are required. As such, he has become an entrepreneur and his son, who is now working with him, will continue his work.

The village is very affluent and almost every family can easily bear the cost of installing a hand pump for their exclusive use. In addition, they can afford to maintain these pumps as well. The only problem is that hand pumps are not on their list of priorities. There is also little understanding of the connection between water and disease. Children in the village normally have severe stomach problems and two died last year of dehydration.

There are two tractors in the village belonging to the larger proprietors. They were purchased ten years ago and are immaculately maintained. Recently they have been overhauled at a cost of 10,000 rupees each in Mirpurkhas. Other peasants hire these tractors from their owners at 60 rupees per hour. All minor repair to these tractors is done by the self trained *mistri* of the village, Mohammad Iqbal.

The villagers are looking forward to the installation of hand pumps in their villages but feel that as the government is putting up the pumps it should also finance its maintenance. If they were to put them up themselves, then only the responsibility of maintenance would be theirs.

Near the peasants' village are the houses of their labourers. Five families live there. These *haris* are not allowed to use the village wells and must go to the water course to collect water. They are not part of the village committee and will not benefit in anyway through the RDD/

UNICEF programme. Even if a separate pump is installed for them they feel that they will not be allowed to use it, and if they are they will not be allowed to maintain it; and as a result it will fall into disuse. These *haris* are the poorest of the poor, as they are bonded labour and owe the village community over 20,000 rupees. Given the meagre sum they receive from their masters, this sum never decreases. However, Jumma who is one of these *haris*, is hopeful of the future. He feels that job opportunities for cash are increasing and also people are becoming more mobile and less shy of moving to urban areas where conditions are different.

Extracts from the author's field notes prepared for the UNICEF's 'Report on a Joint Assessment of the Sindh Rural Water Supply Project', 1986.

PUNJAB 1992

We have been looking at urban issues for the past three weeks. However, their close links with economic conditions in the rural areas have surfaced again and again. So we have visited various villages in the Faisalabad and Sargodha areas. What has struck me is how much these villages have changed since I was a child when I used to spend my winter vacations in my uncle's village near Mian Channu.

Very few people now wear the *themad*. The *shalwar qameez* has replaced it. The colourful dresses with embroidery that women used to wear have also become rare and now you cannot always tell the caste or status of a woman by the clothes she wears. Fodder cutting machines are now all automatic electricity run affairs and so are milk churning ones for extracting butter. Tractors are everywhere and their engines are also used for threshing and drawing water. Suzuki vans and tractor trolleys transport people and goods and bullock carts are on their way out. There are fertilizer and pesticide depots, generators and pumps, *parchoon* outlets and nylon ropes have completely replaced date palm fibre ones. The village well is no longer used. It has been replaced for the most part by hand pumps within the home and in many cases by electric motors installed on a bore. There are schools, both for boys and girls, impressive mosques and improved road networks.

However, this air of affluence is misleading. The necessary physical infrastructure for accommodating mechanization has not evolved, creating severe environmental degradation. Suzukis and tractors are serviced in open spaces and their fumes, oil spills, solid waste generated by servicing and noise, create unpleasant conditions. Transport has no proper terminal facilities and vehicles force their way into narrow lanes not meant for them. Solid waste is not lifted since the *chamars* have migrated to the cities or are no longer willing to do 'dirty' work. Electric wires crisscross the streets and roof tops and the enormous quantities of waste water that is generated by an improved water supply system floods the lanes or flows through open channels (often unpaved) into numerous cesspools. There is chaos and it is not only physical. This village affluence has a price: the agriculturists are in debt to *artis* and many artisans to middlemen related to their trade.

The village in the Faisalabad district which we visited yesterday is no different from the villages described above. We wandered about in it for two hours in the late afternoon speaking to everyone. We came in contact with shopkeepers, people working in the fields, the tractor operators, school teachers and transport operators. While we were in the process of doing this a well dressed middle-aged man came and asked us what we were doing. When we explained, he suggested that we meet at his uncle's house where he would gather people who could help us. His uncle, he told us, was Chaudhry Ismail, a notable of the village. We agreed. I was sure that what people had told us and what we would hear at the Chaudhry's residence would be poles apart. I was completely wrong.

It was dusk and a bit chilly by the time we arrived at the Chandhry's house. The air was full of the dust of a Punjab winter. We were taken into a large room where about twelve to fourteen people were gathered. There were a few chairs and four *charpais*. The status of everyone in the room was obvious. The important persons sat on the chairs, the not so important on the *sirhana* of the beds, the less important on the *painti* (or behind the others) and the rest squatted on the floor. Greetings were exchanged, tea and biscuits were served and the discussions began.

Chaudhry Ismail is about seventy years old. He prefers not to speak Urdu, since according to him, it gives him a jaw ache. He is aware of the trauma that changes in the village have caused and defines the present situation in the rural areas of the Punjab as *afra-tafri*.

'You use that term often but what exactly do you mean by it?' I enquire.

'A few weeks back a *dhobi's* daughter married an *Arain*. Everyone objected but in the end the parents agreed. This girl will be a misfit in her husband's home. This will create conflict, break-up of the family, tension. This is one aspect of *afra-tafri* but there are many other.'

'But there must be a reason for the *afra-tafri*?' I ask.

'There is not one but many reasons', he replies. 'When Pakistan was created the Sikhs went away and the Muslims came. They were poor and destitute. They took on any jobs they could so agriculturists worked as *kammis* and *kammis* became merchants and as a result the *biradri* broke down. People were forced to move around with their families looking for work. All sorts of different people started living together. No rules, no regulations, and as a result, no honour.'

'Those were the migrants but what about the locals?' I ask. 'Surely they are different.'

'They have become the same. *Kharboza kharboza to dekh kay rang pakarta hai* (a melon changes colour by being in proximity to another melon) and a bad example is always more powerful than a good one.'

'Are there any other reasons?'

'Yes, hunger for money. People have left farming. They want to work in the cities. They want to be drivers, loom operators, mechanics, shopkeepers. These people earn more than agriculturists and work less. If one brother is a poor farmer and another brother a rich shopkeeper, the family cannot stay united. Poor and rich do not mix especially if you have to buy a TV or a record player. Those families whose members went to work abroad in Saudia and brought back a lot of money are completely finished. They will never be united again. This is *afra-tafri*.'

'As a Chaudhry do you still settle disputes, do you still mediate between people?' I ask.

'Yes, if they come to me—but less and less do. Even if they do, the one in whose favour I decide listens to me while the other goes to court or to the police. Even the *biradri* is no longer willing to pressurize people to listen to their decisions. The system of the *panchayat* for practical purposes does not exist. Now you understand what I am saying. Then you must understand that people come to me because I am old. They would never go to a younger Chaudhry but they may go to the *arti* who funds their agricultural or artisanal production. This is normal since you seek the help of those from whom you benefit.'

'Is there anyone here who lets out tractors on hire?' I enquire.

Abdul Razzak does. He is about forty years old and has done his FA. He has two tractors. He sold his land (he had less than one *murraba*) and invested it in tractors. He earns more from renting out the tractors and trolleys than he did from farming and it is much less work. The tractor rent is 125 rupees per hour if cash payment is made. In most cases payment is made after harvesting when people have money. In case of delayed payments 150 rupees per hour is changed. About thirty farmers per year hire his tractors. In the non-ploughing season he lets out the tractors for threshing, transport (with trolleys attached to them) and for drawing water from canals. He has made enough money in the last six years to become a dealer in fertilizers and pesticides. These too he gives mostly on credit to the farmers and as a result earns 25 to 30 per cent more than he would on cash terms.

'Do you prefer delayed payments?' I enquired of him.

'Of course, it gives me more money on my investment than any bank would.'

'What if your creditors do not repay you?' I ask.

'That will never happen' he says. 'If they do not pay me no one else will give them credit and they cannot do without it.'

Mohammad Pasand is a small farmer who hires Abdul Razzak's tractors and pays him higher rates as he only has sufficient money at harvesting. He also sells his harvest at 60 per cent its market value to an *arti* soon after sowing. Without this arrangement he cannot finance his agricultural activity and cannot survive from sowing to harvesting. He also purchases seeds, fertilizer and pesticide on credit and as a result pays about 25 per cent more for them than the market rate.

'Why do you not use animals for ploughing anymore? It would save you money.' I ask Mohammad Pasand.

'It is more expensive to keep animals than to hire a tractor, even on credit,' he replies, 'especially if the animal is not used for other things like transportation. Almost all transport activity has been replaced by trolleys and pick-ups. Then ploughing with an animal is hard work. It takes time. It requires more than one person. My sons are studying in Faisalabad and my brother works as a Toyota pick-up driver. I have no one to help me. In the old days it was different. Families worked together.'

The Chaudhry nods his head. 'Now do you understand what *afra-tafri* is all about?' he asks, laughs and slaps his thigh a few times.

'How many people in the village sell their produce to the *artis* before harvesting?' I ask Mohammad Pasand.

'Eighty-five paisas in a rupee (85 per cent)' he responds.

'And these 15 per cent who are free from debt, how much of the village lands would they own?'

'About 30 per cent', replies the Chaudhry. 'They employ others to work for them. These others can sometimes make a lot of money, especially in the sowing and harvesting period. In the slack period they do *mazdoori* at markets, on transport, at building sites. I think that many of them are better off than the agriculturists.'

Abdul Razzak disagrees. 'Those that own land spend less,' he says. 'They do not have to worry about grain and dairy products. A *mazdoor* or *beldar* may earn more but he is much poorer. If he does not get his *dayhari* his family starves. He lives on a day-to-day basis. That is why his women too have to do *mazdoori*. Then his biggest problem is a place to live. One or two of his family members have to provide free labour to the agriculturist who permits him to build a shack on his land. And he can be thrown out of there anytime.'

'In the old days no one starved and every one had a place to live.' Says the Chaudhry. 'The agriculturist looked after all the needs of his workers and service providers. They were given grain, a home, a space to live. But then, there was *qanat* (contentment). That is all gone. The *kammis* are becoming the richest people in this area. They have gone to the cities, to Saudia, into business. Most of the problems have been created by them.'

'Dadji', Says the Chaudhry's twenty-three-year-old grandson, 'we have never seen this world you talk about. I do not think it can ever come back.'

'Yes,' says the Chaudhry, 'the wrong type of education has introduced western values. That is the problem. It will never come back.'

'But let us come back to the problems of those who do not borrow from the *artis*.' I say, trying to steer the conversation to development related issues. 'Do they sell their produce directly at the *mandi*?'

'No one can sell their product directly at the *mandi*', says Mohammad Pasand. 'You have to go through an *arti* or his transporter. That is the only way that you can enter a *mandi*. The option is that you can sell it outside the *mandi* at less than half its value like some poor vendors do.'

'Why is this?' I enquire.

'Because the *artis, bayparis* and transporters organizations control the *mandis* and because the administration takes bribes from them and so supports their monopoly.'

'Suppose the state or some other organization starts giving you credit for production and for surviving from sowing to harvesting. Would that solve your problems?' I ask Mohammad Pasand.

'Yes, to a great extent,' he replies, 'but I would still require a grant to pay back about 40,000 rupees that I owe my *arti*, which I borrowed for my daughter's marriage and about 15,000 rupees left over debts. Unless I pay that back I will have to keep selling my produce to him.'

'Why?' I enquire.

'Because no one will buy my produce until I pay this sum back', he responds.

'Suppose you form a cooperative and have your own *mandi*. Will it work?'

'No', says Abdul Razzak, 'it will never work. They do not have the skills for it nor the finances.'

'It is not a matter of skills and finances. We have both. We know how things function. But this can only be done by support from the DC. He should give us land for it in an appropriate place and protect us from the *mandi* operators and corrupt officials in the police and in his organization. If this happens Abdul Razzak will lose business,' says Mohammad Pasand.

'No', says Abdul Razzak, 'I will gain. I will be your transporter.' Everyone laughs and the Chaudhry begs leave to say his prayers.

The conversation continues into the night. We discuss the sociology of the village, the growing power of the entrepreneurs and *artis*, the break-up of the old *biradri* system, new conflicts, local government and their aspirations. I have had this same discussion in numerous villages in Punjab and Sindh and the story, except for minute details is the same except that in Sindh a large part of the *artis*, transporters and *mandi* operators are non-Sindhi and as such the feeling of deprivation and injustice among the agriculturists is much stronger. Also, in Sindh, although the barter economy is dead, the values and structure of the old order survive in large pockets, because most of the members of the entrepreneurial classes are non-Sindhi. If they were Sindhis, I am quite sure that the story would be very different.

Extracts from author's personal diary, December 1992.

SINDH 1997

I have come back to Karachi after a few days in the rural areas of Khairpur district. This time the visit was in connection with the Strategic Review of the NGO Resource Centre (NGORC). We visited the villages of Hussainabad, Jami Buriro, Talpurwala, Sikanderabad and Arbab Solangi. We also stopped in three other villages to discuss conditions in the district with shopkeepers and residents. The story is the same all over again. Why do I not come across the terrible feudal conditions people describe in Sindh, except in small pockets? I see feudal values, I see a feudal-establishment retrogressive nexus, but I also see that feudal institutions do not function anymore; they do not control production and marketing of agricultural produce; they do not develop and maintain agricultural related infrastructure; they do not effectively control property and personal law of the peasants. The peasant today is theoretically *azad*. A new world has been born; a cruel world, a capitalist world, an exploitative world, a world of middlemen and entrepreneurs that is enslaving the rural population, peasants and small landowners alike. My visit to Khairpur has confirmed all that I wrote in 1987. Feudalism is there in pockets but the new cash economy and its actors are universal. They are everywhere and control the financing and marketing of production. Do we have to pass judgement on Pakistan on the basis of shrinking islands of retrogression rather than on the basis of an expanding sea of change, even if it is exploitative? I constantly ask this question.

In all the villages visited, over 30 per cent of the land or more was water logged and unproductive mainly due to the non-maintenance of *saim nalis*. Previously maintenance was done through the administration-landlord-peasant nexus with the peasant providing *beygar*. This *beygar* is no longer possible. The villages visited had small holdings and their production was supported by *artis* and *bayparis* who also arranged for the transportation of the produce. Many landowners worked as labour on the land of others to augment their incomes. There were large landlords in the area but the villagers had nothing much to do with them except during election time. These landlords were also shifting from the *batai* to the *mukato* system since the children of their *haris* were adopting other livelihoods and the children of the landlords were shifting to Karachi. This is a major change in relationships.

The NGORC has formed CBOs in the villages we visited. Much of this work has been done by Zafar Junejo and Rehana Sheikh, two young, educated Sindhis. Their presence in the villages, especially that of Rehana Sheikh, and the fact that they have been able to create effective women's savings and credit groups, who manage their own affairs, is a revolution in itself. They are ideal role models for others.

The CBOs are clear about what they require. They want loans for production (seed, fertilizer, pesticide, tractor hire) and to survive from sowing to harvesting. This they claim will double their incomes and free them from the *artis*. They want loans to buy tractors on a cooperative basis so that they do not have to hire tractors from 'tractor lords' at exorbitant prices. They want loans to purchase buffaloes and cows so that their children can have milk. At present animal purchasing loans are only available from *bayparis* and those who take them have to look after the animals and feed them while the *baypari* is entitled to half the milk, free of cost, that is produced by animal.

Everywhere I enquire, 'But how will you repay all these loans?' And everywhere I received the reply, 'within two harvests.' 'And how will it benefit the landless?' 'They will have better *dayharis* and after all, almost all of them are from within our families.' I wish it was so simple. These loans without effective controls will open the flood gates to a new form of exploitation, this time, of the most vulnerable.

Then there are other issues. It is no longer possible to live off the land, even for someone who owns ten acres, and few do. They need jobs. People are becoming drivers, labourers in the sugar mills, working for the transport and services sector, driving rickshaws. As a result, the peasantry is undergoing a social change. The CBO representatives and the two middle landlords we met are fully conscious of this. As a result of these changes, the primary school teachers in most of the villages visited have emerged as the major lobby against feudal values and torch bearers of Sindhi Nationalism. This is understandable. Given the political and economic exploitation of the Sindhi speaking population of the province, the consolidation of change and nationalism is inseparable.

Extracts from the author's personal diary, 23 January 1997.

5

Changes in NWFP: 1986

This chapter is derived from the author's field notes prepared for the 1986 UNICEF Water Mission of which he was a member. A postscript has been added to summarize the changes that have taken place since 1986.

NWFP 1986

We visited the districts of Karak, Dera Ismail Khan and Mansehra during the field visit to the NWFP as part of a water assessment for UNICEF. Three types of communities were identified during these visits. Each type is related to the system of land tenure, which in turn is related to the geography of the area and the availability of water for agriculture.

The only irrigated lands visited by us were in the Karak district. Irrigation here is from open wells mounted with pumps. Agriculture received a big boost after electricity came to the area twenty years ago as electric pumps could then be used for lifting water where previously the Persian wheel was used.

There are large land holdings of up to 1,000 acres in the area. However, the majority of the area is peasant proprietorship of holdings below three acres. The large land holders have traditionally been the representatives of the people and have been looked upon to settle disputes and mobilize people for any development work. The small holdings of the peasants and low incomes have made a number of people leave for the cities and also for the Middle East. Many of these returned and purchased more land. They have also built new *pucca* houses on their farmlands away from the traditional village. These isolated houses are visible between Karak and Shabbirabad. Given the process of change, they will in the next decade dominate the landscape. This new class does not accept the traditional leadership of the area, and due to its new found affluence is playing an increasing role in the affairs of the village.

Other changes have also taken place. In the village structure, the blacksmith, the barber, the carpenter, the tanner, the potter and the *dom* (minstrel), were not part of the clan system. They could not own land or even a house. For the services they rendered to the community they were looked after by the village. Now these artisans own their own houses and many have purchased land. They have become richer than the small landowners since their labour now has a cash price to it.

This society is in a state of transformation from a feudal to a pre-industrial one, and the agents of change and development can only come from the new affluent classes. The development of agriculture has also brought in the fertilizer and pesticide agencies; tractors are visible everywhere and as such workshops and mechanics for their maintenance must also exist. There is evidence to show that these tractors are let out to the peasants by the 'tractor lords'. Water for irrigation can also be purchased from 'water lords'. Since the Public Health Engineering Department (PHED) water supply systems became operative the people have converted their drinking wells into sources for irrigation.

At Shabbirabad, a town of 4,500, there are three banks, and according to the village population almost all children, girls and boys, go to school. However, preventive health services are almost non-existent in the area. In Latambar village there is even a shop belonging to a qualified chemist.

Keeping in view the picture painted above, the community seems to be ready to receive education and health inputs with a minimum of preparation for them. Involvement of women in programmes, and reaching some of them may also be possible.

The *barani* areas are, however, different. In these areas there are large land holdings with tenant farmers working on them. Small peasant holdings also exist but as agriculture is dependent on the erratic rainfall only, the peasant population is extremely poor. Earnings can be as little as 500 rupees per year per family.

Power is vested in the big landlords of the area and the influence of the religious leaders is considerable. As agriculture is dependent entirely on rains, people raise livestock, mainly goat and sheep. Bohar, a village of 4,000 in Dera Ismail Khan, has an animal population of 20,000 which moves to the river in the drought period. It has no health facilities, preventive or curative, and only fifty male students attend school. However, there are at least three mosques. Clan organizations are strong and are linked in many cases to the village settlement pattern. For example, Bohar is a village of Jaats, and the head of the Jaat clan *panchayat* is also the main *zamindar* of the area. He is also a member of the UC. The artisanal classes in the village do not own land or houses.

The construction of a rainwater tank in the village was arranged by the *zamindar* and its yearly maintenance and cleaning is also organized by him on *beygar*. This tank caters to the needs of the village population and to their animals. Not more than three *matkas* are allowed per house per day from this pond. After the monsoon it dries up in four to five months. If there are no winter rains the population moves to the river flood plains in January. Otherwise, movement invariably takes place in April and the population returns in July after the first monsoon shower. According to the people we spoke to, most of the villages in the *barani* area of erratic rainfall have similar social structures.

Kari Samozai, a large village of 10,000 persons, also in Dera Ismail Khan district, has a different economic set-up from Bohar. Although the area has large land holdings of up to 10,000 acres, the size of the village, the presence of government institutions for health and education, banks and a WAPDA lines man, have given some independence to the village population from the feudal system. The village has a number of merchants who do business with the towns, selling animals and buying cloth and other industrial goods for sale in the villages. However, such villages are few and far between, and it is doubtful whether their social attitudes are any different from those of the other villages in the area. It is important to note here that one of the main reasons for Shamozai's development is that the chief of the Istarana tribe lives here. He is important politically, is educated, and has taken an interest in the affairs of the village.

The traditional leadership of the landlord and the *imam*, paternalistic in nature, is deeply entrenched. Women are segregated completely and there is no doubt that at this stage they cannot be involved in any programmes and cannot even be reached effectively. In these circumstances can the traditional leadership be an agent for change and that too of a change which will eat away at its power? A lady doctor working for the Dera Ismail Khan District Health Department discreetly expressed her doubts about it.

Again, the Mansehra district is different too. It is a *barani* area where rainfall is regular. Apart from a few feudal holdings, the system of land tenure is peasant proprietorship. The land holdings are small and incomes from them low, but since the population is free from overt feudal controls they seek employment in urban centres in Pakistan, in the Middle East and in Europe. A large number of them join the army. This process has been continuing for the past four decades and has resulted in further consolidating a cash economy at the village level. In Karachi and along the National Highway many motor mechanics, welders, lathe machine operators, electricians and plumbers come from this part of the country. Contact with the rest of the world, the fact that the area is politically important and has received attention, and given its social structure which is free from the control of retrogressive leadership at the micro level, have all created an awareness which has made the local government system workable and viable. The positive reaction of the village communities to the water programme and the school building programme, are proofs of this awareness and organizational potential.

In these areas the local government and the political institutions themselves can be agents of change. As a matter of fact the change has already taken place in the minds of the community and needs only to be tapped and directed appropriately.

WATER AND HEALTH

In the minds of the people of the areas we visited, there is a close relationship between water and health but little understanding of how water gets contaminated and how this contamination can be prevented. Among the community leaders and the officials of the line departments (including the health department), the issue of contamination, is of minor importance. The only exception to this was the chairman of the Mansehra district council, who was not only very clear on the subject, but also had plans for promoting this understanding in the villages. He fully appreciated the role women can play in creating awareness of this problem. However, regular water has made a difference to the quality of life in the villages and hence to the possibility of affecting health positively.

This was borne out by interviews at the Badaber refugee camp at Shabbirabad, at Samozai, at Kata Khel and at Mansehra. In all cases the population spoken to said that bathing and the regular washing of utensils was a low priority before the water system became operative. At Mansehra the district officer, Bahadur Shah explained to us that *bazaars* in the small towns and large villages used to be called *Kala* (black) *Bazaars*, because the people were unwashed and wore dirty clothes. They bathed only once in winter, and once in two weeks in summer. Women bathed even less frequently. This has now changed due to the government's water schemes.

Since the PHED water schemes became operative in Mehrabi and Kari Samozai, people do not take their animals to the river during the yearly drought period. The original water sources, augmented by the PHED schemes are enough for their requirements. Since they have now become settled populations, they can think in terms of education for their children and of developing commerce and trade. It is doubtful if there would have been operative schools, health centres with EPI programmes, and a business class in Samozai, if the population had remained migratory.

After the installation of water schemes, in certain cases, the old water source has been utilized for developing agriculture. This is especially true of the Karak district. The result has been an increase in income levels for some areas.

To cart water from long distances people used animals, mainly donkeys and camels. The camel was also used for ploughing whereas the donkey was entirely a 'beast of burden'. Since the water schemes came into being, many people have sold their animals if the community tank is not too far away from their homes. Thus they save on the maintenance cost of these animals. Others who used to pay professional carriers for transportation of water, also make a saving. People find it cheaper to hire a tractor for ploughing their land than maintaining a camel. As such a camel who does not carry water can be considered redundant.

However, there are problems associated with the water supply schemes. Where community tanks with taps have been installed, they generate a lot of waste water. In many cases this forms a large pool near the community tank. In Mehrabi, the population stands in this stagnant water, which is used by animals for drinking, and fills their utensils. In such cases the guinea worm problem must certainly exist. Similarly waste water from house connections collects in the lanes. To overcome this problem the PHED has taken to providing underground tanks from which water is drawn out with a rope and bucket. This system, however, leads to the contamination of the water in the tank by the insertion of unclean utensils.

In Mansehra, the district council, to tackle the waste water problem has initiated a scheme of paving the streets and making open surface drains on either side of them. These will in the long run create more problems. All waste water will flow into the mountain streams and riverlets, which are also a source of drinking water for other villages; and it will not be possible to stop people from connecting their toilets to these drains in the future.

The women are against the water supply schemes, especially the ones where house connections are given. All the people, leaders and officials are of this view, and it is a source of great amusement to them. Whereas before women went out to fetch water from long distances, now their activities are restricted to the neighbourhood, and in many cases to the home. Movement, social interaction, and a visual contact with the environment have all been curtailed. It is important to ask as to what effect these restrictions have on the health of women and on their immediate environment, their homes and their children?

In some cases people are used to drinking rainwater, which they consider to be 'sweet'. Subsoil water may not be considered 'sweet'. Therefore, in Kari Samozai, where there is a PHED water supply scheme with over 600 house connections, drinking water is still obtained from the rainwater pond and carried to the houses by the women. The PHED water is used only for washing and cooking and for animal consumption. This is in spite of the fact that the pond is contaminated with animal excreta and is filthy. Of the fourteen boys gathered at the pool three had guinea worms.

The village population says that the PHED water causes diarrhoea and so they do not wish to use it. Dr Abdul Rauf of the RHC at Samozai says that he also had the same complaint when he began his service in the village. After two months he got used to the water and now drinks it without any side effects. Mr Aziz, a PHED executive engineer in Dera Ismail Khan, says that the water at Samozai being bad for health is a myth fabricated by women so that they can continue to go out of their houses and neighbourhoods to get water from the village pond. Mr Aziz is very serious when he says this.

When people fall ill they usually go to the village *mullah* for treatment. He prescribes charms, special prayers, and at times even penance. In certain cases he may feel that the patient has been taken over by a *jinn*, in which case he acts as an exorcist. Visits to the shrines of holy men and offerings to them are common. At the same time a doctor is also approached for treatment. However, if the patient is a woman, it is unlikely that she will be taken to a doctor although a male member might consult with the doctor explaining the symptoms and receiving directions for her cure. The above holds less true for areas like Mansehra where peasant proprietorship coupled with strong urban influences exist. But Dr Abdul Rauf feels that things are changing. The younger generation is different. It believes more in medicines than in holy men and *mullahs* but finds it difficult to disobey the older generation.

There are many traditional treatments and taboos for various diseases. For example, during measles no bathing is permitted and an injection is strongly forbidden. The patient must not be exposed to light either. These attitudes conflict with medical treatment, and doctors like Abdul Rauf at Samozai are incapable of convincing people that their centuries old beliefs are incorrect. Again, the doctors feel that with education these old beliefs are also being questioned and once the younger generation comes of age they will follow the advice of the medical profession.

The EPI programme is the most successful extension programme of the health department in the districts visited. Although villagers do get their children to take the first shot they seldom come for the second, if as a result of the vaccination the child catches fever or has a reaction. An understanding of the reasons for the reaction are not known and are not communicated to the people. If they were, things would be different.

The segregation of women in most areas of the NWFP is very severe. The only way of reaching a woman is through her male family members through proxy. Even urban women cannot reach them easily as they are considered a bad influence on their rural sisters. This nature of segregation makes it difficult for the existing health services to function. Women in rural areas do not come forward to be trained as lady health visitors or community health workers. They find it difficult to attend medical training courses away from home. As doctors, they do not wish to be posted at the NWFP rural health centres. They are not willing to be school teachers in rural areas either. However, all the women working in the Karak district are convinced that a change is taking place and very soon women would become active in development projects.

POSTSCRIPT 2008

Since 1986 when the above text was written, the more developed rural areas of the NWFP were changing and the trends identified above, consolidating. CBOs were developing in the rural areas; and lady doctors, teachers and lady health visitors (LHVs) were just starting to manage health and education programmes. Demand for and building of girls' schools increased in a big way. Since 1995 the Aurat Publication and Information Service Foundation (commonly known as the Aurat Foundation), began its programmes in a number of districts in the NWFP. These programmes consisted of political education for women, the setting up of district resource centres for the capacity building of women councillors and the establishment of women's information network centres. Rural women participate in and, in many cases, manage these programmes. In certain cases, there was a strong reaction against the local young women and men who supported the Aurat Foundation programmes and became their activists. They were threatened with violence and were told that the programme was 'spoiling' their women and would eventually destroy peace within the family. In many cases, there was a clear division between the older and the younger generation on this issue. In the local body elections of 2002, many of these young women and men activists and their supporters won the elections and became councillors in their areas. Some of the women have eventually been elected to the provincial assembly.

These changes were considered irreversible by many observers, including myself and were aided by development programmes and projects operated by international agencies and international and national NGOs. Many of these programmes were the result of the importance that the NWFP had acquired due to the Afghan War and the migration of refugees from Afghanistan. Other trends identified in the above text had also continued. The numbers of tractors increased, the bazaars expanded, transport multiplied and the new business community and entrepreneurs were acquiring the potential for eventually becoming a political power in their areas.

However since 1995, the effectiveness of the conservative religious-cum-political movements in the NWFP increased substantially and considerably modified the process of change that was taking place. The opposition of these movements to working women led to a sharp decline in the number of women working or opting to work as LHVs and teachers in the rural areas. Effective movements by the religious parties were also launched against the use of iodized salts (they were considered contraceptive) and against family planning. There was also considerable resistance to permitting women to register as voters. Due to this resistance, almost all the local chapters of political parties have, under pressure from conservative elements, endorsed *jirga* rulings on the ban on women standing for elections or voting. In most cases, this decision by the political parties is in violation of their stated party ideologies.

After 9/11 and the US invasion in Afghanistan, the influence of the religious right has increased and the trends they set in motion have multiplied manifold. Working women have had their throats slit; girls' schools have been routinely attacked or blown up; NGO offices have been attacked since these NGOs are seen as western collaborators; cinemas and video shops have been burnt; threatening letters have been written to social and political activists and often these threats have been carried out; and barbers have been punished for shaving off beards. In addition, due to political uncertainty and insecurity, Punjab *arthis* are no longer active in the disturbed agricultural areas; and in the non-disturbed areas they have increased their commissions and interest rates. As a result, agricultural income and produce has declined. Uncertainty has also led to the weakening of the effectiveness of state institutions. Because of this, ecologically damaging in landuse changes have taken place, since whoever has the power now determines how land is used. The above state of affairs has also created obstacles in the seasonal migration of the nomadic groups I encountered in the Karak district in 1986. More recently, American attacks from across the border have increased insecurity and further strengthened the political base of the religious right. The districts covered in this chapter are not the directly 'disturbed' districts. However, because of uncertain conditions and insecurity, the socio-political and economic trends are similar to what has been identified above.

In spite of what is mentioned in the previous paragraph, the number of women studying in colleges and in the university in Peshawar have increased and they come from all over the province. In 1987, Peshawar University had one hostel for women. In 1991 this number had increased to three, and there are seven hostels today. The number of women working in offices in Peshawar has also increased. There is evidence to suggest that this is because young men support their sisters in their desire to study. There are other contradictions as well. In 1997, in spite of the *jirgas'* decision not to allow women to vote, the Aurat Foundation, with local support, was able to effectively lobby for women voting. This would perhaps not be possible today. However, it is important to note that three Aurat Foundation women information network centres continue to operate in the Tribal Areas. Again, in Lower Dir district, the Anjuman Behbood-e-Khawateen (ABK) put up women candidates for the local body elections in 2001 and 2006 and got women to vote, in spite of the agreement between eight political parties that women would have no vote and would not be permitted to stand for elections. The local administration supported the decisions of the eight parties. As a result of the struggle of the ABK, women backed by men from their families voted, stood for elections and won a number of seats in the local councils. Recently, again after considerable struggle, women have been allowed to sit in the council chamber with the men and participate in policy debates. From this and other available evidence it seems that the internal dynamics of social change conflict with the political ideology of the conservative elements in the NWFP.

Source: Media reports and conversations in June 2008 with Shad Begum, District Councillor Lower Dir and member of the ABK; Rakhshanda Naz, Chief Coordinating Officer, Aurat Foundation and Shaukat Ali Sharrar, board member of two important Swat NGOs, Hujra and the Swat Participatory Council.

6

Changes in Rural Sindh: 1986

Highway robberies; kidnappings; carrying of unlicensed guns in the streets; private armies; an impotent administration; closed universities; non-collection of revenue; failure to maintain canals, drainage channels and roads; migration of middle landlords and capitalists to the larger cities; fear, uncertainty and pessimism: This is the situation in the rural areas of Sindh, and it cannot be explained away as a law and order problem as it so often is.

Over the last fifteen years enormous social and economic changes have taken place in Sindh, resulting in the emergence of a new Sindhi middle class, in both the rural and urban areas. These changes have also led to increased mobility of the population, introduced mechanization in transport and agriculture, and made the traditional *wadera*-administration alliance unworkable. They have created a new awareness in the peasants and supplanted the feudal barter system with a thriving cash economy.

In the absence, under martial law, of a political dialogue for the last nine years, state institutions have failed to assimilate this change, or make necessary modifications in their functioning to accommodate it. As a result, they are disintegrating and the authority of the government no longer exists. This disintegration of the state is the real cause for the present anarchy in Sindh.

Before the mid-1960s, rural society in Sindh was entirely feudal and the system had vitality and viable institutions. The *waderas* and *jagirdar* controlled all agricultural lands. Independent peasants, as in the Punjab, were almost unknown. Carpenters, blacksmiths, barbers, mat makers, tanners, were paid in rice and wheat by the village population. Cloth was spun on the *khaddi* in the village or brought in by bullock carts from the smaller towns, and bartered for other goods. Shoes were rare and water was taken from open wells and canals.

The landlord's word was law. He had the power of life and death over his serfs. He recruited them as labour, as and when he desired, without any emoluments and saw to it that they received only enough to live on. All surplus was taken by him and he handed out penalties and punishments to those who opposed him.

In addition to the landlord, there were tribal *sardars* and religious *pirs*. The tribal *sardars* received a yearly tax from their clan members, and in exchange settled their disputes and quarrels, punishing the guilty party with a fine. This fine could take the form of anything from a maund of rice to appropriating the women of the party at fault. This clan system however, gave the people a sense of belonging and protection, in an otherwise hostile social environment.

The *pirs* promoted and catered to the superstitions of the people, who made regular offerings to them and sought their advice in all personal and religious affairs. Most of them, in addition to being spiritual leaders, were also big landlords and, as such, a formidable force, something that the people could not even think of challenging.

The complete control exercised by the feudal system over every aspect of life in the rural areas freed the administration from the burden of maintaining law and order. In all aspects of government, the advice and help of the local landlord was sought, and in the vast majority of cases the administration turned a blind eye to the violations of law carried out by the landlord—mostly relating to the eviction of peasants, the non-enforcement of *haq-e-shifa* (right of pre-emption), the punishments imposed on the peasants by the *wadera*, and the violation of human rights as enshrined in state laws and constitutions. In exchange, the landlord guaranteed safe roads and freedom from crime and dissent. Thus whole districts could be governed by a handful of policemen, and canals and drainage channels maintained by labour supplied by the feudals. In fact, it was not possible for the state line departments to recruit labour directly, and very often it had to be imported from other parts of the country: the landlord did not want his *haris* to be corrupted by working for cash payments, and under the control of outsiders.

The most important role played by the feudals, however, was political. They controlled the votes, and thus they were able to give the establishment the results it desired in any election. Dissent in the cities was swamped by the voting power of the rural areas, where no dissent was possible. Anyone who rebelled against the system was hounded out and forced to become a *dacoit* (an outlaw) in the jungles.

There were no roads, except for the National Highway and its off-shoots, and the means of transportation was limited to the bullock cart and camel caravans. Thus the outreach of the *mandi* towns was small, and agricultural surpluses had no market. For example, it was easier for Karachi to get grain from the Punjab, than from Dadu or Larkana. Cotton ginning and rice husking were done mechanically in the larger urban centres, and city-produced goods did not find their way into the rural markets. There were no schools, no hospitals or dispensaries, and telecommunications were poor.

These conditions made it difficult, if not impossible, for a middle class to emerge from the rural areas and establish links with the city economy, as had happened earlier in some other parts of Pakistan. The *mohajir* and Punjabi business class filled this void, and joined hands with the *wadera* and the establishment to keep things as they were.

In the Ayub era, many new ideas and institutions were introduced in rural Sindh. Population planning, the Village Aid Programme, agricultural extension services, telecommunications, attempts at road building, hand pumps, agricultural development banks, were promoted. However, the population was not mobilized, nor was any attempt made to raise its level of awareness. The result was that only those aspects of these programmes which suited the feudals were adopted and the others discarded. Thus, budget allocations for roads and schools were frequently allowed to lapse and large loans from the Agricultural Development Bank, Pakistan (ADBP) misused.

Yet these programmes had an impact on the sociology of the rural areas. A large number of children from the feudal families went to schools and universities in Karachi, Lahore and Hyderabad. Travelling became more acceptable, and the more enterprising among the peasants sought jobs in the expanding line departments and government rest houses. Many went to Karachi to work in mills, and came into contact with trade union movements. The 1965 Pakistan–India war brought about the transistor revolution, and for many village people the world became a smaller place. Feudalism, with the tyranny of its barter economy, remained intact, but the rural population became aware of a larger world outside its perimeters.

But it was only with the advent of the PPP and the political movement led by Zulfikar Ali Bhutto between 1967 and 1971 that the foundation for a major change in the rural areas of Sindh was laid. Attempts to consolidate it politically were also made at this time.

Before Mr Bhutto unleashed his rhetoric on the situation in Sindh, the *wadera* was the 'father and protector' and the *haris* were his 'children.' By the time he had finished his first tour of the province, the *waderas* had become the *zalim* and the *hari* the *mazlum*. Previously, the *hari* was not supposed to have any rights; now he was told that they would be given to him, and that there was no law, divine or man-made, that could prevent this happening. A large number of newly-dubbed *zalims* joined the PPP and in their strongholds and from their platforms, radical slogans were raised. A major psychological change occurred in the rural population; it is doubtful if it could have been so sudden or so complete, without the presence of a large number of feudals in the ranks of the PPP.

After Mr Bhutto came to power major development projects were undertaken in Sindh. Roads and telecommunications systems were built and the villagers worked for cash wages on these projects. Along with the roads came the Suzuki revolution: the outreach of the small *mandi* towns increased and, as a result, their size and affluence also increased. Easy access to agricultural loans, mechanized agriculture, and a whole infrastructure was required to cater to the maintenance and operation of tractors, trailers and Suzukis. The supply of electricity expanded, and in the changed socio-political climate, cotton ginning and rice husking units were put up, even in the villages, providing jobs to the peasantry.

Education also expanded and with the founding of new colleges and schools, an increasing number of villagers became doctors and engineers. The hectic development activity of the seventies accommodated them. In addition, job opportunities, so long denied to the people of rural Sindh, became more accessible, and in the process, another avenue of interaction between the urban and rural areas became possible.

Branches of banks and insurance companies were established in even the remotest areas, and local people, patronized by their Member Provincial Assemblies (MPAs) or Member National Assembly (MNAs), were encouraged to man them. Agricultural extension services expanded, the use of fertilizer and pesticides became common and savings increased. The power of the vote had been demonstrated in 1971, and the feudal realized that if he were to win again, he had to be a part of this process of change.

It was because of these developments that the Sindhi middle class expanded and became a political force. Bankers, traders, transporters, tractor lords, factory owners, and the proletariat that served them were no longer the dependants of the feudal system, and it was natural for them to establish direct links with the rural population. So the barter economy died, and as a result a major change took place in class relations in Sindh, a change that would also redefine the *wadera*-administration alliance.

These socio-economic changes in Sindh spelt death for the feudal system. There were instances of *haris* fighting eviction and succeeding. There were cases of *haq-i-shifa* filed by peasants against their landlords. The custom of touching the feet of 'superiors', common in pre-Bhutto days, declined. Peasants sat together and discussed not only politics in general, but also whether they should vote for their landlord or not. Village artisans migrated to the cities and the hereditary occupational structure gave way to the *shagirdi* system. Traditional village entertainers, like *Jogis* and *Langas* were replaced by TV and transistor radios, and they, in their turn, became agriculturists and labourers. In some cases, clansmen stopped paying the yearly tax to their tribal chief, and young men openly questioned the supernatural power of their *pirs*. Although the areas around the larger cities and the highways of Sindh had changed only slowly over a long period of time, its vast hinterland was suddenly torpedoed into the twentieth century during the Bhutto era. Such colossal and sudden changes are bound to create friction. In the Bhutto period, this friction was absorbed by two factors: firstly, that as the change was new, its long-term implications were not really understood by those affected by it, and secondly, that the feudals who were in power were supervising this change and thought that by supporting it, even with reservations, they could continue to enjoy political power. Both these factors disappeared with the coup of 1977, which brought Gen. Ziaul Haq to power and put the country under martial law.

The coup of July 5 and the fiasco of the elections planned for October 1977 highlighted the fact that the *wadera* could no longer guarantee the establishment the results that it wanted in an election. It made it obvious to even the most dull-witted observer of the political scene that the feudals, with a few exceptions, were the political hostages of their *haris*.

Under martial law, the feudals of Sindh lost their political power, and having lost their hold on their peasantry as well, a search for a new relationship with the establishment began. The new middle class also suffered, as it no longer enjoyed the patronage of the state. The socio-economic change which had begun in the mid-sixties continued, but in the absence of politics no interaction between the various classes and the establishment was possible, and hence there were no modifications and adjustments in the administration to accommodate change. The gulf between the people and the state increased, and with it inefficiency, corruption, unemployment and lawlessness.

Things came to a head during the Movement for Restoration of Democracy of 1983. The feudals and the middle class joined hands, but as the movement developed, it became obvious that the middle class had much more political backing than was envisaged. It was not a coincidence that the greatest confrontation took place in the expanding market towns of Moro and Qazi Ahmed, and in traditionally backward areas where change had been the most rapid, such as Dadu and Mehar.

The impotence of the administration to deal with the 'law and order' situation arising out of the movement was clearly demonstrated, even in areas where it had full feudal support. As a result, it lost whatever little credibility it still had. Subsequent army action in certain areas of Sindh forced a number of activists to seek refuge in the forests with *dacoits*. It is rumoured that they tried to politicize the *dacoits*, but in the process were either liquidated by them or became *dacoits* themselves.

The collapse of the administrations, the power demonstrated by the middle class, the growing law and order situation, all created a sense of insecurity in the feudals of Sindh, and as a result it became necessary for them to keep a much larger number of armed retainers than they had previously required. Since the impotence of the administration had been demonstrated, disputes common to rural life began to be settled through the power of the gun. Thus, there are areas where the age old system of getting water by *wara* or turn, has been done away with. The landlord with the most guns has his way.

Such a situation has its own dynamics. The number of guns required to keep one landlord ahead of the other increases every day. The Afghan connection caters to this need and the Kalashnikov has become a common sight in Sindh. Many gangs, originally formed only to protect landlords, have now also taken to *dacoity*, and they terrorise the population. The situation has deteriorated to such an extent that it is not uncommon to see local MPAs driving around surrounded by three or four jeeploads of armed men, many of them with guns of a prohibited bore.

This situation makes it difficult for government functionaries to access land revenue or *abiana*. In certain cases where revenue has not been paid, the government finds it impossible to take any action for its recovery. It is commonly believed that government officials have developed cordial relations with the new power in Sindh, the *dacoits*, and in the present conditions it would be unrealistic to expect otherwise.

Small landlords, businessmen and professionals who cannot command guns to protect themselves are regularly kidnapped and held for ransom, with the result that they are moving out of the area. Some political people in Larkana see in this forced exodus of capital and business an attempt at the reassertion of feudalism.

But the peasant cannot leave. Nor can the small trader or artisan. Nor can the doctors and engineers who belong to the villages, for they cannot get jobs anywhere else in the country. The feudal system which once linked their parents to the establishment is on its last legs. The political activity of the seventies, which did the same thing, is dead and buried. So to fill the void created by the death of previous institutions many villages have formed organizations and got them registered as welfare associations. Their elected office bearers lobby with government organizations for the establishment of schools, dispensaries, roads, bridges, water supply and sanitation. They contact NGOs and concerned professionals for technical help and assistance. They look after law and order in the village and its environs. Some of them have even set up health and education services themselves, and run them partially at their own cost. In some cases they have also captured the union council, defeating the *wadera* of the area.

These village associations are few and far between. However, their number is bound to increase rapidly as they are, for the present, the only hope of consolidating change and creating new relationships which reflect the existing socio-economic situation. They fully realize that the key to their success lies in their capturing the union councils.

Meanwhile, the situation in Sindh will steadily get worse, until the demise of feudalism is institutionalized, and the new classes that have emerged are accommodated politically: an accommodation which will have to be in proportion to their power.

7

Social Changes and the Rural Built Environment

The current housing crisis in Pakistan is the result of the breakdown of the traditional social order which made land, skills and material available to the rural population.

While the housing crisis in the country's urban sector has received a fair amount of media attention in recent years, the problems of housing the rural population have merited far less attention. This is unfortunate as the housing crisis in the rural areas is acute, and unless proper research is carried out and remedial measures are taken, it can only grow worse with time.

The population of Pakistan increases at the rate of 3.2 (1981 Census) per cent per year. To accommodate this increase, 520,000 new housing units are required every year. Of these, 250,000 units are required for the rural areas of the country. However, no more than thirty per cent of the required number are actually constructed, mainly because the cost of access to land for the rural poor is far beyond their financial and social means. Of the units that are constructed, the vast majority are of poor design and of even poorer construction quality. This is because artisanal skills and traditional building materials required for construction are no longer available at affordable prices. Because of these factors, densities on existing plots are increasing, thereby adversely affecting the rural built environment, and the existing housing stock is rapidly deteriorating due to lack of maintenance.

The reason for this crisis is that the old social economy, which organized and governed rural society in Pakistan, and made land, skills and materials available to the village population, has disintegrated due to major social and economic changes, and no new grassroot institutions that can take care of these aspects of life have as yet developed.

Under the old social order, every village had a chunk of land which belonged to the community. This community land was known as *shamlaat* or *ashaish* and was controlled and managed by the feudal, tribal or clan order that controlled the village community. This land was used for cattle grazing; for forest reserves that provided timber to the community for house building and fuel; and for the physical expansion of the village. In this way, land for housing was guaranteed to the rural poor under the old system.

In the past, every village had families of hereditary artisans working for it. The main artisans were masons, carpenters, mat-makers, potters, tanners, barbers, *dhobis*, water carriers and entertainers. They were housed and maintained by the village community which also took care of the expenses incurred for their family weddings and burial of their relatives. These artisans could be called upon to serve any member of the community who contributed agricultural or dairy products, seasonally, for their maintenance. Cash was not used at all in this relationship, nor was the quantum of work done by the craftsman a measure of the payment they received. Artisan families belonging to one village were normally not permitted to work in other settlements, and apart from following their trade, they did no other work.

Most community land had trees on it and also reserves of wattle and reeds. These were jealously protected and a variable quota was reserved for fuel and construction purposes for different families according to their social status. Use of these trees and reserves for commercial purposes was not permitted and wastage was prevented. Mud was excavated from specific areas on community lands and the depressions so caused were used as ponds for the watering and washing of animals.

Previously, the village population had a considerable amount of leisure after harvesting and sowing. These periods were utilized for repairing and improving the house. In the monsoon belt, *lepai* after the rains was a regular ritual. In many areas of Pakistan, nomads from Afghanistan or Balochistan came down to the plains in winter. They were experts in mud-wall-erection and plastering. They helped in putting up new construction and in maintaining the old. However, leisure is a fast-disappearing aspect of life in the rural areas; most families, in order to survive, have to supplement their agricultural incomes by working in other sectors. The nomads, meanwhile, have ceased to visit the plains. Their movements have been curtailed by frontier restrictions and changes in their own socio-economic structure.

The design of houses and the planning of villages followed systems that had been developed over centuries. They catered to social and economic activity both at the family and community level. Thus a tanner's house was different from that of a barber. Due to centuries of experience, village artisans were experts in the use of traditional materials, and had developed techniques that responded to the climate of the area.

Before the turn of the century, all exchange relations in the rural economy were based on barter. It was because of this factor that social and economic mobility for the rural population was difficult, if not impossible; caste distinctions remained intact and the economic self-sufficiency of the village was ensured. The introduction of cash as a means of exchange, along with massive urban growth and industrialization has destroyed the political structure of the rural areas and made village self-sufficiency impossible.

At different stages after the First World War, industrially-produced goods started to find their way into the rural economy and by the 1960s village artisans in the more developed areas began to calculate the labour they put into production in rupees per man day. Mechanization, fertilizers, new variety of seeds and pesticides, all acquired through cash transactions, followed. New modes of transport revolutionized marketing and since the generation of cash became the main objective, all rural produce that did not have an industrially-produced alternative became a marketable commodity.

With the break-up of the old rural structure and social cohesion, many village community lands have been encroached upon by the influential classes. Where such encroachment has not taken place, they are either a subject of dispute or are not administered. In many places, the communities have leased them out to outsiders or even sold them. Due to these factors, the acquisition of affordable land for housing has become very difficult for rural people, especially in the agricultural areas where land values are high.

Given the conditions described above, craftsmen migrated to the urban areas where they could earn more in cash terms, and in most rural areas the old system of village communities maintaining artisans is dead or dying. This change has had three effects. One, it has made social and economic mobility possible, thus putting an end to the hereditary artisanal tradition and this in turn has adversely affected the competence of the craftsmen. Two, it has created an acute shortage of artisans in most rural areas. And three, it has put the hiring of skills beyond the reach of the rural poor and lower middle income groups. Thus, new houses are of much poorer quality than the older ones and are devoid of surface decorations and details that characterize the older houses.

The demand for cash has also led to the sale by the village community, or its traditional chiefs, of forests and plantations on community lands. This has raised the price of timber and reeds and, in the absence of effective village government, made the rural communities dependent on contractors for meeting their demand for construction material.

A large number of villages have now become semi-urban and this trend is likely to continue. Electricity, piped water schemes and sewerage systems are being demanded and acquired. Mechanized transport has to be catered to, and with a change in production techniques and relationships, the old pattern of planning a home, or the village itself, will have to undergo changes. In a haphazard manner these changes have already begun, and the copying of urban styles reflects the unequal relationship that the rural areas have with urban settlements.

All these factors have made it impossible for the poor in the rural areas to acquire land, purchase building materials or hire skilled labour for constructing a house. This, along with the break up of traditional structures and the absence of new appropriate institutions, has marginalized them. As a result, in many areas, landless labour is forced to work at much less than half the minimum wage, or even bond themselves to landlords, so that they may have a place to stay. In such cases, their families do *begar* for their benefactors. So, while cash has broken down old feudal relations, the new order has created a new set of problems for the poor. These problems can, to some extent, be overcome if access to land for house building is made available.

There is a complete lack of research and information on the nature or extent of change related to the housing sector in the rural areas. Issues like land-use changes (very important in the case of central Punjab); changes in densities; degradation of housing stock; accumulated deficit estimates in housing; performance of the housing industry; development of new functions due to change in production methods and marketing have yet to be researched. Without an understanding of these issues it is difficult to formulate a policy for rural housing. A database, however, does exist in the form of the 1980 housing census, and needs to be built upon and analyzed.

8

Khajji Cooperatives and the Culture of Globalization

Anwar Rashid is the director of the Orangi Charitable Trust (OCT). The OCT is one of the OPP institutions established by the celebrated social scientist, Akhtar Hameed Khan. The OCT operates a credit programme through which it provides loans to farmers and fishermen. These loans are used collectively by farmers' cooperatives or grass root NGOs for the purchase of seeds, fertilizer, pesticide, tractor hire, and to survive from sowing to harvesting. These cooperatives and NGOs also on-lend these loans to individual producers. These loans have replaced the loans that the producers took from middlemen at interest rates as high as 10 per cent per month. One of the cooperatives that has benefited from the OCT programme is the Khajji (dates) Cooperative Society (KCS) of date growers in the Khairpur district of Sindh.

Anwar Rashid has written a small book on OCT's relationship with the KCS. Date farming is carried out on 62,000 acres in the Khairpur district where there are 1.977 million date trees. These trees produce 125,000 metric tons of dates and as such date farming is a major economic and employment activity in the Khairpur district.[1] Most of the dates are grown on small land holdings of between two to ten acres. However, the financing of production and control of marketing of dates is controlled by middlemen who provide loans at high rates of interest to the producers for purchase of fertilizer and other chemicals required for production and also for the producers' survival from pruning to harvesting. Even after the produce has been delivered to the middlemen, payment for it is made two months later when an increase in the market price of dates has taken place.

Date growers individually work out the loans they require for production purposes and for survival, and the middleman provides them the money at an interest rate of 10 per cent per month. In addition, on the value of the produce he charges 10 per cent as commission and 2 per cent as *dallali* or brokerage fee. Thus, on a produce value of Rs100,000, Rs10,000 is deducted as commission and Rs2,000 as *dallali* and the producer gets Rs88,000. An additional 10 per cent per month is deducted on loans which have been taken. The OCT gave an initial loan of Rs193,450 to the KCS as a result of which a group of 25 producers saved over Rs350,000 in purchases related to date production. The programme has expanded manifold since then and the cooperative now consists of 338 members.[2]

In Pakistan, there are numerous *tanzeems* (organizations) and cooperatives that have been created or built-up by 'well meaning' NGOs and development practitioners, often with foreign funds. Most of them become ineffective after their funding is withdrawn or they get engaged in issues that are important to their donors.[3] The important question is how was the KCS established and why has it become increasingly effective? The answers to these questions are provided by the life and involvements of Qurban Buriro, one of the two early activists of the KCS.

Qurban's father was a date grower. His farm was on three acres in the Khairpur district and consisted of 150 to 200 trees. He died when Qurban was 14 years old. After that Qurban looked after the trees. Initially, he contracted out the management at Rs150 per tree but soon realized that if he did this himself, he could manage to get Rs600 to Rs700 per tree. Self-management brought him into touch with the middleman system. Unlike the sons of other date growers, Qurban acquired an education. He graduated in Economics from the Lateef University in 2002. The graduation made him eligible for government and NGO employment and he joined the Poverty Eradication Network (PEN), an NGO based in Khairpur. Later, he worked for the Indus Resource Centre (IRC), another Khairpur based NGO. According to Qurban, the date growers of Khairpur have never questioned the middleman system. They have accepted it as normal. He also says that had he not acquired a university education, he would not have worked for PEN and IRC. And had he not worked for these NGOs, he and his friends would not have been able to develop the vision which led to the creation and expansion of the KCS. One sees this relationship between the effectiveness of local organizations and the education and exposure of young activists from poor exploited communities to new ideas, all over Pakistan.

A number of important changes are taking place in the date production and marketing business. For one, the cost of production has gone up. Dap fertilizer which cost Rs1,400 six months ago now comes for Rs3,100. *Rangkot,* the local name for a chemical used in the production process, was Rs3,500 for 50 kg last year. It costs now Rs7,300. These increases have reduced the profit margin for producers since the market price has not increased in proportion to production costs. Middlemen however have been able to increase their profits in spite of production cost increases. Qurban does not know the exact reasons for the increase in production costs but he is aware that this is due to the removal of subsidies on agriculture by the government. He correctly attributes the removal of these subsidies to structural adjustment and to WTO conditionalities. According to him, the other date growers also think on similar lines.

Anwar Rashid and Qurban Buriro are currently working on a new project. Dates are purchased by middlemen at Rs800 per 40 kg at the time of harvesting. Three months later the price goes up to Rs1,200. If the OCT gives a loan to the growers so that they can hold on to the sale of their produce for three months, the producers can benefit by an increase of 50 per cent in the sale price. The OCT interest rate is 18 per cent per year which means that it will be 6 per cent for four months or Rs48 for a loan of Rs800. So on each 40 kg the producer will make a profit of Rs352 (Rs400 profit minus Rs48 interest). Anwar Rashid and Qurban Buriro feel that if the state provides a loan facility of Rs2 billion, the poverty of the date growers and their dependents will be eradicated.

Other changes are also taking place in the date business. Previously, the vast majority of middlemen operating in the Khairpur district were Hindu *Banyas* from Sindh. Over the past two to three years, middlemen from the Punjab have started to come to Khairpur to purchase dates. They have also set up a storage facility for 5,000 to 6,000 maunds (one maund is about 40 kg) in Hussainabad in the Khairpur district. They charge 6 per cent as commission as opposed to the 10 per cent charged by the Sindhi middlemen. In addition, the date grower can store his produce here, but he can sell it whenever he wishes to. The Lahore middlemen have no objection to Khairpur producers taking their produce individually or collectively to Lahore. If they do that, the Punjab middlemen provide them with free board and lodging and the free use of the telephone.

Allah Rakha is a middleman in the Khajji market in Karachi. According to him, the reason why the Punjab middlemen have become active is related to the communication revolution and the Pakistan government's reaction to the WTO regime. Export of any produce has now become a very simple affair. Red-tapism has been removed and expenses on the export process have been considerably reduced. Punjabi middlemen are better organized, connected and educated and thus able to benefit from these opportunities. Most of the date produce purchased by the Punjab middlemen goes to India and Afghanistan. Dubai is also a major market through which it is diverted to different countries. Afghanistan is near the Punjab while one can now export to India legally only through Wagah.

Almost all information regarding the purchasers and sellers and their requirements are available on the Internet. The Indian purchasers use the Internet extensively for searching the market and making deals. So do purchasers from other countries. Middlemen and traders who can access the Internet and communicate through it are now the real beneficiaries. The Punjabis are way ahead of the Sindhis in the use of these new communication processes. As Allah Rakha puts it 'the world has changed and those who use the new tools are the ones who will control trade and commerce'. Allah Rakha has done his matriculation but he cannot read and write English properly and as such he cannot access the Internet. However, he has got his son enrolled in a computer programming course whose fee is Rs62,000 per semester. This investment, he says, will help him access the international market and to deal with the requirements that globalization has imposed on all trade and commerce.

Allah Rakha is sceptical about the possibility of grower's cooperatives replacing middlemen. 'They are uneducated people with no business sense. How can they replace us? Even if they do, it will take at least 20 years and in those 20 years we are told international companies will be producing and marketing produce. No small landowners and no middlemen.'

Source: Author's conversations with Anwar Rashid, Qurban Buriro and Allah Rakha in June 2008.

NOTES

1. Anwar Rashid, *Khajji Cooperative Society*, Ushba Publishing International, 2005.
2. Ibid.
3. For details see Akbar Zaidi, *Issues in Pakistan's Economy*, OUP, 2005 and Arif Hasan, *Working With Communities*, City Press Karachi, 2001.

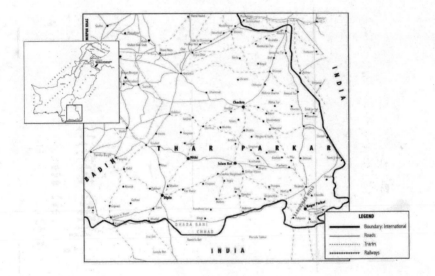

PART THREE: THE DESERT

Pakistan has many desert areas. Tharparkar is the best known of them all. There are a number of reasons for this. Tharparkar has a comparatively large population and the desert can still support it and the livestock that is an integral part of its economy. Its artisanal skills produce exquisite handicrafts which are valued by the elite and middle classes. It is comparatively close to Karachi. Like other deserts, it is often hit by droughts. Due to a mix of these reasons, unlike other desert regions, it has been of considerable interest to NGOs and politicians.

In 1987, the effects of a long drought in Tharparkar created near famine conditions in the desert. UNICEF and Save the Children Fund (SCF) UK were involved in relief operations along with the Government of Sindh. Collectively they appointed me as a consultant to review their programmes and to assess the drought and famine conditions. It was obvious from the very beginning that drought was not the cause of the famine. Droughts are a common occurrence in Tharparkar as in other deserts. Famine was the result of the inability of the desert populations to deal with drought conditions due to major social and economic changes that had taken place in the last two decades. The result of this consultancy was a report, extracts from which constitute Chapter 9.

The report's recommendations led to the setting up of the Tharparkar Rural Development Project (TRDP) which was supported by SCF UK. Since then it has been upgraded to a national NGO and named 'Thardeep'. The Project is basically a research and extension effort and has initiated many development programmes in which the desert communities are involved. In 1992, I was asked by the Government of Sindh, SCF and UNICEF to evaluate the work of the TRDP. Chapter 10 is derived from this evaluation. I have added a postscript to this chapter so as to identify the changes that have taken place between 1992 and 2007, when I last visited Tharparkar for any length of time.

9

Tharparkar: 1987

The desert area of Tharparkar district, generally known as Thar, consists of the *talukas* of Mithi, Chachro and Nagar and parts of the Diplo and Umerkot *talukas*. The total area of the desert is 22,000 square kilometres and the population is between 0.7 to 0.8 million.[1] The animal population is estimated at 1.5 to 1.8 million.[2] Except for the south-eastern part of the Nagar *taluka*, the desert consists of sand dunes between which are flat plains where agriculture can take place.

Agriculture in the desert is entirely dependent on rainfall. This rainfall occurs between July and September and in normal years varies between 200 to 300 millimetres.[3] Sowing is done immediately after the first rains. The main crop is *bajra* (millet) and it matures in seventy to seventy-five days. However, more than one shower, preferably three, is required to produce a good crop. Consequently a smaller quantity of rain spread over two months produces better results than one heavy shower. In addition to millet, which formed, until recently, the staple diet of the people, *till* (sesame), *gowar* (fodder) and cluster beans are grown. The stalks of the crop are used as supplementary feed for the animals.

After the rains, the Thar desert supports extensive grass growth which provides high value feed to livestock. In drought years, however, sheep and cattle are forced to migrate. Goats, donkeys and camels can manage to survive on shrubs such as *ak* (*Callotropis procera*), *booh* (*Aerva tomentosa*), *phog* (*Calligonum*) and *khip* (*Leptadenia*). Depending on the intensity of rainfall, grass in the pasture land can grow up to three feet high and can be cut and stored as fodder for the animals.

WATER

All water sources in the desert are charged by the rains. These water sources consist of wells, *tarais* and covered tanks. In different areas of the desert wells behave differently. Certain wells retain fresh water in spite of long periods of drought. Others become brackish by February or March every year in spite of heavy summer rains, in which case the population has to cart water from perennial fresh water wells which may be six to eight miles away, or migrate with their livestock to the barrage areas. Wells behave in this manner in a small part of Thar and are mainly to be found in the Chachro and Umerkot *talukas* and a small part of Parkar in the Nagarparkar *taluka*. Of the twenty-four places visited only four faced this problem. However, in periods of successive drought (for example, 1951 to 1955) the amount of water in some perennial fresh water wells also falls and people can only withdraw small quantities at a time. The depth of the wells also varies from 20 to 30 feet in certain areas of the Diplo and Nagar *talukas* to over 200 feet in certain areas of the Chachro *taluka*.

All settlements in the desert have their *tarais* or ponds, where rain water collects. A *tarai* is a natural depression between sand dunes. Water in large *tarais* can, if the monsoons are adequate, last for over six months. The animals are watered at the *tarai*, and shallow wells are dug in the *tarais* once the surface water has evaporated. In the larger *tarais*, permanent deep wells are sunk with platforms raised above the *tarai* water level around them. These wells in the *tarais* constitute the most reliable sources of potable water in the desert. The *tarais* are also convenient as animal watering points. As long as there is water in them, water for animals does not need to be drawn from wells. The storage capacity of *tarais* is sometimes increased by building embankments in appropriate places on their periphery and by desilting them annually or bi-annually. Traditionally, the village population, organized by the *Thakur* of the settlement, would undertake the maintenance of the embankments and the desilting of the *tarai*.

In villages where perennial sources of fresh water are unreliable, or far away from the settlements, people also construct covered, surface water tanks. These are really miniature *tarais* with a thatched roof on them and belong to extended families and not to the whole community. They are used exclusively for human consumption and seldom last for more than four months.

Rainfall figures show that every four to six years a drought period of two to three years sets in. Thus, there were major drought periods between 1951 and 1956; 1962 and 1963; 1968 and 1969; 1979 and 1981 and again 1985 to 1987. The worst recorded drought occurred between 1951 and 1956 when there was no rain at all in most of Thar except in 1954, when it was abnormally heavy.[4]

1981 to 1984 were exceptionally good rainfall years in Thar. Showers were almost evenly spread out over July, August and September and so agricultural yields were high. In 1985, however, rainfall in large parts of Umerkot and Chachro *talukas* was as low as 30 millimetres. This rainfall, again, was spread out over two months and a crop was possible in most areas of the two *talukas*. In Nagar, Mithi and Diplo rain was normal in 1985 and there was no drought. In 1986, the monsoons failed on two counts. First, rainfall was low. Second, it all occurred in the last week of July and the first week of August, making agriculture impossible. Pasture yield was also far poorer than in the preceding years. In 1987 the monsoons failed again and the press reported that due to the drought, famine conditions prevailed in Thar.

THE DROUGHT

The villages visited in the Mithi, Nagar, Diplo and the south-eastern portions of the Chachro *talukas* had a normal crop in 1985. However, production in 1986 dropped by over 70 per cent and there has been no crop in 1987. The villages visited between Chachro and Khinsar, and between Khinsar and Umerkot, give a different picture. Agricultural production in these villages in 1985 was less than 50 per cent of 1984. In 1986 it was no more than 10 per cent of the 1984 average.[5] Farmers fear that if the fields are not cultivated next year, then the top soil will be carried away by the desert winds, reducing the productivity of the land.

From time immemorial, the desert population has migrated to the irrigated areas or the flood plains of the Indus during the dry season, between February and June. In this period, the wheat is harvested in the irrigated areas and the desert population provides labour for this harvesting. The migrants are accompanied by their cattle. It is generally agreed by the elders in the villages that before 1972 it was rare for the Tharis to be paid cash for the labour they provided. They were given protection, provided grazing grounds for their cattle and allowed to take back the wheat stalks to the desert as fodder for their animals. In addition, they sold *ghee* (clarified butter) to the irrigated areas for cash. It is held that the irrigated areas depended entirely on Thari *ghee* before *vanaspati* replaced it in the seventies. Tharis also provided labour for cotton picking in central Sindh. They received a part of the cotton crop as payment. This cotton was carried back to the desert and turned into cloth on handlooms by the *Meghwars* in the desert settlements. The cotton picking season, however, coincided with the good months in the desert and so this migration was usually small. In the seventies, sugarcane production was introduced in the irrigated areas and Thari migrant labour is now used for its harvesting, which takes place between October and January.

Not all the castes from the desert migrate to the barrage areas. The Thakurs and the Nooris, who constitute the upper castes, do not migrate at all. Their cattle is taken across to the barrage lands by people hired for the purpose. Previously, they were paid in food, milk and *ghee*, but now they are paid in cash. The Kohli caste, who are agriculturists and share croppers, migrate with their animals. It is estimated that in the sugarcane harvesting period 50 per cent of all Kohlis with their families and animals migrate to the irrigated areas. It is further estimated that 90 per cent of them migrate for wheat harvesting. The migration of the Bhil caste seems to be smaller, and a minority among them migrate with their families. Muslim castes such as the Bajirs do not normally migrate with their families, except in drought years. One can safely assume that in normal years 15 per cent of the population migrates in the sugarcane harvesting and cotton picking seasons. This increases to well over 40 per cent in the wheat harvesting season. In certain areas such as Nagarparkar where there is a large Kohli population, and in certain parts of the Chachro *taluka*, where there are water problems, migration can be as high at 70 per cent in the dry season.

The larger migration in 1987 affected the labour market in the barrage areas in both agriculture and trade. Labourers in the animal markets in Mirpurkhas and Judho complain that it is no longer easy for them to get daily jobs at the normal rate of 30 rupees per day. Thari migrants are willing to work for as little as 15 rupees per day. Similarly, an excess of migrant Thari labour has brought down the rate of agricultural labour from 20 to 15 rupees or, in some cases, even less. The rate of sugarcane harvesting per maund has also fallen by 20 per cent. In spite of low wages there is considerable unemployment and there are also other problems. Pasture land is insufficient in the barrage areas for the large number of Thari cattle that has moved to the irrigated areas because of the drought. Fodder is not scarce nor has its price gone up, but due to the decrease in wages and the larger requirements this year, the immigrants cannot afford to buy it. In addition, the Thari population has to now send back money to dependants in the desert for the purchase of grain for everyday use.

In good years, livestock migrate to the barrage area with those castes who migrate with their families. According to estimates made as a result of conversations with the Tharis in the barrage areas and in the desert, no more than 20 per cent of the total livestock moves out in years of normal rainfall. On the contrary, in exceptionally good years livestock from the barrage is brought over to graze in the desert. The 20 per cent migration that does take place begins in February and the animals return in time for the first rains in July.

In 1986 there was a 50 per cent increase in the movement of animals from certain parts of the Chachro and Umerkot *talukas*. This migration took place in March and the animals returned in July. According to the villagers, this migration took place because the pasture land had not been adequately replenished because of meagre rains in 1985. However, the human and animal population faced no major problem as a result of this movement. Other parts of Thar were unaffected. In 1986, there were meagre rains all over Thar and the grasslands were depleted by March 1987. A large proportion of the cattle was shifted to the barrage areas. However, the sheep, goats and some cattle necessary for fulfilling the milk needs of the people were kept and maintained in the desert. The condition of these animals deteriorated and by July they had become very weak. They were not shifted for two reasons. One, because the people waited for rain, and two, because they were assured, by certain quarters, of government assistance. When it did not rain, the population started shifting cattle and other livestock to the barrage area in late August. In many cases, this movement took place in September.

Almost 96 per cent of all livestock deaths occurred during their movement to the barrage lands as the cattle had become too weak to make this journey. People who were able to transport their animals by GMCs (six-wheel drive trucks) were able to save them. However, the cost of transportation by GMC is exorbitant. A number of livestock were also saved through rail transportation from certain parts of the Umerkot *taluka*.

THE PROCESS OF CHANGE

In 1961 the population of Thar was 396,993. In 1981 it had increased to 774,617. That means that in twenty years it increased by 95 per cent, or at a rate of 4.75 per cent a year. Thus the rate of increase was 1.55 per cent higher than the national average of 3.2 per cent. During this twenty-year period the urban population increased by 362 per cent and the rural by 86 per cent.[6] In addition to natural growth there has also been a migration into Thar from Indian Rajasthan. Four hundred families were settled in Nagar after the 1965 war and an additional three thousand in the Chachro taluka.

According to the figures of the animal husbandry department at Mirpurkhas there were 445,240 animals in the desert in 1976.[7] In 1986 this figure stood at 1,268,960, an increase of 185 per cent. The figures sound incredible, but the residents of the settlements visited also give similar figures for the increase of animal heads in their villages. The largest increase, 538 per cent, has been in sheep. This is because of the expanding trade in wool and the growing dependence of the Karachi and Hyderabad cottage industry on it.

This growth has put pressure on land. Under the settlement carried out by the British colonial government, large tracts of land were identified and preserved as pasture lands or gowcher (cow grazing lands). The thakurs (upper caste Hindus who owned most of the land in Thar) and patels (village headmen) were responsible for protecting these lands from cultivation and deforestation. This alliance between the feudal order and the government worked as long as the thakurs and patels had power. However, major social and economic changes that have taken pace in the desert over the last twenty-five years have all but demolished the old social order, and changed its relationship with the state institutions. As a result, most of the gowcher lands have been taken over by important persons in the area. However, what government records do not show is that much of these lands have been encroached upon. An increase of only 15 per cent in the total cultivated area is shown in government records between 1981 and 1986.[8] On the other hand, people in all the settlements visited complained that 50 to 80 per cent of these lands were now under the plough. In some villages the people said that gowcher lands had simply ceased to exist. In addition, there was general consensus among the villagers that trees from the gowcher land had been cut for firewood and house construction, and that the phog shrub, which holds the soil together, had been used in a big way for making dry hedges around the ever-increasing houses and settlements. This depletion has been on so large a scale that large tracts of land have been turned into absolute desert.

According to the land grant policy of the government a one-year contract for cultivating gowcher or government wasteland can be acquired by local landlords. This contract is known as yaksala or 'yearly'.

If the landlord can hold this land for five years through yearly leases, then he can buy it at 15 rupees per acre. According to the residents of Thar, large tracts of good pasture land have been taken over by local landlords under this policy, thus depriving the local population of grazing areas. Also, after the 1965 and 1971 wars a large number of Muslim refugees moved into Thar.[9] They were given twelve acres of land per family from government wasteland. As per government records this land amounted to 42,000 acres. According to the local population the refugees occupied double the land allotted to them.

The older residents of the settlements visited remember the days when there were large tracts of pastureland in the now irrigated areas. In dry seasons, when the Thari pasturelands were depleted, the cattle moved to the pasturelands in the Badin district. In the barrage areas also there were large uncultivated spaces to which the desert population could move its animals while it worked as agricultural labour for wheat harvesting or cotton picking. The entire Badin district was colonized by the canals from the Ghulam Mohammad Barrage in the mid and late fifties, and extensions of the Jumrao canal system have brought a larger part of the non-Thar part of Tharparkar under cultivation. Thus, in addition to having lost their pasturelands in the desert, the Tharis have also lost the possibility of grazing their animals in the neighbouring areas.

The economy of Thar before the 1960s was a subsistence one. Before the 1960s the people's transactions with each other, and with the outside world, were based on barter. The desert people produced almost everything they needed for their subsistence. Cloth, shoes, blankets were all manufactured locally. Food consisted entirely of millet bread (*bajray ki roti*) and yogurt or *lassi*. Tea, biscuits, city-made clothes and shoes were unknown. Shops in villages were non-existent. Animals were rarely sold for cash and the only source of monetary income was from the sale of *ghee* (clarified butter) to the barrage lands. In fact, a large part of Sindh depended on *ghee* from the desert. Middlemen, however, did not go into the desert in search of *ghee* but purchased it from the Tharis working in the barrage areas during the wheat harvesting season. Land belonged entirely to the upper castes who controlled every aspect of life in the villages. They mobilized the people for maintenance of embankments and *tarais* and protected government wasteland from encroachment and deforestation. However, from 1947 onwards, changes slowly started to take place in the desert. In the post-1965 period, cash was introduced extensively as a means of exchange, and after 1972 the

Box: People Prefer Tarais and the Government Hand Pumps

Kabul Khanna Goth in the Thar desert consists of about 100 houses and over 1,000 animals. The village cluster is built on the hillocks and two wells in a depression, about two furlongs from the cluster, serve the population. There is a_tarai about one mile from the village.

In summer, the water disappears from the wells and has to be extracted in small quantities from the wet sand that remains. Alternatively, people dig wells in the *tarai*. These wells are of a temporary nature and sometimes become inoperative in the later summer months, in which case the villagers are forced to migrate with their animals to the barrage lands.

The people are aware of the advantages of a hand pump at their wells. However, they feel that the fly-wheel type hand pumps which were installed in their villages in 1973 are difficult to operate. They also informed us that the fly-wheel type hand pumps were abandoned because they failed to provide water in the drought season and not because of maintenance problems. Hand pumps are welcome, but there must be a guarantee that they provide water the year round, otherwise the people do not want them. The villagers are more interested in developing their *tarais* than installing hand pumps at the wells. They feel that if the *tarai* can be cleaned out and some protective construction can be made against its silting, then its water retention can be improved and as such the wells near it or in it can perhaps become perennial. Before the *tarai* used to be regularly cleaned out by the villagers as the owner of the village, Kabul Khanna, was interested in agriculture and cattle. He used to organize the people and get them to work. If investment was required (it seldom was) he made it, and recovered it from the people. Now he has gone into commerce and trade. The villagers have no tradition of communal work except through the *zamindar's* initiative and authority.

Another village, Khisar Goth consists of 500 houses and the population owns about 25,000 animals. There are wells in the depression near the village. The wells become almost dry in summer and so the major part of the population is forced to migrate. About fifteen kilometres away there are wells which never go dry, but do become brackish, and animals are usually shifted there in late summer. Every year a large number of animals (about 5,000) are sold at Umerkot for the Karachi market from this village.

Here again the villagers prefer development of the *tarai* to installation of hand pumps. Again the disintegration of the village social structure has made it impossible to maintain the *tarai* properly. Before, the *wadera* through *beygar* organized the maintenance. Now he has gone into commerce. The villagers do not blame him as there is very little that one earns from agriculture and livestock as compared to business. Three years ago the *tarai* was cleaned by some government agency through the UC with the help of a tractor. The silt was pushed to the edges of the *tarai* instead of being removed, and it came back with the rains. To a question as to why the people did not point out this shortcoming while the work was going on, Arbab Ali, a Khisar shopkeeper, replied that they do not interfere in government matters.

Source: *Report on a Joint Assessment of Sindh Rural Water Supply Project*, March 1986.

integration of Thar's economy with the Karachi and Hyderabad market began. There are a number of reasons for these changes.

The creation of Pakistan as an Islamic state in 1947 had a major psychological impact on the sociology of Thar. The old order, dominated by the Hindu higher castes, had to hand over some of its power to the Muslim landlords. This weakened the government-feudal relationship and made encroachments on government waste lands possible. Then came the creation of the Ghulam Mohammad Barrage in the fifties and the subsequent colonization of pasture land adjacent to the desert. This further deprived the Tharis of grazing tracts. Thus their relationship with the landlords of the barrage areas changed as their dependence on barrage agricultural produce for feeding their animals increased. In addition, the colonization through the Ghulam Mohammad Barrage and extension of the Jumrao Canal system also introduced a new sort of farmer in the barrage areas. This farmer had links with the outside world, was not a native of the soil, and through official patronage could receive government loans for agriculture. Consequently, his relationship with the migrant Tharis was bound to be different from that of the older landlords. It was through these new landlords that cash payments to the Thari seasonal agricultural labour were introduced.

SOCIAL DISINTEGRATION

During the Ayub era major changes were attempted in the barrage areas. New varieties of seed and fertilizer were introduced. Loans for agricultural purposes were made available and mechanization of agriculture was promoted. Although these measures were not entirely successful during the tenure of the Ayub government, they laid the basis for future developments and had a major impact on the thinking of the people. At the same time, development projects on a small scale, such as the erection of windmills for pumping out water and the building of dams in Nagar, were undertaken. In addition, through the Basic Democracies System, people elected their own representatives. Through these developments the people of Thar, so long isolated from the mainstream of economic and political life in Sindh, came into contact with the outside world. Industrially manufactured vegetable oil as a substitute for Thari *ghee*, factory-produced shoes, cloth and agricultural implements, also made their appearance in Thar along with tea, biscuits and white sugar. The most powerful impact on the social structure of

Thar, however, came with the 1965 Indo-Pakistan war. As a result of the war many higher-caste Hindus fled to India and their lands were given to their lower-caste Hindu *haris*. Muslims from Indian Rajasthan also moved into Thar. This further weakened the *thakurs* and *patels* and intensified the disintegration of the old order. At this time, mechanized transport through GMCs increased from about six to ten trucks in 1964, to over twenty-five in 1967.

After the 1971 war Thar was occupied by India. In 1972 it was handed back to Pakistan. A large number of the remaining Hindu merchants and landlords migrated to India and the process of social disintegration begun in 1965 was completed. The post-war economy of Thar was in a shambles and the city traders stepped in to colonize Thar. All the shops in the villages visited were opened after 1972, and the majority of them after 1980. Middlemen started visiting the desert to collect wool, animals and handicrafts and Tharis started using city-made shoes, clothes, soap, matches and other consumer items. Tea replaced *lassi* as the main beverage and wheat bread became popular.

The changes described above were accompanied by changes in the barrage lands as well. Industrially manufactured *ghee* replaced Thari *ghee*. Mechanization of transport and improvement in roads, along with an increase in the price of agricultural produce, changed the economy of the barrage areas. Tharis were now paid in cash for their labour and they needed this cash for purchasing the necessities of life. By 1974, one can safely say that Thar had been colonized by the city market forces and its dependence on cash was complete.

As a result of the social and economic changes that have taken place, the Tharis' eating and dressing habits have also changed. Vegetables, meat and tea are now part of their diet. The vast majority purchase industrially manufactured shoes and clothes. Since cash is needed for these items, *bajra* is no longer stored for bad years but sold in the nearby markets or to wandering middlemen. Similarly, livestock has become a marketable commodity and everything possible is done to increase its quantity. This change is so enormous that Hindus, who previously for religious reasons did not sell cattle for slaughter, now have no qualms in doing so.

Middlemen are now an important economic power in the desert. They are the suppliers of essential items, money-lenders and purchasers of produce. The dependence of the population on them has increased to such an extent that whatever power the *thakurs* and *patels* may have retained is dying out.

The search for social mobility among the desert population is obvious in their new aspirations. Where schools are available an increasing number of lower caste Hindus and Muslims send their children to them. In all the villages visited there is a demand for hospitals and medicines. The Meghwars have stopped producing leather and now animal skins are sold directly to the city markets. The reason is that tanning is considered to be a 'dirty' job and tanners have traditionally been considered 'untouchables'. The Meghwars have given up tanning with the hope of improving their social status. Similarly, there are young Kohli doctors and engineers in the desert and an increasing number of Tharis are going into trade in the expanding market towns of Thar. Before 1961, Umerkot was the only town in the desert.

These economic changes have resulted in the breakdown of social cohesion. Caste barriers have weakened and the village populations insist that the government through the Union Councils (UC) or other institutions should look after the *tarais* and embankments or dig wells as they have no faith in *Thakurs*, *Patels* and *Mukhis*.

DESERTIFICATION

The demographic, social and economic changes that have taken place in the desert have resulted in the desertification of Thar. The process of desertification and the reasons for it can be clearly identified.

Due to the increase of population larger areas of land are required for cultivation. This has led to the disappearance of pasture land and an end of the system of crop rotation. Previously 50 per cent of agricultural land was cultivated and the remaining was set aside for animal grazing. The animal droppings fertilized this remaining land and the following year the cultivated part was set aside for grazing. This system produced higher yields and also provided extra pasture lands. This system of crop rotation is no longer followed.

On one hand, the animal population has increased by 185 per cent. On the other, pasture lands have decreased considerably, both in the desert and in the neighbouring areas. Thus overgrazing of the pasture land has taken place. Older residents in the villages report that twenty years ago grass would grow up to 5 feet high after a good monsoon year. It could be cut and stacked for over three years. Now it hardly reaches a height of two feet and there is never a sufficient quantity available for storage for more than one season. In addition, there is a general consensus among the older residents of the settlements visited that animals today are of a far inferior quality than their counterparts of ten years ago. According to the UNDP consultant's report, 'Review of Strategy and Plans for the Development of Arid Zones of Sindh Province' (February 1987), the appropriate stocking ratio for excellent range-land condition is quoted as 30 cattle equivalent units per 100 hectare. In Thar, the stocking ratio is 68 head per 100 hectare in degraded range-land. The report feels that the range-lands in Thar in their present poor condition are incapable of supporting the current livestock population.

There are many indications of desertification in Thar. Trees that normally grow in good soil conditions such as Khejri (*Prosopis cineraria*), Rohiro (*Tecoma undulata*) and Beri (*Zizyphus mauritiana*) have almost disappeared. Trees and shrubs which have replaced them are the Ak (*Calotropis procera*) and *Aristida funiculata*. Both are multiplying rapidly and are indicative of degraded rangeland. In addition, the *Phog* species (*Calligonum polygonoides*) has also become scarce, and between Chachro, Khinsar and Umerkot has almost disappeared. *Phog* is an important soil stabilizer and in the areas where it has become scarce, soil erosion is taking place. This is obvious from the fact that the roots of almost all large trees are visible and the main trunk begins a good one to two feet above the present earth level. Because of selective grazing, it seems that only shrubs and trees that are unpalatable to the animal population are likely to survive. Unfortunately, these plants are not good soil stabilizers.

As a result of desertification the land will not be able to meet the demands of the animal population even in good years. If animal husbandry has to continue to be a source of livelihood for the population of Thar, then either fodder will have to be imported to the desert, or a massive programme for range land management and rehabilitation will have to be undertaken. In the absence of these programmes the people of Thar will have to depend increasingly on the barrage areas and the towns in Sindh for jobs, and a remittance economy will emerge in the desert.

Transportation in the desert before the 1950s was entirely by animals or private jeeps. The first GMCs (six-wheel drive trucks) started plying in 1956. These carried only passengers and were two in number. By 1967 these had increased to twenty-five, but still they catered mainly to passengers to and from the desert. In the mid-seventies there was a big increase in the GMCs and there are now over 100 plying from Naukot to the desert and over fifty from Umerkot.[10] The increase in their number took place not only because of an increase in passenger traffic but more so because of the need to transport grain and daily necessities of life from and to Thar. The urban centres of Thar and their markets developed and expanded as a result of this mechanised transport.

Maintenance costs of GMCs is about 35,000 to 50,000 rupees per year. Fuel consumption is about one litre of diesel for every one and a quarter kilometre. An average GMC can carry up to 7,000 kilos. Two wheel drives capable of carrying the same weight on normal roads would require no more than 10,000 rupees as maintenance costs and would cover four kilometres in one litre of diesel.[11] Thus the cost of maintenance and operation would be reduced to less than one-third of the present costs if a road system was built in Thar. One can easily imagine the benefits this would bring to the people of Thar and the extent to which it would help mitigate the effects of drought.

ARTISANAL SKILLS

The Meghwar caste in Thar manufactures shawls from cotton and silk thread; blankets from sheep wool; rugs and cloth made from animal hair. All these items are prepared on primitive handlooms which the artisans manufacture themselves. Raw material, except for cotton and silk thread, which are imported from Karachi and Hyderabad, are produced locally. Wool is prepared from fleece on a spinning wheel by women; animal hair thread is manufactured by men in their spare time, while socializing or walking. Although production for local use had dropped over the years, according to Hera Mal, a middleman from Karachi, it has increased twenty times since 1968 for the Karachi market. For the past two years the market has been static. In addition, the daily earnings of Thari skilled workers are well below the Pakistan average or the minimum wage suggested by the Government of Pakistan. For instance, for making a blanket (khatta) an artisan earns about 40 rupees for two days' labour on the loom and an additional two days for manufacturing wool on the wheel. Similarly, the manufacture of a rug takes over ten days and the time required for making animal hair thread for the rug takes an additional ten days. Profit for the artisan is between 100 to 150 rupees. A silk shawl, whose fibre is imported from the cities, fetches the best profits. An artisan finishes it in one day and makes a profit of 20 to 30 rupees.[12] The shawl manufacture was introduced in Thar by middlemen from the cities and the demand for

Thari shawls is on the increase. All production takes place in the homes, and centres are not required. Middlemen go to the villages with orders, advance cash payments and raw materials, where required, and then go again to collect the finished goods. Artisans who do not require a loan, often take their goods to the *taluka* headquarters and sell them to shopkeepers directly, thus making an extra profit. No scientific study of the handicraft industry in Thar has been made to-date. Figures related to production, earnings, number of artisans, and market possibilities are not available. However, one can safely say that if the present trends continue, the relationship between the artisans, Thari middlemen and the Karachi market will consolidate primarily to the benefit of the Karachi shopkeepers.

Conclusion

A number of areas in Pakistan have become unproductive as a result of deforestation, overgrazing, pressure of population, breakdown of the old social order and the absence of new institutions. The population of these areas now supplements its income by remittances from the cities or by employment as contract labour in irrigated areas. Dir, the northern reaches of Swat and the Dera Ismail Khan district of the NWFP, are examples of this pattern. Makran is another, but in its case remittances come from the Gulf. If Thar is to be saved from a similar fate, then the long-term intervention plan must seek, as a priority, the creation of new and viable social institutions, without which no appropriate development can be sustained.

Notes

1. Government of Pakistan, *Population Census Reports 1981*, Population Census Organization, Islamabad.
2. DC Tharparkar, *Report of Relief Measure for Calamity Affected Areas*, 1987.
3. UNICEF, Water Resource Survey for Tharparkar 1979 and metrological records at the Mukhtarkar's offices at the taluka headquarters.
4. Ibid.
5. Government of Sindh, *Crop Acreage Statistics of Sindh 1981–82 and 1985–86*, Department of Agriculture.
6. Government of Pakistan, *Population Census Reports*, Population Census Organization, Islamabad.
7. Figures provided to the author by the Animal Husbandry Department of the Government of Sindh at Mirpurkhas
8. Government of Sindh, *Crop Acreage Statistics of Sindh 1981–82 and 1985–86*; Department of Agriculture.

9. Figures provided by the Mukhtarkar's office in Mithi.
10. Information provided by Seth Juma Khan, owner of a transport company at Umerkot and Seth Bharomal, the largest transporter at Naukot.
11. Ibid.
12. Worked out from information provided by middlemen and artisans in Mithi, Islamkot bazaar and Sorek-jo-Tar village.

10

Thar Revisited: 1992

Major changes have taken place in the towns and villages of Thar since 1987. In the towns, such as Islamkot and Mithi, a large number of new shops have opened; old *katcha* structures have been replaced by *pucca* ones; and a fairly large number of shacks and houses have been constructed through encroachments on government land by migrants from the rural areas. These encroachments have been informally promoted by government functionaries and are protected by them.

The shops in the town *bazaars* have a larger volume and variety of city produced and imported consumer goods such as biscuits, transistors, soap, henna, textiles, ready-made garments and medicines. An important addition is the availability of newspapers and magazines for sale, which in 1987 was non-existent. Shopkeepers claimed that sale of factory produced food stuffs, such as tea, biscuits, *ghee*, powdered milk, was fast increasing and that an increasing number of Tharis were taking to wearing ready-made garments, something very rare in the past. The changes in the physical nature of the *bazaars* certainly pointed to this as well since there was an air of considerable affluence as compared to 1987–88.

However, the towns have become more unhygienic. There is still no sewerage system and almost all neighbourhoods have their cesspools which are increasing in size. The open drains are not maintained and the streets and open spaces are littered with organic waste and polythene bags. An increase in the number of vehicles, and hence in the services sector to them, is also a major pollutant.

In the rural settlements the picture is not dissimilar. In all the villages visited a few of the residents (their number is increasing) have demolished their Thari huts and replaced them with semi-*pucca*, or in some cases, with *pucca* structures. Mud utensils, common in 1987, have to a considerable extent been replaced by aluminium, stainless steel and plastic ones. Most *kumhars* (potters) now work at other skills and many of them have migrated to the urban areas and become richer than the higher caste agriculturists of their villages. In addition, a few village shops, non-existent in 1987–88, have come up.

What the future holds for the rural settlements can be seen at the Meghwar Para at the Jogi Marhi village where a large number of *pucca* houses have been built in the last five years. Their construction has been financed from remittances from the barrage areas and urban centres and from the wages of children working in the carpet trade.

EDUCATION

Between 1985–86 and 1990–91 there has also been a major increase in the number of schools and teachers in the four *talukas* of the Thar district. However, there has not been a corresponding increase in the number of students, except for enrolment at the mosque schools. Since 1985–86, the number of female students at the primary level has increased by over 300 per cent. Although impressive in percentage terms, this figure constitutes no more than 9 per cent of all school age going girls in the Thar district. In 1989, this figure was 7 per cent.[1]

In 1985–86, there were only two girls' middle schools in the district. Now there are seven. However, there are no girls' middle schools in the Diplo and Nagar *talukas*. Moreover, the girls' high school at Diplo, which was operating in 1987, remains the only one in the whole district. The number of students at the school has fallen from 240 in 1985–86, to 131 in 1991–92.[2]

Due to the absence of girls' high schools and an acute shortage of girls' middle schools in the district, women teachers and paramedical staff cannot be locally recruited. The absence of girls' middle and high schools also means that the only way women can receive education is by going away from their village to a place where there is a school. This is simply not possible in the vast majority of cases and in the recent past, the law and order problems in the province have created an additional psychological barrier to girls moving away from their village or travelling. This is the reason given for the drop in the number of girl students at the high school in Diplo.

HEALTHCARE

Between 1987 and 1991, there has been a major increase in the Government of Sindh provided health facilities in Thar. In addition, the Mithi *taluka* hospital has been upgraded to a civil hospital, and as opposed to a total of 98 beds available in hospitals, Rural Health Centres (RHCs) and district council dispensaries in 1987, there are 124 beds available today. Similarly, the number of doctors working at the health facilities has increased from 38 to 69. On the other hand, the number of nurses has increased only from 9 to 11 and the increase in the number of other paramedical and technical staff is not anywhere in relation to the increase in the number of doctors. These statistics do not indicate that there has been much of an improvement in the provision of health services to the Thar district. However, immunization coverage has increased in the Thar district from well below 5 per cent in 1987 to 22 per cent in 1989 to 34 per cent in 1992. This is a major achievement.[3]

There has been an increase in the number of private medical practitioners, some of them quacks, in the larger Thar settlements. They prescribe patent medicines and as such there has been, according to the shopkeepers that stock these medicines, an over 200 per cent increase in their import and use in the last five years.

There has been no visible hygiene related improvement in environmental conditions or the attitudes of people. If anything, the conditions in the larger settlements have deteriorated due to pressure of population, generation of solid waste and waste water, and a break down of the social structure.

ENVIRONMENT

In 1987, when I visited the desert, the region was drought stricken whereas this visit was immediately after one of the heaviest monsoons Thar has experienced in over a decade. Therefore, it is not proper to compare the two situations. However, a number of changes have occurred in the attitudes of the Tharis towards their natural environment and especially towards trees.

In 1987, none of the notables (except one) or the drought afflicted population showed any major interest in tree plantation or preservation. There was a conviction that desertification could only be averted by adopting the agricultural techniques of the barrage areas and for that it was felt that there was sufficient subsoil water at depths that hand dug wells could not reach. This time the emphasis in all conversations was on protecting trees and *gowcher* lands. In addition, in large tracks of the areas visited, local *panchayats* or *baras* (elders) had reasserted their traditional roles of protecting and planting trees and of fining persons who felled trees without permission. However, this activity is only taking place in areas where the social structure is still somewhat intact, such as at Mithrio Soomra. In other areas, such as the village of Lunio, trees are cut with impunity, although the *baras* have tried to impose controls and fines; and at Juglar no attempt to protect trees in the *gowchers* is being made.

Whereas on the one hand attempts to protect the trees are being made, on the other hand demand for fuel leads to the felling of a large number of trees. Previously people used timber from their own farmlands or from small shrubs in the *gowchers* as fuel. However, an increasing number of people collect it and supply it commercially to the more affluent residents in the rural areas or sell it at the *tals* (timber mart) in the urban settlements. The quantity of timber being used as fuel has increased due to the pressure of population and a change in eating and cooking habits among an increasing number of Tharis.

Similarly, while the district administration has discontinued its policy of giving out *gowcher* lands on lease, the villagers insist that encroachment on *gowcher* lands for agricultural purposes continues. In the village of Jogi Murhi the residents insist that the *gowcher* land had been reduced from about 2,000 acres to less than 150 acres in a period of thirty years and that every variety of tree is felled and used for fuel.

There seems to be considerable weight in what the villagers say because although the cropped area has fallen in the Thar district between 1988–89 and 1990–91, the cultivated area has increased by 11.37 per cent in spite of government policy and the fact that Thar has suffered from a major drought for the past eight years.[4]

Economic Changes

The most important indicator of social and economic change in the Thar region is the increase in transport activity and its nature. In 1987, there were three jeep taxis in Thar. Today there are over 35 and they charge 500 rupees per day.[5] They claim that there is no shortage of business and there is room for more taxis. The taxi clients are all locals and often fodder, consumer items and Thari dairy products are also transported in the taxis.

There has been no addition to the number of GMCs plying on the *katcha* roads in Thar and nor have any new routes been developed. However, the number of trips on almost all the routes have more than doubled in the last five years and fares have increased by an average of

66 per cent. Cost of maintaining and operating a GMC has also more than doubled. The GMC operators feel that they can easily charge higher fares and people can afford to pay them, but this is forbidden by the government. Discussions with GMC drivers also indicate that an increasing number of animals are transported by GMCs from Thar to the barrage area markets. Previously this movement on GMCs was rare.

Workshops, spare part shops for vehicles, hotels and tea shops to serve the transport staff and passengers did not exist in the desert in 1987. Now there are over 40 such establishments in Mithi, and according to the shopkeepers, they have generated over 250 jobs. The average daily wage for such jobs is 30 rupees. As Kirpal, a waiter in a Mithi teashop put it, 'before one had to go out of Thar to earn such a huge amount.'

At the Islamkot truck terminal as well there was a feeling that as electricity was now easily available, welding facilities, lathe works and related activities would soon be established. Everyone at the terminal felt that there was a need for such functions.

The number of carpet looms has also registered an increase in the last five years. There were carpet looms at more than 50 per cent of the villages visited during the field trip. In all cases the weavers were children who had been trained by a local who had earlier received training at Islamkot when it used to be a major carpet manufacturing centre. According to the relatives of the children working at the looms, their average earnings are 700 rupees per month. The number of looms is steadily increasing and about 80 per cent of the boys who work on them come from the Meghwar community. For example, at the Jogri Murki settlement there were two looms in 1987, twelve in 1988, and forty-one in 1990. Over eighty persons work on these looms. In the Lunio settlement, there are ten looms with thirty children working on them. The hours of work vary between ten and fourteen per day and the conditions of work are unhealthy because of a lack of light and cross ventilation.[6]

Families whose children are working on the looms, have lost interest in agriculture and the children are quite definite that they will not ever be agriculturists. In addition, these families are distinctly more affluent than their neighbours.

The looms are all owned by entrepreneurs and middle men from the urban areas of Thar. Initially, they were installed in the urban settlements where the children were brought from the rural areas and lived in large groups in one room with grown-ups. Many of them became drug addicts and alcoholics. The move to the villages was made because it cut the middleman's overhead costs and made this activity a more low profile one, thus reducing government and public awareness concerning it and interference in it.

A remittance economy is also fast developing in Thar. Since time immemorial Tharis have migrated along with their animals to the barrage areas in the dry season, or in periods of drought, to work as farm hands. This migration was primarily for feeding and watering their animals, selling their dairy products and surviving drought conditions. However, between 1987 and 1992, an ever increasing number of Tharis migrated to the urban areas outside Thar to work as masons, tailor masters in garment factories, domestic servants, labour in sugar factories, and as employees in government departments. They earn anything between 1,000 to 4,000 rupees per month. Villagers claim that families who receive remittance money from the cities have lost interest in agriculture and in many cases let out their land to others rather than cultivate it themselves.

In Jogi Marhi, there are over fifteen persons out of a population of 800, working in the cities, most of them as tailor masters in garment factories or as masons. Younger boys are being groomed to leave.[7] Since only the Meghwars in Thar possess artisanal skills, and their 'low caste' status gives them greater mobility in a decaying social system, the vast majority of skilled out-migrants belong to this caste.

In addition to this migration, the Thar elite have also abandoned the desert since 1987. They live in Karachi or Hyderabad with their families where they are engaged in business or 'service' and visit the desert only in the 'in season'. Many Tharis have also established shops in the cities where they sell Thari handicrafts and employ Tharis as assistants. A number of such shop owners operate through middle men in the desert, or themselves act as middle men. According to the Islamkot shop owners there are at least ten to fifteen such operators in the Islamkot-Diplo area alone.

There has also been an increase in animal population since 1987. This can only be estimated as there has been no livestock census in Thar since 1986. The census established a growth rate of 8.4 per cent per year. The villagers feel that since 1987 the rate of growth has been much more as people, during the drought period, realized that animals were the only reliable source of income. The TRDP survey of the animal population in the TRDP project area in 1989 and again in 1992 has established a 258 per cent increase between 1989 and 1992.[8] The major increase has been in cows. If this is true (and there is no reason why it should not be), then the livestock to rangeland ratio for Thar, which was already more than twice of what it should ideally be in 1987, has gone up (it was 68 per 100 hectare when it should be 30 per 100 hectare). This means that if the desert has to regenerate, animals will have to be stall fed and a lot more trees will need to be planted.

Many villagers feel that they could afford to stall feed their animals if there was a market for their dairy products, their animals and a cheaper source of fodder. They point out that the only saleable dairy product is *ghee*, which middlemen buy from them at half the market price. Alternatively, they have to take small quantities of it themselves to the urban areas. The general feeling is that if roads could be constructed, fodder prices would fall and *ghee* and animal prices would go up. Most villagers who owned animals were certain that it was the animals that sustained them during the drought years and not agricultural activity. It was pointed out, more than once, that a poor man was one who owned no cattle or goats.

Due to the long drought, agricultural activity in the desert has reduced considerably. The more aware and vocal villagers feel that agriculture will not go back to the pre-1987 position as people have found alternative sources of income and have started considering it a subsidiary activity. However, the older generation definitely feels otherwise and has a strong attachment to farming.

Artisanal activity in Thar has also increased since 1987 to cater to the city markets. It is entirely financed and managed by Thari middlemen and increasingly uses city produced raw materials. As a result, the production of *khata* and *kharal* has fallen (in some areas they are not produced anymore), and that of shawls has gone up. Tharis no longer make thread out of their wool but export it raw. The price of Thari wool has increased by 150 per cent between 1987 and 1992.[9] Similarly, leather is no longer manufactured or worked in Thar in any substantial quantity but hides and skins are sent to Karachi and Hyderabad in increasing numbers. This is because the Meghwars no longer want to do this 'dirty' work and nor can they be forced by the upper castes to do it.

The exploitation of Thar's mineral wealth has increased. Since 1987 granite is being extracted in Nagar, and according to transporters, the volume of China clay being carried to Mirpurkhas has more than tripled in the last three years. However, the general feeling among all Tharis met during the field trip, is that this activity has not benefited the

Tharis. The labour employed, both at the China clay and granite mines, is from other parts of Pakistan.

It is rumoured that large deposits of coal have been discovered near Bhatian-ji-Jeri in Thar. The government geologists established camp in that area earlier in 1992 and conducted drilling operations. The people of the area do not believe that there are any coal deposits and if they are, they are sure that they, like the people near the granite mines in Nagar, will not benefit from them. The DC sees no possibility of coal extraction operations beginning in the near future.

Eighty per cent of the Thari households in the TRDP project area are in debt to moneylenders. Sixty-three per cent of households in the project area have debts of more than 4,000 rupees and 65 per cent of Thari households in the project area pay 3 per cent per month as interest on their debts. Seventy-five per cent of the households in debt have borrowed money for food and 25 per cent for other needs. This situation was established by the TRDP baseline survey of 1989[10]. Since there is no previous survey nor a survey after that date, the trends in debt cannot be ascertained. However, as average earning according to the survey is only 4,954 rupees per year, and about 46 per cent of this is spent on food, there is no way that these debts can be repaid. According to the villagers spoken to during the field trip, the vast majority of these debts were incurred during the previous drought and only those persons who are working regularly in the cities or the barrage areas, those whose children (more than one) work at the carpet looms, or those who can sell enough cattle, can repay these debts.

ADMINISTRATIVE CHANGES

The recent decision to create a new Thar district with Mithi as its headquarters, has already had a major impact on Thar's sociology, economics and politics. Mithi has visibly expanded. Taxis have multiplied, over forty new shops and tea houses have been established, and according to an estimate by the Deputy District Education Officer, over three hundred government jobs will be generated for the residents of Thar. In addition, the volume of traffic between Naukot and Mithi has increased, a petrol station has been set up, and there is talk of shifting the GMCs to Mithi from Naukot. A saw mill, welding facilities and lathe machines have also been established. Normal trucks and buses now operate from the barrage areas and animals are now being transported from Mithi in two-wheel drive vehicles, thus reducing transport costs by about 40 per cent.

In addition, the residents of Thar will no longer go to Mirpurkhas to settle their government related affairs or disputes and the local politicians, with the administrative power nearer to them, will be able to assert themselves more forcefully. This will definitely improve the functioning of government and political institutions and give the people a greater sense of belonging.

Given the population of Thar district and per capita government investments in other areas of the country, the Government of Sindh (GoS) has made considerable investments in the development of infrastructure and social services in Thar. However, the GoS has not developed roads in the district and has not extended electrification. These two components of infrastructure are essential for economically consolidating the social revolution that is taking place in the district.

Government interventions, like elsewhere in Pakistan, are also not compatible with the social, economic and geographical conditions of Thar and as such are either not sustainable or do not benefit the people of the region. For example, the water schemes that have been developed will face severe maintenance problems due to financial and technical reasons, unless local level institutions can be made to finance, operate and maintain them. Similarly, the veterinary services of the GoS, for all practical purposes, cannot be made use of by the villagers since they are centrally located and have no effective outreach facilities or extension agents in the settlement. Again, the education curriculum in the schools has no relevance to Thar conditions and the centralized nature of the education department makes local action difficult if not impossible; and the government's healthcare input is almost entirely curative in nature.

Another example of inappropriate government policy is the ADBP loans for the desert. It seems that almost all the loans have been used for the purchase of tractors and some for the installation of tube wells. The use of tractors will produce desertification in Thar as tractors will uproot trees and shrubs and turn up the soil from a depth that a plough pulled by a donkey or a camel cannot. Similarly, tube wells of an excessively large size will deplete the already meagre subsoil aquifer. Moreover, almost all loans are made to affluent people.

SOCIAL REPERCUSSIONS

The physical and economic changes in the desert have had major social repercussions. The traditional social structure based on caste, feudal relations and the *panchayats* has broken down and the extended family is under stress. As a result, there is no longer an institutional arrangement for any form of collective action. In addition, the elite, who organized this collective action and controlled the institutions, are leaving the desert and developing economic interests elsewhere.

The artisanal classes, traditionally considered 'low caste', are becoming increasingly affluent because of the commercial potential of the skills they possess, and as such politically powerful. They are also taking to education, and since they have fewer social taboos and restrictions than the other castes, they have adjusted to the changes around them more easily. This process, which was just beginning in 1987, is now well on its way, and the Meghwar community is very definitely developing on the lines of the *kammis* of the Punjab, who now economically dominate the Syeds and Chaudhries of their areas and control the local bodies.

The links with the cities through the remittance economy and middle men, have introduced urban values in Thar as a whole. This, along with the development of the carpet industry, has diminished the importance of agriculture in the minds of the Tharis. Almost all the young boys spoken to during the field trip wanted to work at the loom, go to the city, or join government service. They did not want to be farmers. In addition, an increasing number of women wish to wear *shalwar-kameez* instead of their traditional clothes, and some have given up their traditional ornaments and bangles as well. Children now play cricket, even in the villages (they did not in 1987), and for them Imran Khan is a well known name.

Many Tharis do not wish to do intensive work anymore as they now measure all labour inputs in cash terms (that is enough to put them off agriculture). Many also know the daily wages in Karachi and Islamabad for skilled and unskilled work and the sale price in these cities of the goods they produce. Thus, the main complaints of the villagers spoken to during the field trip, were the labour involved in pulling out water; the difficulty involved in walking animals to the market; the difficulty of digging wells; the small returns in agricultural activity and artisanal work against labour inputs; and above all 'government indifference' to the absence of roads and electricity. There is a complete understanding in the older generation that the old social order is dead and that, as Nagaram, the retired headmaster in Jogi Marhi put it, 'everyone can now go their own way'.

In addition, a proportionately high number of Tharis are receiving higher education and becoming doctors, engineers and graduates in social sciences. Many of them are returning to Thar because of difficulties in getting jobs in suitable positions. Their presence in the desert is bringing about attitudinal changes in their homes and neighbourhoods and speeding up the process of social change. In addition, they are increasingly taking over and manning the various government departments in the district.

In the various visits to Thar since 1968, one has noticed that the primary school teachers are the most aware and concerned citizens of the region. Before they were reluctant to express their views openly because of the fear of the 'powers that be'. However, today that fear has gone. It is felt that they, along with the young graduates, can be major agents of change that can balance out the exploitation of the people of Thar by the market forces.

The social change taking place in Thar is irreversible. Agriculture, because of recurring drought, the introduction of a cash economy and the demise of the old social order, can no longer meet the economic needs of the Tharis. They should consider a good harvest simply as a bonus. Their assured earnings can only be from animals, artisanal work, trade related activities, services sector employment and from remittances. If they can develop the attitudes and skills to relate to these changes and to the market economy that is propelling them, they will prosper and survive. If they cannot do so, they will be exploited and fall further into debt, at least for the time being.

To create a more equitable relationship between the market economy and the Tharis, the development of physical and institutional infrastructure is essential. Roads, appropriate and sufficient credit and technical support mechanisms, easily accessible veterinary services, and markets for their produce, are a few essentials.

POSTSCRIPT: 2007

I have visited Thar several times since the TRDP evaluation of 1992. My last visit was in November 2007. The trends I identified in 1992 have continued and consolidated. The urban population has increased considerably. According to the 1998 Census, the population of Mithi for example, was 19,524. In 2007, it had increased to over 50,000.[11] This large migration and the remittances it sends back to the villages has had a major impact both in the urban and rural areas. In the rural areas interest in agriculture has declined. Lifestyles have changed. Families whose members have migrated to the cities use steel and china crockery instead of earthenware. The traditional dress, even in the case of women, has or is being replaced by the urban *shalwar-kameez*. Before the upper castes did not allow lower castes, especially women, to dress well. That is no longer possible. Money from the cities has built better houses and festivities are strongly influenced by urban culture and music. Dowries, which were all made by village artisans, now invariably consist of industrially manufactured items. Almost every family, except for the bhils and kohlis, have mobile phones and wherever roads are being built motorcycles are replacing donkeys and camels. Loans for these motorbikes are being negotiated. The poor can now be defined as those who through remittance money or urban based trade have not acquired these assets and culture.

The reasons for migrating from Mithi to the larger cities of Sindh are better working conditions and more money. Migration from Mithi has also catered to the demand created by the building of roads, petrol and CNG stations and small tea shops, eating places and utility stores that have sprung up to serve the newly created transport sector. Tharis are now replacing Pathans in these jobs along the highways. A large number of Tharis are also working as tailors in the garment industry in Karachi and an increasing number are seeking employment as domestic servants in the larger Sindh cities, especially in Karachi and Hyderabad.

Another reason given for migration from Mithi is for higher education, especially for girls. It is also felt that the future of educated girls lies not in Mithi but in the larger cities. This is an incentive to migrate and for this Hyderabad is preferred since Karachi is not considered a Sindhi city anymore. A demand for Thari handicrafts has also led to the opening of outlets in the major cities of Sindh and in Islamabad and Lahore. This has given incentive to migration to these cities and created links for the Tharis with the job markets in other urban areas.

The migration of the Hindu upper caste, the government's response to the 1987 drought and the building of roads has brought considerable financial benefits to the Lohanas and the Memons. They are increasingly going into education and because of the TRDP their women, and those of the artisanal castes, have also taken to education and to jobs in offices. However, the Rajputs and the Baloch still dominate Tharparkar politically, due to which the newly educated and affluent classes feel oppressed. In numerous conversations, this has been given as a reason for migration.

The caste system is on its way out. People of different castes now eat together. Kohli girls, previously considered untouchables, now work in the homes of the upper castes. The Meghwars have become the best educated community in Tharparkar and the majority of Thari professionals belong to their caste. The building of roads and the making of Mithi the district headquarters has led to a revolution in transport. There are now 275 jeep taxis, 50 Qingqis and 50 car taxis in Mithi alone. This has led to the creation of terminals, guest houses, and eating places. In addition more than 300 government jobs have been created as a result of these changes and real estate prices have increased.

The culture of shopping has also undergone a change. Previously, shops were in residential neighbourhoods. Now, they are being built in officially and informally designated 'commercial areas'. Nestle's milk and mineral water are available at all shops and eating places and persons who have migrated are looked up to and considered as role models for other young people. Young women who have got jobs at the TRDP are also considered as role models by other young women.

The large–scale migration to Mithi has resulted in the creation of informal settlements. These settlements are sometimes at a small distance from the town where land values are comparatively less. These settlements have problems of water and sewage disposal. They are growing fast since there are no formal housing schemes for low income groups. Meanwhile, remittance money is being invested in building houses on the pattern of Hyderabad and Karachi expressing an increasing rich-poor divide.

The road network has also made the importation of fodder for animals cheaper. Therefore, migration to the irrigated areas during the dry seasons is being replaced by migration to areas along the road where transportation and hence fodder is available. Also, there is considerable evidence to suggest that Kohlis who use to migrate seasonally to the irrigated areas are no longer coming back to Tharparkar. A new society and class structure is being created. The intellectuals of Mithi feel that they live in a state of social anarchy and doctors claim that depression and mental illnesses have increased as a result.

People migrate to the other cities of Sindh with the help of their friends, relatives and family members who are already there. The two main destinations are Karachi and Hyderabad and since they are not too far away the link of the migrant with his family remains intact. Remittances therefore need no bank accounts and are made directly by the migrant when he visits or through other migrants from his neighbourhood or village. A large number of families also migrate collectively to Mithi. Through their links with middlemen they negotiate with the *patwari* who allows them to settle on government land. They know that they are not owners of the land but they hope that once they build their houses they will be able to negotiate some sort of regularization with the government. Although they claim that they have made no payments for this land, there is evidence to suggest that ad hoc payments are made from time to time to relevant government officials and the police. The main reason given for these collective migrations are education of children (especially girls), freedom from an oppressive society and better facilities in the urban areas.

Though social change has taken place the power of the traditional elite still holds. This is because the merchant classes do not have a tradition of contesting elections which are invariably contested and won by the traditional elite. Before devolution in 2001, the bureaucracy was a major player in the governance and development of Tharparkar. After devolution the elected *nazims* and *naib nazims* are the dominant power and at the district level they belong to elite families. This is resented by the residents of Mithi as it evident from a number of conversations the author had in this town.

An example of the change that has taken place was given in conversations with estate agents. They pointed out a number of plots which the bureaucracy in the pre-devolution days had identified for public utilities and amenities. After devolution, their landuse was changed by the elected *nazims* and they have been converted for commercial use and have been purchased at below market rates by relatives of the political representatives.

Source: Interviews carried out by the author in Tharparkar in November 2007 for the preparation of an International Institute for Environment and Development (IIED), UK sponsored report on 'Migration and Small Towns in Pakistan'.

NOTES

1. Worked out from: (1) tables provided by the District Education Officer (M&F), District Tharparkar and (2) Statistical Brochure District Field Officer, Bureau of Statistics, Mirpurkhas, 1991.
2. Ibid.
3. Worked out from Statistical Brochure District Field Officer, Bureau of Statistics, Mirpurkhas, 1991.
4. Ibid.
5. Interviews with taxi owners and drivers.
6. Interviews with loom owners in the village.
7. Ibid.
8. Worked out from TRDP, *Survey of Animal Population in TRDP Project Area 1989 and 1992.*
9. Interviews of artisans and middlemen at Jogi Mahri village and Islamkot bazaar. Also interviews with animal *hari* dealers in Islamkot bazaar.
10. TRDP base line survey 1989.
11. Author's interview with Dr Sono Khanghrani, Director TRDP for the IIED Study on 'Migration and Small Towns in Pakistan' in Mithi on 3 November 2007.

PART FOUR: THE RIVER IN SINDH

The Indus River was the main communication artery of what is today Pakistan. Boats carried men, cargo and agricultural produce all the way from Kalabagh in the north to Keti Bunder in the delta region and back again. The delta meanwhile traded with the Indian, Gulf and African coasts. Almost all the major towns were located along the Indus and its tributaries, and if they were not (for the rivers changed course often) they had *bunders* or ports a few kilometres away. The delta region was the richest area of the Indus Valley and almost all agriculture was carried out on the flood plains of the rivers. There were considerable tamarisk forests along the rivers and mangroves in the delta region. But this was all before the railway, roads and barrages were built.

The communities that were (and still are) involved in fishing and transporting people and cargo on the rivers are known as Mohanas and Mirbars. Folklore has it that they are the oldest inhabitants of the Indus Valley. There has also been speculation that they are the descendants of the people of the Indus Valley Civilization and that Mohenjodaro is a deformation of Mohana-jo-daro or the mound of the Mohanas. All over Pakistan there are settlements whose names are associated with the name Mohana.

Both the Mohanas and the delta region of the Indus have been severely affected by the building of dams and barrages and by the emergence of a cash economy and the values that accompany it. Environmental changes have also taken place as a result. The effect on the Mohanas is described in Chapter 11 and the effect on the delta region is described in Chapter 12. A postscript has been added to Chapter 12 to describe the changes that have taken place in the delta and the coastal areas of the Thatta district between 1989 and 2007, the Kalabagh Dam controversy and the emergence of new social and political movements.

11

Mohanas: 1968 and 1986

We arrived in Kashmore at seven in the morning (without being kidnapped) and made straight for the river bank where the Mohana settlement is located. The last time I was here was in 1968 when Mushtaq and I travelled from Kashmore to Sukkur in a Mohana boat. The settlement was much larger now and the number of boats were much fewer. There were a number of *pucca* houses whereas none existed before. I enquired from people about Bhuro, the Mohana who had transported us to Sukkur in his boat more than eighteen years ago. No one seemed to know him. At last an old man informed us in a matter of fact manner that he had died some years ago but his son Suleman lived on a boat at the lower end of the *bunder*. After considerable enquiry we located Suleman's boat and I recognized it as the one that had taken by us to Sukkur in 1968. Suleman did not recognize us but he did remember the journey we had undertaken with his father. He was about eight years old at that time.

After much discussion and debate Suleman agreed to take us to Sukkur. The journey lasted three days. The whole experience was very different to that of 1968 because many changes had taken place in the physical environment along the Indus and in the lifestyle of the Mohana family whose guests we were.

The old mud and lattice architecture of the small towns along the river has given way to a number of concrete buildings. Quite a few ugly overhead water tanks (probably PHED schemes) disturb the landscape and badly maintained school, administrative and health buildings have cropped up. There are fewer trees now (but may be that is my imagination) and far less water in the river. There are fewer boats plying on the Indus (perhaps because of the scare of *dacoits*) and those that are, are laden exclusively with timber, unlike before. But more important, the Mohanas have changed.

When we began our journey Suleman said a Quranic *dua* and made an offering of rice and sugar to Khawja Khizar, the guide of travellers on the river, whose protection the Muslim Mohanas seek during their voyages. In 1968 Bhuro had also said a Quranic *dua* and made a similar offering, but to Darya Lal, the Hindu water deity. I remember that I asked him if he was a Muslim or a Hindu and he had replied that he was a Muslim. 'Then why do you make an offering to Darya Lal?' I enquired. He replied, 'There is one destination (*manzil*) but many roads (*rah*) to it. I try and follow all the roads for one can never be sure.' I remember how pleased I was with that response.

I related this incident to Suleman. He responded 'Please forgive my father. He was an ignorant man. He was not educated and aware.' So the mullahs have got to the Mohanas as well and so has city culture that goes with them which is reflected in more ways than one. In 1968 almost all Mohanas, men and women, wore *kurtas* and *tehmats*. The *tehmats* of the women came down to their heels at the back and from the front they were one *balish* above the ankle. Now the vast majority of Mohana men and many Mohana women wear *shalwar qameez awami* suits. Mohanas previously lived almost entirely on boats but now the majority live on the shore and an increasing number have started working as labour in the Sukkur markets. The boat makers among the Mohanas have moved to the cities (particularly to Karachi) where they work as carpenters for cane and timber furniture makers and they send back money to their families. This is because boat making has declined. Many Mohanas now work in government departments as caretakers and *darogas* and five have also become doctors and engineers, or so Suleman and his uncle say. Also, since 1982, the Sukkur and Kashmore Mohanas have started migrating to Karachi during the fishing season to work as *khalasis* at the fish harbour. Every year this seasonal migration increases. A number of Mohana families have also settled in Karachi. 'Why?' I ask Suleman's uncle. 'Why not?' he responds, 'In Karachi there are reliable jobs and you can send your children to school. You cannot do it here. You cannot earn any money on the river. You cannot be free.'

'How about before', I persist.

'Before was different. You did not need much money. Needs were very limited. There was no tea and biscuits and you could trade fish for milk and *ghee*. Now it is not possible. The Gujjars want cash and they now eat vegetable and meat. They do not want fish. Also they sell their product to the city people. There is a big demand for their goods. For cooking you need timber and that cannot be purchased by fish anymore. You need money for everything.'

Suleman is planning to sell his boat and buy a house in Sukkur so that his younger son can go to school. He has boat making skills which a Sukkur furniture maker is willing to hire at a good price. Also, since Mohana women do not observe *purdah* they are looked down upon and he does not want his daughters to be considered improper. 'So will you put them in *purdah*?' I ask. 'Yes', he says 'it is good for all of us. It will give us *izzat.*'

On arriving in Sukkur we wandered along the *bunder* and finally settled down to have a long conversation with eighty-year-old Allah Rakha, a Saraiki speaking Mohana who has a large boat which he built in 1973 at a cost of 80,000 rupees. For building the boat he took a loan from a *bara* or elder. A *bara* according to him is a Mohana who has acquired land. He repaid the loan in six years. The repayment was possible because like all Saraiki speaking Mohanas he is not a fisherman but a cargo carrier. He spoke of the days when his uncles' boat used to travel from Kalabagh to Ketti Bunder before the dams and barrages were built on the river. They considered carrying timber (which is all that they do now) an insult in those days and only carried wheat and rice. But at that time most agriculture, unlike now, was in the *katcho* areas and so river transport made sense. It was also safe in those days as the British had armed river police patrolling the river. Now, the river banks are the abode of dacoits and Mohanas for their protection have started to keep guns. The present day river police are worse than the dacoits.

According to Allah Rakha his group of Mohanas have no *punchayat* system. The *bara* deals with their problems and administers justice. People listen to him because he gives them loans and protection. However, Mohanas who work in Karachi or as market labour and carpenters do not respect the advice of the *bara* and even some younger *sir phiras* do not go to his *katcheries*. This trend is increasing.

Allah Rakha says that he has seen the river trade and its transportation system die. 'It is the age of roads and trucks. The Mohanas, who are the descendants of the family who made Noah's Ark, will soon cease to exist.'

'But why should they cease to exist?' I ask him.

'This is an age of education. Mohanas who get educated give up their *quom* and call themselves Soomos. The Pirzadas of Sukkur are also Mohanas who have changed their name but are aware of their Mohana origins. No *quom* today can exist without educated people.'

Throughout his conversation Allah Rakha constantly stressed that the Saraiki Mohanas were *boog* (cargo) carriers whereas the Sindhi Mohanas were fishermen and as such inferior.

While we were talking to Allah Rakha two young men dressed in clean *shalwar qameez* came and introduced themselves as belonging to a committee that the Sukkur Bunder Mohanas have formed to struggle for better economic conditions. Three other young Mohanas from two neighbouring boats joined us and a lively discussion took place in which Allah Rakha did not participate. He listened with a blank expression on his face and played with his moustache. The gist of what I could gather from the discussion is given below.

Boats have become too expensive and so the Mohanas have been forced to move onto the land with the result that the water front has become a *katchi abadi* which every government wishes to bulldoze. Every time they wish to bulldoze it they offer the Mohanas plots far away from the river which means far away from work. The Mohanas do not object to being moved onto the river bank opposite Sukkur city since they can come to the city side by boat. But this would be inconvenient and time consuming for Mohanas who do *mazdoori* (labour) and almost every Mohana family has at least one member doing *mazdoori* in Sukkur. Resistance to moving from the Sukkur side of the river front has been supported by the fishing contractors who saw shifting as a problem for acquiring Mohana labour. This brought us to the subject of fishing contracts. Fishing in the river is not permitted since fishing rights are auctioned out every year. The contractors who get these rights are *waderas* and merchants since they are the only ones who can make full payments for them. They do nothing but employ staff to manage the Mohanas. Mohanas provide labour, boats and nets. The contractor takes care of transport, ice, administrative matters and *bhatta* (illegal gratification) to government officials. Fish goes to Punjab as well, by train. Monahas get 50 per cent of the local sale price of the fish and the contractor gets the rest. Thus the contractor makes big money for doing almost nothing as compared to the Mohanas.

Till the 1950s—before General Ayub Khan's regime—fishing contracts could go to the Mohanas. They used to get together, pool their resources and bid in an auction. The administration used to take payment from them in instalments so that Mohanas could afford to get the contract. Thus the Mohanas were richer. At least they owned the fish they caught. In Bhutto's time an attempt to revert to the pre-Ayub system was made but the *waderas* were able to sabotage it.

When Mohanas need to make a boat they get a loan from the contractor. Although no interest is charged on the loan, the Mohana becomes a slave of the contractor. He works for him free on other than fishing jobs; gets paid less than his share of fish money; and his family can be called at any time to assist the servants of the *waderas* at his residence without payment. The contractors try and turn this debt into a life long slavery. According to these young men, their elders have told them that when the Hindu *Banyas* left in 1947 they owned the Mohana community as they were all in debt to them.

Another problem that was discussed is related to the fact that the contractors are now non-Mohanas and by virtue of being contractors, they have become the *baras*. Being non-Mohanas, they are not particularly interested in the welfare of the community or in settling its disputes and problems. They only wish to exploit it. Due to these reasons, social cohesion among the Mohanas is breaking down.

The five young men are quite clear as to what they want for the Mohanas. Contracts for fishing should be given only to Mohanas. They want cheap timber and government loans for boat making. They want duty free nylon string for net making. They want land along the river banks for housing. 'The future of the Mohanas' they say, 'is along the river, rather than on the river.'

In 1986 I had visited the *Ziarat* of Khwaja Khizar or the Zinda Pir near Bukkar (in Sindh province). I had been informed that there used to be a throne there protected by serpents. My young hosts informed me that the *Ziarat* had been washed away by the floods. At this Allah Rakha broke his silence and said that this tragedy was the result of the Mohanas giving up their profession and that more tragedies were in the offing. The young men said that they saw no relationship between the two issues and then continued with their discussion.

Khawaja Khizar figures prominently in all Mohana celebrations related to births, marriages, commencement of voyages, the launching of a boat, or a large fish catch. Some times these occasions are accompanied by singing and dancing in which all Mohanas, men and women, used to participate as the women did not observe *purdah*. However, the participation of women is now discouraged and such celebrations are no longer held as often as they were. The musicians at these events have always been Mohanas as well, although now the system of hiring *langas* has begun.

The extent to which middle class values have affected the thinking of the younger Mohanas surfaced when we discussed drugs and alcohol.

I enquired whether the Mohanas consumed *charas,* opium or alcohol. In many voyages on the Indus I had seen Mohanas use them frequently. The young men said that the Mohanas were free from these bad habits. Allah Rakha again spoke up, 'Seventy-five per cent of Mohanas take these (twelve *annas* in a rupee).' The young men ignored this statement.

In the evening we visited Seth Dilomal at his Bunder Road house overlooking the river. Seth Dilomal was a forest contractor. According to him, till the mid-sixties forests were mainly in the *katcha* areas and therefore boats were the only means for transporting timber. Now these forests have disappeared. In the fifties and sixties he employed the Mohanas extensively for transporting timber. He looks down on them. According to him Mohanas have always had to depend on permission from the landlords of the *katcho* area for movement of their boats upstream since they pull them with ropes while walking along the banks. They have had to purchase this permission by giving their women to the *katcho waderas.* This is why their women are not respected and the Mohanas are considered *beghairat.* According to Seth Dilomal, things have not changed.

Later at night I sat in my hotel room overlooking the Indus and contemplated the enormous changes that a change from a barter to cash economy has brought about in the last eighteen years. Should one support this inevitable process of change and help in its more equitable institutionalization or remain wedded to unrealistic idealism? I do not know. The more I see of Pakistan and what is happening to it, the more confused I get. It is so easy being dogmatic, it blinds one to reality and leads nowhere.

Extracts from the author's personal diary dated 3 March 1988.

12

The Indus Delta: 1989

This picture of the Indus Delta in the Thatta district was put together in 1989 through observations and interviews of school teachers, community elders, formal and informal transporters, middlemen; boat hands and contractors in the fishing industry, timber merchants and herders, shopkeepers and vendors, farmers, government officials, elected councillors, representatives of NGOs, CBOs and workers and middlemen in the Karachi Fish Harbour, and Keti Bunder residents. Since 1989 major changes have taken place in the district and are described in the Postscript at the end of the chapter.

Thatta district is divided into nine *talukas*. Of these Gorabari, Keti Bunder, Kharochan, Shah Bunder and Mirpur Sakro are coastal *talukas*, while Jati, Mirpur Bathoro, Sujawal and Thatta are non-coastal *talukas*.

The coastal *talukas* for the most part form a part of the Indus delta. This area consists of the Indus distributaries which discharge into numerous creeks that crisscross the shore. All settlements are built on the mud flats between these channels. Before the dams and barrages on the Indus were built, fresh river water flushed this area. Now the sea has crept in. As a result, the agricultural lands in the delta have been badly affected by water-logging and salinity. Share-croppers on these lands have moved to other areas of the district in search of better agricultural land. In the Keti Bunder *taluka*, residents feel that about 25 per cent of the *taluka* population has migrated due to this reason in the last twenty years. Many members of both agricultural and fishing communities have migrated to Karachi permanently, along with their families, due to the environmental degradation that has taken place. They now work in the fisheries in Ibrahim Hyderi or at the fish harbour in Karachi.

From March to June is the prawn catching season. During this period there is a big demand for *khalasis* in Karachi. It is estimated by the residents of the Keti Bunder *taluka* that 15 to 20 per cent of the adult male population engaged in fishing migrates to Karachi and Ibrahim Hyderi in response to this demand. The extent of this migration falls as one moves eastwards and it is estimated that only a few families go to Karachi from the Sir Creek on the Indian frontier. Again, between September to March is the *gand* season. During this period the sea is calm and almost 60 per cent of the population engaged in fishing, along with their families, move to the banks of the creeks near the open sea so as to catch *gand*. Older community members agree that before the commercialization of fishing in the early sixties, these migrations did not take place.

SOCIO-ECONOMIC CONDITIONS

The people of the delta regions belong to various clans and tribes. Traditionally these clans and tribes had hereditary productive activities. For example, the Khaskhelis were agriculturists; the Jats were pastoral people, breeders of camels and suppliers of timber for fuel; the Memons and Shidis were merchants and traders; the Dablas were fishermen. In addition, there were artisans such as carpenters (*wados*), barbers (*nai*), potters (*kumaras*). These served the clan communities and in exchange were maintained by them. This maintenance involved a house, expenses for social occasions such as marriages and feasts and a seasonal share in the agricultural or fishing produce. All economic relationship between the clans was based on barter. Cash transactions only took place between the *sardars* and *waderas*, and through them with the outside world. This system guaranteed not only the economic independence of the village but also the supremacy of the feudal class.

The *sardar*, along with the major *waderas* of the area, wielded authority over his people, organized them for maintenance of infrastructure and production, and represented them in their dealings with the state. In addition, he determined their relationship with other clans and with the hereditary artisans and administered justice. Those clans, whose productive activities required intensive organization for production and extensive maintenance of infrastructure, were politically stronger and more cohesive, such as the Khaskhelis. Fishing, before the 1960s, was not a major activity and required almost no organization or infrastructure maintenance. As such the Dablas were a weak and exploited community and since they had no clan government of their own they were subservient to the more powerful clans. The vast majority of the population, irrespective of the clan they belonged to, were permitted to live only at subsistence level by their chiefs.

Major changes have taken place in the social order described above. The authority of the tribal chiefs and landlords has broken down. The artisans are no longer dependent on the village structure for their survival, nor do they receive payments in agricultural produce. Many of them have migrated to the urban areas and since they now work for cash their labour cannot be afforded by the rural population. Clan affiliation no longer determines the productive activity one is engaged in. Poorer Khaskhelis, Jats and Shidis have started working as fishermen, since it is economically more profitable. Memons, however, remain merchants and middlemen. Members of all clans now aspire for education and government jobs, something that was the domain entirely of Memons and Hindu Amils. People see state institutions, inadequate as they are, and the new entrepreneurs who have emerged, as substituting the functions of their *sardars* and *waderas*.

In addition, cultural changes have also taken place. Traditional singers and dancers, belonging to the Langa castes, do not perform at feasts and marriages. Westernized bands and pop singers from the cities, complete with furniture and city food, have replaced them. The result is that many Langas, along with Jogis, have migrated to the cities or turned to fishing. Similarly, rituals performed at the launching of a boat, birth of a child and on the night of the full moon have been abandoned. The *malakhro*, or wrestling competitions, which were held with great fanfare have ceased. Instead children play cricket on the mud flats. Although feudal relations have broken down, elected councillors, chairmen of UCs, MNAs and MPAs still belong to the upper-classes of the traditionally more powerful clans.

The main reason for the changes described above is that the economic independence of the village is no more. Cash has become the principal means of exchange and this has led to the replacement of feudal relations, which were the cornerstone of the old social economy, by crude capital relations. This change has been facilitated by water logging and salinity, and by the development of fisheries through government intervention in the 1960s. The former conditions have made agriculture difficult and unprofitable and rendered a large number of peasants jobless. The latter circumstance i.e. development of fisheries by the government, has given incentives to entrepreneurship, provided credit facilities to the people, and made social mobility possible. Roads, mechanized transportation, populist political movements, and the accessibility to the media and the urban areas have also played their role.

Productive activity in the coastal areas can be divided into three broad classifications: Fishing and related activities, in which an estimated 90 per cent of the population is involved; agriculture and forestry, in which 8 per cent of the population is involved; and the services sector, in which 2 per cent of the population is involved.

Khalasis are fishermen who do not own boats but work as hired hands on the boats of others. The population that migrates seasonally to Karachi and Ibrahim Hyderi consists for the most part of *khalasis*. After deductions have been made from the catch for a share of net, boat, engine, share of the owner himself, cost of diesel and food, the remaining proceeds are divided equally among the *khalasis*. This share is known as *patti*. The shares of different elements and persons involved are: net six *pattis;* boat two *pattis*; engine six *pattis*; owner one *patti*; and khalasi one *patti*.

Average earnings of a *khalasi* in the Keti Bunder area are no more than 6,000 rupees a year. Over 70 per cent of the population engaged in fishing are *khalasis*. Many of them also possess small boats of 6 to 10 feet length which they operate with the assistance of family members. However, with these boats they cannot earn even a subsistence livelihood. One such boat owner, Mohammad Ibrahim, now works for a middleman at 1,000 rupees a month and says that as a result his income has more than doubled. Almost none of the *khalasi* children go to school or have their health problems attended to.

According to the local population, about 25 per cent of the population engaged in fishing own boats larger than 20 feet. These boats require hired hands and in certain seasons go out to the open sea. Boat-owners are of two kinds. Those who have built their boats by taking credit from middlemen and are perpetually in debt and those whose boats are free of debt. The former constitute over 90 per cent of the boat-owners.

Those who have borrowed money from middlemen for the construction of their boats and the engines are obliged to sell their produce to these middlemen at prices considerably lower than the market rate. In addition, large mechanized boats, in order to be fully utilized, require large nets, ice for storing the catch if they go into the open sea for several days, and food supplies for the crew. Credit for these is again taken from the middlemen. Thus, the debt is never paid off and in most cases increases with every season. Such boat-owners earn twice as much as the *khalasis* and have a social status as they are employers of labour. However, their children do not attend school either and their attitudes to health are similar to those of the *khalasis*.

The boat-owners who have not borrowed money from middlemen for constructing a boat, belong to the wealthier classes. They do not go out to the sea themselves but engage experienced *nakhudas* or captains. They are also able to finance nets, ice, diesel for the boat and provisions for the crew. As such, they are free to sell their produce in the open market.

Bayparis are middlemen in the fishing industry. They purchase the fish from the fishermen and then sell it to the Karachi market. They also make arrangements for providing credit to the boat-owners and supply nets, ice and provisions for the crew. Transportation of the catch, whether by sea or road, is also arranged by them. All *bayparis* belong to the delta area and the majority of the financially powerful ones belong to the Memon clan. Credit for fishermen is given to the *bayparis* by Karachi entrepreneurs. In exchange the *baypari* has to sell the fish he purchases from the fishermen at 20 per cent less than the market price to the entrepreneur. In addition, he keeps the accounts of the credit and manages the interests of the entrepreneur in the area. Abdul Karim Memon, a *baypari* of Keti Bunder, gave credit of 250,000 rupees in 1988 to the Dablas of the creeks around the settlement. He does not hope to recover any of it but this investment guarantees him a continued supply of fish at well below market rates. Depending on the scale of their operations, *bayparis* can earn anything from 120,000 to 720,000 rupees a year. In the Keti Bunder area there are five *baypari* families.

There are only four or five boat-makers left in the Keti Bunder area. Most have migrated to Ibrahim Hyderi and Karachi, where they work for big contractors. Those that are still in the Keti Bunder settlement have little work. This is because it is cheaper to have a large boat constructed in Karachi and cruise it down to the settlement than pay the cost of transportation of timber from Karachi.

According to local accounts, over 85 per cent of people engaged in agriculture are *haris*. The rest are small land-owners possessing four to ten acres. The Jats of the region, in addition to being cultivators, cut timber and sell it for fuel, manufacture matting for roofs and floors of houses, and breed camels. The camels, in most cases, belong to the wealthier among them, with the poorer Jats looking after them. Camel breeding in the Indus delta has increased substantially over the years and delta camels are sold at all the *melas* and *urs* in Sindh. *Haris* do not earn even a fraction of the cash they require for production and survival. However, about 30 per cent of their grain needs are taken care of by their share of what they produce.

Two per cent of the population is involved in providing support services to the major activities. The support activity which employs the largest number of people is transportation. Local transportation involves the carting of fish from the creek shores to the high ground for sorting, drying, weighing and transfer to trucks and pick-ups for their journey to Karachi. This is done entirely by donkey-carts. Similarly, water from the water source to the house, where it is not carried by boat or by the women themselves, is carted by donkeys. A pair of donkeys cost 1,000 rupees and eat fodder worth twenty rupees per day. Average savings of donkey-cart operators are twenty to thirty rupees a day. A small number of people are engaged with the transporters that operate pick-up trucks between Keti Bunder and Karachi. These work as labour for loading and unloading, cleaners and record-keepers. Their earnings vary from 800 to 1,500 rupees a month. The pick-ups bring diesel, ice, grain and consumer goods to the delta and take back fish and prawns. In addition, there are shopkeepers, government employees and small-scale contractors. Their number is negligible and they exist only in larger settlements. However, they have considerable influence in the community.

Due to the absence of a proper all weather road network, the cost of all consumer goods in the delta's coastal areas is on average 30 per cent higher than in those areas of the district which are better connected to Karachi or the district headquarters.

Housing And Infrastructure

Almost all housing in the delta is constructed of a *lai* frame with lattice-work walls of the same material, plastered over with mud. In areas where *lai* is difficult to acquire, *timmar* is used instead. The people, however, have a preference for *lai* as it is easier to work with and is not twisted like *timmar*. The roof is pitched and finished with reed thatch. The floors are compacted earth covered with mats. In some cases the latticed walls are not plastered over but are covered with reed mats. These mats are made by the Jats and are purchased from their settlements. Due to salinity the earth plaster near the plinth is quickly corroded and the residents complain that the timber frame in the local soil conditions weathers badly.

Houses usually consist of one or two rooms and accommodate a nuclear family. The extended family shares an open space around which its sub-families build their huts. In smaller settlements, all residents belong to the same clan. Larger settlements may have a number of clans living in them in which case the settlement is divided on a clan basis into *mohallas* or *paras*. Cooking is done in a semi-open kitchen. It has low walls to protect the *choola* or stove from the south-west wind, and a roof. Latrines, if they are built at all, are placed far away from the houses. Water is stored in earthenware pots, which were previously built by the local *kumaras*, but are now imported from the nearest urban settlement. Plastic water-coolers are also becoming popular. Traditionally, cooking was done in earthenware pots. These are slowly being replaced by city-manufactured aluminium utensils.

Richer people in the delta have now started to build their houses in cement concrete blocks and asbestos cement roofs. Reinforced concrete roofs are also used but in rare cases. Supports for the asbestos roofing are provided by bamboo poles or steel channels, both imported from Karachi. The houses of the affluent have courtyards, *verandahs* and latrines, so that greater privacy is ensured, and tend to imitate the style of the houses of the middle-classes in the large urban areas of the province. Cement for these houses is imported from Karachi and costs 98 rupees a bag as opposed to a Karachi price of 79 rupees. Aggregate comes from Jimpir or Thatta, about 40 miles away. Since these concrete structures are badly affected by salinity and rising damp, more and more houses have started using stone foundations and plinth walls. This stone comes from Jung Shahi, over 60 miles away, and its cost works out to 50 per cent more than for similar cement concrete work. Government buildings in more recent years are built entirely of stone. Salinity and water-logging are both the result of the creeping in of the sea and perennial irrigation which have been created by the building of dams and barrages.

Most of the land in the coastal belt belongs to the government. The people live on the land but do not own it. Permanent settlements, like Keti Bunder, are thus *katchi abadis* or squatter settlements. There is no move to give the people living here tenure rights. In areas where state authority is present, such as Keti Bunder and Shah Bunder, people seek the permission of the local authority or revenue department to occupy land for housing. However, more important than this permission is the permission from the residents of the area where one intends to build the house. Normally residents do not permit other than their clan or family members to live next to them. Some residents, no more than 5 per cent, do have a 99 year lease in the Keti Bunder settlement. This was given to them by the Keti Bunder Town Committee before it was dissolved in 1932.

Before the construction of dams and barrages which have dried up the Indus delta, water was easily available from the numerous distributaries of the river. These have now become saline as the sea has crept in. Water in the delta belt is therefore acquired from those delta channels which are still operative or from the nearest perennial canals. These are many miles from the coastal settlements. Water is brought from these places by boat, in most cases by the users themselves, and is used only for drinking and cooking. In the dry season most river water is highly saline.

In the early 1970s, the government initiated piped water schemes for larger coastal settlements like Keti Bunder and Shah Bunder as the Indus mouths on which these settlements were situated had long since become saline. Water was pumped from perennial canals to surface tanks in the settlements through many miles of pipeline. Most of the settlements along these pipelines have also acquired water connections and many villages have shifted their locations so as to be near the pipeline. However, no more than 15 per cent of the coastal people receive water from such piped water schemes. These schemes are managed by the District Councils or the PHED. People pay only for house connections at 30 rupees per month. Water from the stand-posts at the surface water reservoirs is free. UNICEF has also been involved in the water sector in the delta. The present water line to Keti Bunder and Shah Bunder were added to by the UNICEF in 1986. However, these piped water schemes do not function efficiently and when they break down people revert to their traditional sources. Even while they function, water from these schemes is inadequate.

There is no system of excreta or waste water disposal in the coastal settlements. Adults, males and females, excrete in the open, away from the settlements while the children excrete in the settlements. In some settlements families do put up mat walls to enclose a small space near the sea which is used as a latrine. The tide, when it rises, carries the excreta away. In the settlements where piped water has arrived, the disposal of waste water poses problems as there is no drainage system. The result is that these settlements are full of large stagnant pools of foul water in which flies and mosquitoes breed and children play. The UNICEF tried to introduce its pit latrine system through an extension effort in the area. However, it was unsuccessful as the subsoil water is only two to four feet below the surface. Traditionally, *lai* was used as fuel by almost the entire delta region. It was brought to the settlements by Jats on camel-back and exchanged for fish, agricultural produce or cash. The poorer sections of the population gathered their own firewood from the forests. This pattern for the most part is still the same, except that the Jats now only sell firewood for cash and *lai* is not easily available everywhere. For this reason, people living near or in the *timmar* marshes use *timmar* as a source of fuel. *Timmar* is more difficult to gather than *lai* due to marshy conditions and hence very little, as compared to *lai* can be collected in a day. Cost of *timmar* in the market is twelve to fifteen rupees a maund as compared to ten rupees for *lai*, provided it is available. In the Keti Bunder settlement there are only two families that gather *timmar* for sale as compared to over ten who deal in *lai*.

The delta region supports extensive grasses and shrubs which are palatable to buffalo, cows, camels and donkeys. These include *sohand* grass in the saline creeks and *pal* grass and the *lana* shrub where sweet water is available. *Sohand* and pal is eaten by buffalo and cows, and the *lana* shrub, along with *timmar* leaves, are eaten by camels. Buffalo, cows and donkeys, however, require supplementary feeds of *khalli* and *bhoosa*. These are imported from Karachi. With the decrease of river water in the delta there has been a marked decrease in the quantity and quality of pal and *lana*. Local people feel that both these species will be extinct with the passage of time. Due to these reasons the quantity of livestock in the delta areas has declined, except for camels, who need no supplementary feed and little fresh water.

KETI BUNDER

Keti Bunder has a population of 3,000[1] and is situated on the Ochto mouth of the Indus, which enters the sea through the Hajamro creek, 10 kilometres from the settlement. The area around the settlement consists of mud flats and is crisscrossed with water channels, giving the place the appearance of a marsh. Towards the west of Keti Bunder on the opposite bank of the Ochto, there is some vegetation. This consists mainly of *sohand* grass and *lana* shrubs in the immediate vicinity of the settlement and *timmar* at a distance of 4 to 5 kilometres. Keti Bunder is 50 kilometres from Mirpur Sakro and about 138 kilometres from Karachi.

From Karachi to Gharo there is a good metalled road which passes through Mirpur Sakro. After Gharo, the road is bad, and ten miles from Keti Bunder it turns into a dirt track, passing for the main part through an area which is badly affected by salinity and water logging. In the rainy season, or when tides are exceptionally high, the road is either washed away or becomes unusable due to sagging. At such times, the settlement becomes inaccessible by road. To the west, along this dirt track, are a number of small settlements. This is because the water line to Keti Bunder runs along this track and people have moved here so as to be near a source of water. Two buses leave for and two arrive from Karachi every day in Keti Bunder. They are operated by two separate families of the settlement.

The dirt track enters Keti Bunder from the east. The first buildings one comes across as one enters the settlement are the two schools constructed by the government, Union Council offices and a Basic Health Unit. All three buildings are in reinforced concrete construction and in standard government of Sindh style. The structures are badly affected by damp and salinity. A couple of dilapidated structures, in colonial style, face these new buildings. Residents say that these housed the Town Committee in the days when Keti Bunder was a large town. Later the road forks into two. One arm leads into the *bazaar* and the other to the 'jetty'. The *bazaar* consists of sixteen shops. Of these two are tea houses, five are general merchants and the rest sell cloth, sweetmeats or are owned by tailors and cobblers. The shops are built of *timmar* or *lai* lattice work plastered with mud. The roofs are pitched and finished with thatch. The roads are not metalled. The area around the *bazaar* is divided into *mohallas* or neighbourhoods. The *mohalla* of the Memons has concrete block houses with asbestos roofs, whereas the rest of the settlement has dilapidated houses which are similar in construction to the shops. There are two concrete surface water tanks with taps in them for water collection. One of these has been out of order for a long time. About 30 per cent of the population has house connections. Around the surface water tank and in the open spaces, there are stagnant pools of foul water. This is because there can be no gravity flow waste water disposal system in Keti Bunder as the level of the water in the river, at high tide, is as high as the settlement itself. The Union Council has erected protective *bunds*, by stone pitching, along the river to the west and the swamp to the east, to save Keti Bunder from flooding in the rainy season or through excessively high monsoon tides.

The jetty is just a 1 kilometre road of compacted earth along the *bund*. To one side of it is the marsh and on the other the Ochto river. A concrete surface water tank connected to the Keti Bunder water supply system has been erected to serve the people and boats at the jetty. Storage rooms, belonging to various *bayparis*, have been constructed, along with quarters for their caretakers. These storehouses are for diesel, nets, provisions for the sea-going crew and storage of fish in locally manufactured ice boxes. The construction is of local materials. In the open spaces on the jetty, one finds *timmar* stocks, which arrive here by boat; vendors of fruit and vegetables; and scales for weighing the catch as it comes in. At high tide the boats can come right up to the *bund*, but at low tide one has to walk about 20 metres through soft mud to get to the boat. Pick-ups that transport the catch to Karachi and donkeys and donkey-carts which bring the fish from the boat to the drying yards, or to the *bayparis'* store houses, are always visible.

Keti Bunder has one primary girls school in which 35 girls study. There is one teacher who is a resident of Mirpur Sakro. There is a boys' primary school and a boys' middle school as well. The former has 65 students and the latter 25. Keti Bunder has 20 to 25 matriculates (high school graduates) who studied in Karachi and Thatta as there is no high school in the settlement. One resident of Keti Bunder is a doctor and another an engineer. Both graduated from Karachi where they now work. Almost all of the matriculates and both the professionals belong to the Memon clan. In addition, Keti Bunder has one Basic Health Unit with a male doctor and a compounder. However, there is no lady health visitor or midwife although there are three traditional birth attendants in the settlement.

There is no electricity in Keti Bunder. However, there are three generators in the settlement, two of which rent out electricity to about twelve families. The third generator is at the mosque, and four shops, in addition to the mosque, use it. The shopkeepers pay for its maintenance and operation. Garbage is collected and dumped at·a central place by a sweeper employed by the Union Council. He also cleans the few latrines that exist.

Keti Bunder is the Union Council headquarters and the Union Council chairman lives here. In addition, there is a coastguard station on the entrance to the settlement with ten to twelve guards stationed in it. The purpose of this post is to prevent smuggling of contraband goods from the sea. The residents, however, feel that this post serves no purpose except to create harassment for the people.

ECOLOGY

Before dams and barrages were built in the Indus valley the delta area was crisscrossed by the distributaries of the Indus. The discharge from the river was large enough to affect the ocean currents up to over a hundred miles from the shore. Due to this enormous quantity of fresh water and the silt the river brought with it, the delta lands were the richest in what is today Pakistan. They supported extensive *lai* and *timmar* forests and grasses which were excellent feed for animals. Timber was a major export from the delta to Muscat, Aden and the Kutch peninsula. Charcoal-making and breeding of buffalo were important activities and were the domain of the Jat tribes. Agriculture was seasonal and yields were high. It was carried out when the rivers receded. Rice was the main crop and most of it was exported by boat to the coastal regions of India and the Gulf. The harbours of Keti Bunder and Shah Bunder, as such, were full of boats from Dawarka, Gumti, Muscat and the Persian Gulf ports. Populations of these delta ports were well over 15,000.[2] Fishing was then a minor activity and was carried on only by the Dabla clans.

In the 1890s the Punjab irrigation system was established. This harnessed the waters of the four major eastern tributaries of the Indus for perennial irrigation. The impact of this act on the delta was minimal, as these tributaries contributed only 25 per cent of the water in the Indus. In 1932, the Sukkur Barrage was built on the river. As a result, fresh water reduced considerably in the Indus delta. In 1958, the Ghulam Mohammad Barrage became operative and in the early sixties the Tarbela Dam was constructed. Whatever water was left in the river was siphoned off to colonize new land and transform many old inundation systems into perennial ones. Thus, fresh water no longer flowed down the Indus delta channels except for a few weeks in late summer, and that too if the floods were exceptionally high. And also the mouths of the delta became part of the sea. In addition, the Ghulam Mohammad Barrage introduced perennial irrigation in parts of the delta region.

Major ecological changes took place as a result of the sea moving into the delta channels. With the disappearance of fresh river water, agriculture in the coastal belt was no longer possible. Fresh water for drinking purposes became difficult to acquire. This affected both human and animal life. Slowly the *lai* forests diminished as they could not grow in sea water or saline soil conditions. The *timmar* forests also diminished due to the absence of fresh water flushing the marshes. The delta grasses and shrubs, on which the animals fed, were affected as well. They declined both in quality and quantity. These changes forced the agricultural and pastoral communities to migrate to the newly colonized barrage areas in the Sujawal, Jati and Thatta *talukas*. The *dowhs* unfolded their sails and left for good, as there was little or no rice left to export and no water to drink. Buffalo, which consume large quantities of fresh water, declined in number. Today, an area which produced a surplus of dairy products till the late fifties has to depend on imported powdered milk to meet the needs of its rural population. The urban centres declined and Shah Bunder and Keti Bunder are now no more than large hamlets. The Dablas and camels, and the Jats that looked after them, stayed on to force a livelihood out of the saline waters and *timmar* swamps.

After the Ghulam Mohammad Barrage was built certain areas of the delta *talukas* acquired perennial irrigation. Initially, this led to the cutting down of large tracks of forests so as to make way for agriculture. However, developing a proper drainage system for the irrigation channels posed problems because the delta area was far too flat. As a result, water logging and salinity set in and ancient orchards perished. Given these soil conditions, people have started to plant coconuts and bananas in large numbers instead of the traditional mango and guava. Sugarcane has also become an important crop. Whether these new crops and plants will be successful or how they will affect the ecology of the area, remains to be seen. They do not, however, affect the fishing communities living on the shores of the saline water channels, except in that the perennial canals have become a source for the few piped water schemes that serve some of them.

In the early 1960s the Government of Pakistan established the Department of Fisheries. This department introduced new nets, provided small loans for boat-building and motors, and gave incentives to people to involve themselves in this industry. This move coincided with the development of large scale poultry farming in the Karachi area and led to the establishment of poultry feed factories. These factories now turn enormous quantities of fish into poultry feed. In the late sixties, a demand for Pakistani prawn, lobster and fish was established in the international market and has grown ever since. These factors led to the creation of middlemen in the regions where traditionally fishing took place. As a result, large mechanized boats that could go out into the open sea replaced the traditional sail-boats;

new nets and fishing techniques were introduced and the number of people employed in fishing increased enormously. These changes have had profound social and economic effects on the delta region. They have created seasonal job opportunities for the fishing communities in Karachi. They have raised the awareness level of the people engaged in this trade and badly mauled an already disintegrating social order. On the environmental side, the residents of the coastal settlements feel that fish life is being depleted by the Karachi trawlers who drag their nets a few miles from shore and carry off all fish, irrespective of age and size. The unwanted fish is thrown back into the sea and its stench drives away other fish from the area.

COLLECTIVE EFFORTS

Although the most important aspects of the old clan order and village government have broken down, no new grassroot or state institutions have sprung up to replace them. In this state of social anarchy, cooperative efforts are almost never attempted without motivation from some external source; and if they are, they are seldom successful. The same is true for the delta region. Collective efforts for infrastructure maintenance through the local government are not uncommon. However, these are managed by the councillors and chairman, who are usually members of the affluent community, in a patriarchal manner. Thus, we see in Keti Bunder, the management and operation of a water supply and garbage collection system with no participation in the process by the poorer section of the population. However, at the initiative taken by the Union Council chairman, the entire settlement of Keti Bunder last year contributed labour or money for strengthening the protective *bunds* along the approach road. It is unimaginable that this work could have been done if the Union Council chairman had not been an affluent Memon businessman with close family ties with the *bayparis* who economically dominate the population. The fundamental problem here is that the peasants and the fishermen are no longer subservient to any order, system or government, and in these circumstances find it difficult to work with one another.

The people of Keti Bunder and its surrounding settlements, especially the shopkeepers, traders and boat-owners, have observed the degradation of their environment and understand the reasons for it. For instance, it is generally felt that fish-life is decreasing because of the increase in the number of trawlers and their fishing systems; mangroves are dying because of lack of fresh water in the river; salinity and water logging are the dual result of the sea having crept in and perennial agriculture. However, none of the residents have thought about the reasons for some of these problems nor are they particularly bothered about possible solutions.

The above are extracts from the author's field notes and reports prepared for the UN ESCAP sponsored Coastal Environmental Management Plan for Pakistan, 1989.

POSTSCRIPT 2008

The social and economic conditions in the delta region have changed considerably since 1989. The trends identified in 1989 have consolidated themselves and new trends related to the WTO regime are now emerging. Some of the new trends are described in the Introduction to Part Five, 'The Coast'. There has been a considerable increase in commercial fishing as a result of which a depletion of fish life is taking place and increasingly fishermen now work for big commercial interests. Because of this, subsistence fishing is on the way out and fishermen often have to buy fish from the middlemen from their own catch, if they wish to have fish as food.[3]

An increasing lack of water in the delta due to siphoning off the Indus for agricultural purposes upstream continues to have an adverse affect on the ecology and the natural resources of the delta region. Since my last visit in 1999 many villages have been forced to move because of a lack of water and migration to Karachi has increased considerably. These migrants, for the most part, live in grossly under-serviced and in tenure terms, insecure informal settlements in Karachi.

The formation and activities of the Pakistan Fisher Folk Forum (an NGO of fishing communities) has highlighted the ecological crisis of the delta and other related issues. Local communities have organized themselves around these issues and held demonstrations and initiated movements against what are perceived as injustices in the commercialization of fishing activities, the government's deep sea fishing policies, the adverse effects on inland fisheries and the delta of the World Bank financed Left and Right Bank Outfall Drains, and against the building of the Kalabagh Dam. The media has taken up these issues in a big way and environmentalists and NGOs have highlighted them through articles, reports and films. As a result, these issues and the Sindh coastal communities have become highly politicized.

NOTES

1. Government of Pakistan: Population Census Reports 1981; Population Census Organization, Islamabad.
2. This decline of population in the Delta Region increased between 1972 and 1982. In Mirpur Sakro, Dero and Gharo Town Committees population decreased by 23.33, 30.28, and 53.16 per cent respectively. Worked out from Government of Pakistan Census Reports.
3. Author's conversations with Muhammad Ali Shah, Chairperson, Pakistan Fisher Folk Forum at his office in Ibrahim Hyderi on 10 June 2008.

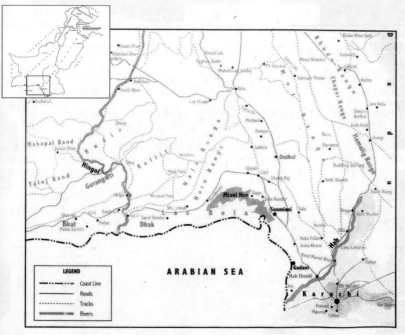

PART FIVE: THE COAST

Pakistan's coast can be divided into three distinct areas. One, the coastal areas of Lasbela and Gwadar districts in Balochistan; two, the coastal areas of Karachi; and three, the coastal areas of Thatta and Badin districts which include the Indus Delta region. This section of the book deals with the first two areas only, while the changes in the Indus delta region are described in Part Four 'The River'.

There are considerable differences between the coastal regions of Balochistan and Karachi. On the Karachi coast and to a great extent in the other coastal regions of Sindh, commercial fishing has already consolidated itself. In the case of the coastal areas of Balochistan this process is underway and is initiating social, cultural and environmental changes with the result that society is in a state of flux. These changes and conditions along the Balochistan coast are described in Chapters 13 and 14. The picture for the Lasbela and Gwadar districts was put together in 1989 through observations and interviews of school teachers, community elders, formal and informal transporters, middlemen, boat hands and contractors in the fishing industry, timber merchants and herders; shopkeepers and vendors, farmers, government officials, elected councillors and residents. The changes that have taken place since 1989 are described in the Postscript at the end of Chapter 14.

In the case of Karachi, its coastal villages have to a great extent been physically integrated into its urban sprawl. However, they are under-developed and poor as compared to most other poor settlements. Even where physical integration has not taken place, they are very much a part of the urban economy of which commercial fishing and related industries are important components. However, clan and tribal associations and culture, though under attack, are still alive and well. Changes in one such village are described in Chapter 15.

All three coastal areas have three things in common. One, they are backward as compared to most other districts of Pakistan with low literacy figures (especially among women), poor social and physical infrastructure facilities (such as roads, health centres, schools, transport, electricity) and skills. Two, the major social and economic changes that have taken place in them are primarily due to the creation of the Fisheries Department by the government of Pakistan with UN Food and Agriculture Organization (FAO) assistance in 1960. The Department promoted the commercialization of fishing, which was until then a subsistence activity for the most part. And three, all three areas depend heavily on Karachi both in terms of economic relations and for logistic and technical support to the fishing industry and related trades.

THE FORMATION OF FISHERMEN FORUMS AND MOVEMENTS*

The Pakistan Fisher Folk Forum (PFF) was formed in May 1998 by young men from fishermen families from the coastal village of Ibrahim Hyderi in Karachi. Initially, the Forum worked on issues related to education, water supply and sanitation. However, they realized that the real issue was livelihoods and the relationship of livelihoods to the exploitation of fishing communities by commercial interests, the pollution of water bodies, the depletion of fish life and mangrove forests and the growing absence of water in the Indus delta. They contacted fishing communities all over Sindh and on the Balochistan coast and also sought advise and support from the Pakistan Institute of Labour Education and Research (PILER), a Karachi based NGO.

The PFF has raised a number of issues and has backed them with public demonstrations and fishermen's movements in which fisher women, for the first time in Pakistan's history, have been prominent. They have achieved a number of successes. First, fisher folk in Pakistan in general and in Sindh and the coastal areas in particular, feel that they have an organization that represents them. This motivates them to organize. The PFF has also successfully challenged the Ranger (a para-military state organization) controlled contract system whereby the Rangers in the Badin-Jati areas managed the fishing related resources. The system was excessively exploitative of local communities. The PFF also became involved in the issues related to the absence of water in the Indus delta. Before the PFF involvement the delta issue was an environmental one. Due to the PFF involvement, it became a 'people's' issue related to livelihoods and security. The PFF has also raised issues related to the inequities in the deep-sea fishing policies of the government and the constant arrest by India and Pakistan of each other fishermen and boats who stray into Indian or Pakistani waters.

As a result of the PFF and other fishermen's organizations, such as the Mahigeer Tahreek which was formed in 2004, issues related to the fishing industry have received considerable media coverage. This and demonstrations and movements, have politicized these issues, taken them to the national and provincial assemblies and attracted the attention of national and international NGOs and IFIs.

The PFF and the Mahigeer Tahreek have both been very active in protesting the sale of islands at the mouth of the Korangi Creek in Karachi by the government of Pakistan to a Dubai based company for real estate development. They have also protested the Defence Housing Authority's Waterfront Project and the development of what is known as the Sugarland City along the western coastal areas of Karachi. The reasons for protesting these developments are that they will deny fishing communities access to the beach and to traditional fishing locations and also adversely affect the flora and fauna of the coastal regions on which fish life and hence livelihoods depend. In addition, a number of fishing villages would be evicted due to real estate development and the proposed development would also add to the pollution of the Karachi coast. Civil society organizations have supported the fishing communities in their struggle.

New challenges have emerged for the fishing industry and its actors due to the WTO hygiene requirements. Pakistani fishing techniques and processes from harvesting to export do not meet these requirements as a result of which there are fears of increased commercialization through foreign trawlers replacing local ones in the Pakistan territorial waters and the setting up of international corporate sector processing plants. As it is, in the last 10 years, increased commercialization and the pushing out of local entrepreneurs from fishing communities by groups from other parts of the country, has adversely affected the livelihood related issues of local fishermen. Increased commercialization is also leading to depletion of fish life and of the flora of the coastal and inland fishing areas. These are the challenges that the coastal areas of Pakistan and the fishing communities face today.

* Author's conversation with Muhammad Ali Shah, Chairperson of the Pakistan Fisher Folk Forum at his office in Ibrahim Hyderi on 10 June 2008.

13

Lasbela District: 1989

Lasbela district is divided into four sub-divisions. Of these Bela and Hub are coastal subdivisions and Dureji and Kanraj are non-coastal. For the most part the coast is hilly, barren and uninhabited. At the estuaries of the mountain streams there are small fishing hamlets. The larger streams are the Hub, which divides Sindh from Balochistan; the Hingol and the Polari. Of these, the first two are perennial. The Polari discharges into an enormous marsh known as Miani-Hor. Around this marsh the major coastal settlements of the district, apart from Gadani, are located.

The people of the coastal region of the Lasbela district belong to various tribes. They are Alyasanis, Rajputs, Mandra, Khashkhelis and members of other Baloch sub-tribes. In other areas of the district these tribes would follow different professions and have their separate clan organizations. In Lasbela, however, due to a lack of agricultural activity, clan groupings have never been organizationally strong, and since agriculture here depends on highly erratic and meagre rainfall, all the clans have been involved in fishing. Thus, there has been constant interaction among the different clans and marriages between their members are not uncommon. Agriculture, however, whenever possible, was carried out by traditionally agriculturist clans such as the Khaskhelis and Rajputs. Few artisanal skills were needed in such a society and these were limited to the making of small boats, carts and primitive agricultural implements. Previously each clan had a leader, or 'jam' whose main function was to settle disputes between clan members or families. The position of the jam was ensured by his comparatively greater prosperity, which was the result of his control over large tracts of usually barren rain-fed agricultural land. Contacts with the outside world were almost non-existent as was government involvement in the area. This state of affairs, and the almost universal poverty that accompanied it, created a fairly democratic and egalitarian social order.

THE NEW WADERAS

After the establishment of the Fisheries Department by the Government of Pakistan, Karachi and Mianwali entrepreneurs became active in the area to exploit its fishing potential. Locals did not have the necessary connections or the know-how to make use of the credit facilities offered by the Government of Pakistan. Also, at that time the physical and political relationships between the coastal regions of Balochistan and Karachi were not developed. Initially the middlemen used their own boats and nets for fishing and employed the local population as *khalasis* or boat hands. Thus mechanized boats and new techniques of fishing were introduced to the people. However, these entrepreneurs found it difficult to manage their affairs on the coast without local support and involvement. This led to their appointing middlemen from the area to be go-betweens between them and the *khalasis* and they disinvested in their boats and nets. Credit is now given to the coastal people by the middlemen who were originally fishermen themselves, for purchase of boats, motors and nets. In exchange the middlemen buy the catch from the boat-owners at half the market price. Many of the middlemen have now become principals of fishing companies and still live in their old settlements. These middlemen are the new *jams* or *waderas*, and since they are the economic power in the area, the old hereditary system of leadership and the democratic society that went with it have ceased to be. The people of Damb Bunder have no love for these company owners and middlemen and consider them exploiters. Since the previous society was not economically a class-ridden one, social mobility in the coastal area of Lasbela has not been too much of a problem or related to class or tribe. Thus, there are many boat-owners who have boats of their own which they have purchased from loans taken directly from the Agricultural Development Bank (ADB). Similarly, there are local truck-owners who transport the catch to Karachi. In some instances, such as in Gadani, loans are given for boats and nets on a commission of 12 to 15 per cent of the value of every catch till twice the value of the loan is repaid. Easy access to Karachi, especially for the Hub sub-division, has also been a major factor in a change of attitudes among the people. For instance, many of the elected councillors and organizers of political parties, in both Damb Bunder and Gadani, do not come from the new affluent class or the old privileged one. Some of them are openly critical of the manner in which fishing is organized and would like to see the emergence of a more equitable system.

The introduction of loans for fishing has increased the productivity and incomes of the population and finished off whatever little involvement they had with agriculture. It has also increased demands for, and dependence on, city-produced consumer goods and a growing involvement in local government affairs and politics. In these changed conditions, it is natural that the people have abandoned a number of old rituals. For example, music, song and dance were common on all festive occasions. The performers were local. Now such festivities are rare, except on marriages, and performers are hired from Karachi for this purpose. Wandering minstrels no longer roam the countryside and collective visits to the tombs of saints seldom take place.

COMMERCIAL FISHING

The introduction of commercial fishing has also had an effect on migration patterns in the district. Before, populations were fairly stable. Migrations today are both permanent and seasonal. Permanent migration, from and within the district, has taken place only to Karachi and the Hub Industrial Estate which is on the Karachi-Balochistan border. In Karachi, the immigrants work at the fisheries (developed as a result of the establishment of the Fisheries Department) and acquire residential land in settlements where their other clan members already live. At the Hub Industrial Estate the immigrants work as unskilled labour. Families from the inaccessible parts of the Balochistan coast have also moved to more accessible areas like Damb Bunder and Gadani and other settlements linked to Karachi by the RCD Highway. For instance, there are three extended families from Hingol who have settled in Damb Bunder. It is generally agreed that this migration is far too small to warrant any attention.

Between June and August the sea is far too rough for boats (other than trawlers) to go into the open sea. For this reason fishing communities from Damb Bunder, Gadani and the Hingol estuary go to Karachi and work as *khalasis* on trawlers. The same happens during the prawn season between March and June. Damb Bunder residents estimate that about 35 per cent of the male population goes to Karachi in these seasons.

Due to the growth of fishing activity on the Lasbela coast the demand for boat hands and transport facilities have increased in the coastal settlements. At Damb Bunder, over 40 per cent *khalasis* come from Uthal, Bela, Lyari and Lakhra. The donkey-cart operators at the beach are almost entirely from Bela. They are agriculturists over there and go back between May and September. This period coincides with the slack period in fishing and is also the sowing season for millet and corn. The true extent of this seasonal migration cannot be estimated through the information available.

Except for a small number of people engaged in forestry, the entire coastal belt is in some way or the other involved in fishing or related activities. An estimated 80 per cent of the coastal population owns its own boats. However, 70 per cent of these boats are small and cannot go out into the open sea. These small boat-owners and those without boats, work as *khalasis* on larger boats, when there is a demand. They get a share of the value of the catch after deductions for the cost of the boat, net, provisions, diesel, engine and the owner share, have been made.

Almost all boat-owners have borrowed money from middlemen for the purchase of their boats, engines and nets. In Damb Bunder they are forced to sell their produce to these middlemen at half the market price. Every year they borrow money again for the purchase of nets, ice, provisions, diesel and repairs. The owner after paying the *khalasis*, overhead expenses and profits for himself still needs to borrow money for the next year to keep the boat in operation. In Gadani, as mentioned earlier, loans are available on a commission of 15 per cent of the value of each catch until twice the value of the loan is paid off. In this case, the loan on a boat is paid off in six to seven years but by that time the engine needs to be overhauled and a new loan may be needed for that.

Bayparis (merchants) purchase fish from the fishermen for the Karachi market. They give loans for boat making, purchasing of nets, engines, provisions, ice and diesel. In the Lasbela area most *bayparis* have registered companies through which they operate and are not dependent on Karachi entrepreneurs and businessmen for financial support. Earnings of the larger companies can run into millions of rupees per year.

LIVELIHOODS

Boat-making is common both in Gadani and Damb Bunder. Mohammad Hashim is an old boat-maker. According to him, timber for this work is imported from Karachi and as the road is good this importation poses no problems. The boat-makers are local people and have been trained 'on site'. They employ apprentices who will carry on this tradition. In

Damb Bunder there are four boat-makers and they always have orders from the settlement itself. Mohammad Hashim has three apprentices working with him. They will become independent but only if they can borrow money for setting up their own yard and purchasing the necessary tools required for building a boat. Mohammad Hashim says that the small boats used before the Fisheries Department came in could be made with ordinary manual tools. However, the new mechanized boats cannot be made in the same way and require some machinery for their construction.

Agriculture is still a source of livelihood for many villages in the Lasbela district. However, cultivation in the coastal belt is rain-fed, and very meagre. Often the rains fail and there is no crop. This activity is carried out by the Jats and the Sheikh clans. The main crop is *bajara* and *jawar*. Apart from agriculture, they also cut timber from the forests along the seasonal torrents and sell them as firewood in the coastal settlements. These forests, in some cases, are over 40 kilometres from the coast and so the firewood has to be transported on camel back. These camels are also used for ploughing the land whenever agriculture is possible. Supplying firewood in the Lasbela district is a more reliable source of income than agriculture, and the earning of a family engaged in this work can be well above the Lasbela average.

A number of activities provide support to the fishing industry in the coastal belt. Donkey-carts carry fish from the boats to the storehouses of the fishing companies and provisions for boat crews from ration shops to the boats. Where donkey-carts cannot operate due to excessive sand, as in Gadani, this work is done by human labour on daily wages. Loans for the purchase of a pair of donkeys and a cart are available from Hindu *banyas* (a trader caste) in Sonmiani. Donkeys and camels also carry water from distant water sources to the coastal settlements and are paid for it by the residents. Trucks and pick-ups bring ice from Vindar (for preservation of the fish catch) and wheat and rice from Karachi; and carry back fish across the Hub River. They employ drivers, cleaners and loaders. The people who perform these functions are entirely from the Lasbela district. This world of new professions and activities did not exist before 1960.

A good road links the major coastal settlements of the district with Karachi. Thus, transport costs are not high and an increase of only 7 to 10 per cent over the Karachi price takes place on major consumer items such as cement, cigarettes and timber for boat-building. Without this road link with Karachi, the relationship between the Karachi and

Mianwali entrepreneurs and the Lasbela locals involved in fisheries, would be an even more unequal one.

The people of the coastal area eat fish with all their meals. Cereals are wheat and rice, which are imported from Karachi. Vegetables are eaten not more than once a month and are also supplied from Karachi. Meat is consumed only once a year, on *Bakra Id*, or on the weddings of the more affluent residents. Import of foodstuffs and grain from Karachi is of recent origin and was rare before the 1970s.

Women in the Lasbela coastal belt are segregated from men outside the extended family or close clan relatives. This determines their position in society. They look after the house, children and animals and wash and stitch clothes. They gather firewood and water, in cases where it does not mean going too far from their settlements or to areas inhabited by other tribes. Gathering of firewood and fetching water are declining as more and more people purchase firewood from Jats and Sheikhs and as the government introduces piped water schemes. Previously, a major activity of women was making fishing nets. This is no longer necessary as almost all nets in use now are ready-made nylon ones. In spite of this women have very little spare time to themselves and almost no social life or outing. Although girls are still seldom sent to school, there is a consciousness that education other than the traditional reading of the Koran is necessary for them. *Imams* and *maulvis* are the main deterrent to a change of attitudes towards women.

HOUSING AND INFRASTRUCTURE

Almost all houses in the Lasbela district, except in Gadani, are constructed of a *lai* frame, with lattice-work walls of the same material, plastered over with mud. In areas where it is more easily available, *timmar* is used instead of *lai*. But even there people have a preference for *lai* as it is easier to work with and is not twisted like *timmar*. The roof is pitched and finished with mats made from fine branches of shrubs. The floors are compacted earth covered with mats. In some cases, no lattice walls are raised and mats, with appropriate *lai* or *timmar* supports act as the walls. In recent years, the slightly more affluent have started using bamboo as a structural member for the roofs. This bamboo is imported from Karachi. Leftover of timber planks and shavings from ship building activity are increasingly used for wall construction. Most of the recent houses have been built in this manner.

Near Gadani, there is a large ship-breaking yard and in the town an intensive ship building activity goes on. A number of houses in Gadani reflect this reality. Scrap from the ship-breaking yard, including lights, steel sheets, and channels, and discarded timber from ship-building have started to dominate domestic architecture. The old method of building houses of mud and *timmer* or *lai* frame is declining for other reasons as well. People are now too busy working in fishing and have little or no time to collect *timmer* and *lai*. In addition, purchasing these timbers is becoming increasingly expensive and bamboo from Karachi is becoming a viable substitute.

Houses usually consist of one or two rooms and accommodate a nuclear family. The extended family shares an open space around which its sub-families build their huts and in which animals, mostly goats, are housed. Cooking is done in a semi-open kitchen. It has low walls to protect the *choola* (stove) from the South-West wind, and a roof. Latrines, if they are built at all, are placed far away from the houses. Water was stored in earthenware pots but now plastic containers from old ships are increasingly used. Traditionally, earthenware pots were used for cooking. These have been replaced, in the accessible settlements, by city manufactured aluminium utensils. The role of the *kumhars* has thus decreased and many of them have also become *khalasis* on the boats of their one time clients.

Richer people in the coastal settlements have now started to build their houses in cement concrete blocks and with asbestos cement sheet roofs. Reinforced concrete roofs are also used but in rare cases. Support for the asbestos roofing is provided by bamboo poles, left over timber from ship building or steel channels from the Gadani ship-breaking yard. The houses of the affluent have courtyards, verandas and latrines, so that greater privacy in ensured. They tend to imitate the style of middle-class houses in the large urban centres of Pakistan. Cement for these houses is imported from Karachi and costs 86 rupees a bag at Damb Bunder, as opposed to a Karachi price of 79 rupees. Aggregate comes from the bed of nearby hill torrents and seasonal rivers. These changes are accentuating the rich-poor divide that the commercialization of fishing and the cash economy have created.

The major part of almost all the coastal settlements are technically speaking, *katchi abadis*, as most residents do not have tenure rights. This is especially true of the expansion that has taken place since the 1960s, which perforce had to take place illegally on state land, as private land was too expensive to purchase and impossible to encroach upon.

There is no government move to regularize these encroachments although there are statements of intent to that effect. Nor are there any schemes to subdivide state lands for housing purposes. If anyone needs land to build a house he encroaches on an area, provided his neighbours-to-be do not object. So as to prevent eviction for illegal squatting he then has to pay a bribe to the *tehsildar* at the relevant *tehsil* headquarters. The sum involved in this illegal gratification depends on the location and size of the plot and the paying capacity of the squatter. Both in Gadani and in Damb Bunder, the demand for regularization of occupation has been an issue in recent local body elections.

As mentioned earlier, most of the coastal settlements are situated at or near the estuaries of seasonal hill torrents. Earth dams are built at regular intervals in the torrents to catch some of this water. It is from wells dug in the beds of these channels that most of the settlements receive their water. If the wells are not more than 5 or 6 kilometres away from the settlement, women carry water from there to their homes on their heads or on donkeys. If the wells are farther than that, water is carried back on donkeys or camels, often by professional water vendors. If it does not rain for a couple of years, the wells become saline, in which case the population simply puts up with having to drink brackish water.

The Government of Balochistan has initiated a number of piped water schemes in the district. These consist of pumping water from improved locations in the beds of the hill torrents, to surface water tanks in the settlements, and sometimes to an overhead water reservoir. A number of persons acquire house connections, although this means paying a charge of 30 to 40 rupees a month. This is considerably cheaper than paying a water vendor. The system, both in Damb Bunder and Gadani, is inoperative 15 to 20 times a year for 3 to 4 days at a stretch. During such periods people revert to their traditional sources of water. Water schemes are managed by District and Union Councils and the Town Committee. The Councillor, Mohammad Ismail of Damb Bunder, gets 30,000 rupees year as a grant from the UC. He spends almost all of this on maintenance and operation of the water scheme in the settlement and the small length of road that exists in this area.

Generally there is no system of latrines and waste water disposal in the settlement. People excrete in the open, some distance from their houses. However, a few affluent families have built latrines. For example, in Damb Bunder, eight families have proper pit latrines and another thirty have bucket latrines. In large settlements, such as Gadani, where population densities are high and it is not easy to excrete in the open without being observed, over 20 per cent of the houses have started to use bucket latrines. A scavenger cleans out these latrines every few days. There is no solid waste management in the settlements with the result that they are littered with plastic bags, tin containers, used nets and other inorganic materials. Luckily, waste water disposal does not pose a major problem as yet, as the soil is sandy and the water seeps through easily.

FUEL AND LIVESTOCK FEED

Lai and *babar* trees grow along the hill torrents or in depressions where rainwater gathers. Often these trees are planted and looked after by clans, such as the Jats, who are also engaged in seasonal agriculture. The branches of these trees are cut and carried to the coastal settlements on camel back. If the distance to the settlement is too long for a daily journey, entire camel caravans, carrying enough fuel to last a month, come and camp outside the settlement. People purchase their stock on a daily or weekly basis from these camel men. Sometimes local middlemen purchase parts of the stock and sell it to their fellow villagers at a higher price. In certain coastal areas there are *devi* forests or clumps near the settlement. Many of these have been planted by the forest department to protect the new metalled roads from sand drifts. Women, of families who cannot afford to purchase fuel from the Jats, collect firewood from this source. *Devi*, however, burns poorly. In more recent years, *Pathan* settlers in Vindar have started making charcoal out of *devi*. This is sold to the coastal settlements and is cheaper than *lai* or *babar* firewood. Ghulam Rasool brings timber from the hill torrents to Damb Bunder and sells it to residents. Previously, he and his family did nothing else and as such much of their time was spent in moving with his camels from the torrents to the settlements and back again. However, he does not wish to do this any more since he wants his children to study and he also feels that in Damb Bunder at least, liquefied petroleum gas (LPG) cylinders will soon make him irrelevant. In other settlements, where people have time on their hands, they can collect firewood themselves.

Since there is no natural vegetation that can sustain animals, except goats and camels, there are very few cows and no buffaloes in the Lasbela coastal settlements. In Damb Bunder for instance, for a population of 2,000, there are only a hundred goats and about ten cows.

Since the natural vegetation is not nourishing enough, the goats give much less than normal amount of milk. The cow-owners import corn and fodder for their animals from Vindar, the *tehsil* headquarters. The people in Damb Bunder and Gadani estimate that it is cheaper by 50 per cent to use powdered milk than feed milk-producing cows. In the Sonmiani *tehsil*, at Naka Kharai, there is a colony of dairy farmers who keep buffalo. Feed for these animals comes from Karachi. All tea shops in Damb Bunder and Sonmiani purchase milk from here but an increasing number of households use powdered milk for domestic consumption.

DAMB BUNDER

Damb Bunder has a population of 2,000,[1] and is situated on the main creek of Miani Hor, a large marsh, which is the estuary of the Porali river. Damb Bunder is in the Vindar *tehsil*. The area around the settlement consists of alternating sand dunes and flats, with clumps of *devi* shrubs. The opposite side of the marsh is visible and contains mangrove forests. Being on the shore of a creek, Damb Bundar is protected from the open sea, so that in the stormy season during the South-West monsoon, boats can be left in the water and remain operative, unlike in settlements on the open sea.

From the RCD highway, about 80 kilometres from Karachi, one turns South-West towards the sea. This metalled road takes one through Sonmiani to Damb Bunder, a distance of about 20 kilometres from the RCD highway. Sonmiani was the original port, famous in history, but physical changes in the coastline, due to erosion by the sea, forced the Sonmiani fishermen to move to Damb Bunder. The road between Sonmiani and Damb Bunder runs in the most part along the Miani Hor. On either side of the road, from the RCD highway to Sonmiani, there are *devi* plantations developed by the forestry department to protect the road from sand drift. Four buses daily ply between Sonmiani and Karachi. They are able to do this thanks to the *devi* plantations. The people of the area understand this and as such they have not damaged the plantations or cut their branches for fuel.

The road from Sonmiani ends at the creek. Its last three hundred meters is the Damb Bunder Bazaar. It consists of ten tea-houses (of which four also serve food), provision stores, cloth-shops and a barber's establishment. Open air storage space for firewood is also a part of this bazaar. Most of the tea-houses belong to people from Sonmiani and are open twenty-four hours of the day, as they cater to fishermen whose boats come and go at all times of the night and day. Towards the north of the bazaar, there are a few dilapidated concrete structures. These are the dispensary, the girls' primary school and the boys' middle school. A mosque, also in concrete, is the most impressive structure in the settlement. Further north, beyond these structures, are concrete block houses which belong to the more affluent Damb Bunder residents. Towards the south and east of these structures, nearer the sea, are the houses of the fishermen. These houses are in clusters with large open spaces in-between. Each cluster accommodates an extended family of six to seven nuclear families. Almost all these houses have timber board walls and thatch roofs. Some have galvanized iron sheet roofs, and a few, asbestos sheet roofs. Still nearer the sea are the homes of migrant *khalasis* and daily wage labourers. These are made of *timmar* or *lai* skeletons with mat walls and roof. Some have used tin, cardboard, or plastic sheets for walls and for roofs as well. In the space between these clusters are store houses of the companies and middlemen. Twenty such establishments exist and consist of a *veranda*, with a large terrace in front of it, where the fish is weighed; a storehouse and a small office. The older structures are of board and the newer ones are of concrete blocks and asbestos sheets. Piles of fish, used nets, plastic bags and damaged cardboard containers litter the water front.

The present settlement is in danger of being destroyed by the action of the sea which is eroding the shore. It has already affected the middle school building. At exceptionally high tides the water now comes right into the settlement. The bazaar is safe as the road there is raised well above the level of the shore. The settlement has shifted twice in the last thirty years because of the action of the sea. To the south of the bazaar, there is a large natural depression where all the garbage gets collected and since the surface water supply tank is also here, there are large pools of stagnant water. There are four boat-makers on the beach and their stocks of timber lie in the open. A lot of materials, in the form of containers, timber, furniture from old ships, purchased or acquired from the ship-breaking yard in Gadani, are in use in the settlement, including fibre-glass boats. Thirty years ago Damb Bunder was a small settlement of thirty to forty houses. These were made of *timmar* lattice-work and mud infill. The present expansion of the village, and the hectic activity one sees here, is the result of the expansion of the fish industry which has extended mechanized boats, new types of nets, and credit facilities for the local fishermen.

Damb Bunder has no electricity. The middlemen and company-owners have diesel generators. They have given connections to the hotels and tea-houses at 8 rupees per day for one tube light. The rest of the population uses kerosene lanterns. One lantern consumes about 20 rupees per month if it is used for four hours each day.

IMPACT ON ENVIRONMENT

The introduction of mechanized boats, nylon nets and credit facilities for the fish industry since 1960, coupled with a local demand for poultry feed and an international demand for Pakistani catch, has had a profound impact on the environment. As a result of these actions populations in the coastal settlements increased considerably as a large number of people turned to fishing. In 1960, 15,785 persons were involved in fishing on the Balochistan coast. By 1970, this figure had increased to 28,600. Sail-boats declined and were almost entirely replaced by mechanized craft between 1980 and 1985.[2] Apart from raising incomes, this expansion established closer links with Karachi. Migration, seasonal and permanent, related to work in the fisheries started to take place. The boat-building industry has also expanded, and with it diesel and oil requirements, which have resulted in the beginnings of marine pollution. These factors have brought about major changes in attitudes. Agriculture and forestry have declined, although people are consuming larger quantities of grain and firewood as compared to, say, ten years ago. This is leading to deforestation and a growing dependence on Karachi for food supply. Physical changes in the settlements have also taken place. The houses are now seldom made of *lai* or *timmar* with a mud infill and thatch roof. Walls are constructed of left over planks and wood shavings from boat-construction and the roofs are of galvanized iron and asbestos sheets, thus reflecting the new economic realities. Plastic bags, PVC crates and containers, nylon nets, rubber tyres, litter the beaches. There is, however, no solid waste management anywhere along the coast. Stagnant pools of waste water are a common site where piped water schemes have been implemented, and since the settlements have increased in area, it is increasingly difficult to go into the wilderness to excrete. This is leading to a demand for toilets within the homes which means a whole new mind-set and a different way of planning a house.

The operation of trawlers from Karachi, off the Lasbela coast, is a source of anxiety to fishermen. According to the fishermen they denude the coast of all fish life, including baby fish and fish eggs. They feel that due to this the quantity of fish is decreasing. The trawlers also dump dead, unwanted fish back into the sea, creating pollution which drives away other fish. By law, the operation of trawlers cannot take place within twelve miles of the Balochistan coast. The residents of Damb Bunder, however, are definite that this law is constantly violated but are not sufficiently organized to fight the violation.

The Hub Industrial Estate in the Lasbela district has attracted a lot of labour from other parts of Pakistan, especially Karachi, and has thus changed the ethnic composition of the Hub subdivision. It has also led to considerable air pollution and farmers in the neighbourhood complain that not only has agriculture been adversely affected, but also their health. As an example of the effects of pollution, people point to the case of Bela Chemicals, five miles from Vindar. Chlorine gas emissions from the factory have completely destroyed fruit gardens and plants. Local residents have had to move from its vicinity as there was no grass left for their animals. People in Damb Bunder have also mentioned that labourers faint regularly in the factory.

Employment activities provided by the ship-breaking yard at Gadani have not attracted the people of the district. Labour at the yard is almost all Pathan and Punjabi. This is resented by the locals who complain that since the ship breaking contractors are not locals, they employ outsiders. The locals, however, do operate animal transport. Still, materials from the destroyed ships have had an effect on the domestic architecture of the coastal belt. Fibre glass life-boats from the ships, suitably mechanized, are also in use for fishing. Fishermen feel that these boats are more suitable for transport than for fishing. In either case they are cheaper and require less maintenance and are more stable in the high seas than the traditional timber boats.

The Hub Dam, on the river Hub, has reduced the flow of water in the river below Lang Laharani, to no more than a trickle. The water from this dam is used for Karachi. The effect of the drying up of the Hub on the coastal communities downstream of Lang Laharani could not be properly ascertained. However, according to the population at Gadani, agriculture on the river banks has declined and the settlements at the estuary no longer have adequate drinking water. It seems that unlike in the past, wells dug by the people near the river estuary now become dry long before the rainy season sets in.

COLLECTIVE EFFORTS

There have been efforts by the fishing community, both in Damb Bunder and in Gadani, to come together to try and tackle the problems that economic and physical change have forced upon them. The *Mahegir Faleh-o-Bahbood Anjuman* was formed in Damb Bunder in 1986. It had 140 members. Its aim was to pressurise the companies and middlemen to accept the system of deducting commission from the value of a catch rather than purchasing the catch at less than market rates, from their creditors. However, the companies and the middlemen put economic pressure on the members of the Anjuman, along with threats of violence, and the organization had to wind up. The organization had the backing of the Pakistan People's Party's local organization. The Party in those days was in the opposition, unlike today. There are no moves afoot to revive this Anjuman. In Gadani, an organization is in the process of being born. Its name is Baloch *Yakmusht* Welfare Association. Its president, Abdul Khaliq, an active member of the Pakistan Peoples Party is the owner of a tea-shop and its secretary is a compounder in the government dispensary in Gadani. The aim of the Association is to involve people in discussion and debate on the conditions in Gadani and then to organize the community in seeking solutions to the problems of the town. It is important to note that the initiative for setting up these organizations, both at Damb Bunder and Gadani, has not come from the previously privileged classes or the new economically powerful ones, and nor does it have their involvement.

The residents of both Damb Bunder and Gadani, who were interviewed, had not only an understanding of the environmental issues that were affecting their lives, but a willingness to do something about those that were affecting them economically. They understood the repercussions of deforestation, the role of trawlers in destroying fish life, and the problems created by piped water schemes and the Hub Dam. They knew and were concerned about the environmental problems being created by Bela Chemicals, and had sent press releases to various newspapers regarding this issue.

The above are extracts from the author's field notes and reports prepared for the UN ESCAP sponsored Coastal Environmental Management Plan for Pakistan, 1989.

POSTSCRIPT 2008

Between 1989, when the above text was written, and 2004 when I last visited the Lasbela district, major changes have taken place in the district. These changes are the result of the continuation of the trends identified in 1989. For one, urban populations have visibly increased. This is borne out by the 1998 Census results as well. According to the 1981 Census, the urban population was 16 per cent and according to the 1998 Census it is 37 per cent of the district population.[3] The number of RCC houses, latrines, and telecommunications, have all increased considerably and television is the major source of information. Census figures also indicate that every second house in the urban areas has satellite television. Bamboo, used for house building, has visibly replaced *lai* and *timmar*. This bamboo is imported from Karachi. The population of the district has also increased by about 80 per cent between 1981 and 1998. There has been an in-migration of 12.8 per cent in the inter census years, 55 per cent of this migration is from Balochistan. Much of the rest is from Karachi. However, these impressive figures have one down side to them. Large scale urbanization has really taken place at Hub, on the Karachi frontier and as such Hub, which has grown at the rate of 17.15 per cent annually between 1981 and 1998, is the largest urban centre in the Lasbela district.[4] It is for all practical purposes an industrial suburb of Karachi.

Electricity has expanded considerably and the new Hub Power Project which has been set up has the potential of supplying the entire district with energy. Health and education facilities have not increased in proportion to the increase in population. However, census figures tell us that literacy which was 5.6 per cent in 1972 has increased to 22.3 per cent in 1998. Female literacy has increased from 1.5 per cent to 14.88 per cent in the same period.[5]

Increase in urban populations, water usage, fishing activities and transport have increased waste water disposal and solid waste related problems. Shops and bazaars have also increased considerably. As such, all urban settlements are far more environmentally degraded than they were in 1989 mainly because government attempts at tackling these problems have been missing or have not been successful and communities have not taken to managing their settlements themselves.

Because of the proximity of Karachi to the urban centres of Lasbela, the economic inter-dependence between the district and Karachi has increased. Conversations in 2004 seem to suggest that the wealthier middlemen and influentials have moved their families to Karachi and have also made investments in fishing related businesses in the city. The reason for this move is to get their children educated and to make them a part of big-city culture.

Workers in the fish industry and *khalasis* are trying to form organizations to protect their interests against exploitation by big businesses. Some of the initiators of these organizations are active members of the PFF and have participated in PFF organized demonstrations in Karachi and Badin. These developments are the natural result of the social changes that were taking place in 1989 when I visited the coastal areas.

In 2003, the coastal highway from Karachi to Gwadar was completed. This has facilitated traffic between Karachi and the coastal areas of the Lasbela district due to which land values along the coast have increased and Karachi real estate companies and entrepreneurs are looking for investment opportunities. Already eating places have been established to cater to Karachi weekend visitors. Due to the construction of the road there is evidence to suggest that the involvement of Karachi entrepreneurs and companies related to the fishing industry has increased.

NOTES

1. Government of Pakistan: *Population Census Reports 1981*; Population Census Organization, Islamabad.
2. Government of Pakistan, *Handbook of Marine Fisheries Department*, Volume 14, Ministry of Food and Agriculture, 1985.
3. Government of Pakistan: *Population Census Reports 1998*; Population Census Organization, Islamabad.
4. Ibid.
5. Ibid.

14

Gwadar District: 1989

Gwadar is divided into two sub-divisions. These are the Gwadar sub-division and the Pasni sub-division. Both these subdivisions are coastal. The district stretches from the Iranian frontier in the West to the boundary of Lasbela district in the East. As in the case of Lasbela, habitation is normally found where hill torrents or rivers meet the sea. Major rivers are Dasht, with Jiwani at its mouth, and Shadi with Pasni near its estuary. For the most part the coast is barren and uninhabited and has no metalled roads, at all, linking it to other areas of the province or to Karachi.

As in the case of the Lasbela district, tribal and clan organizations in Gwadar district were never very strong. This was because agriculture was meagre and depended solely on erratic and insufficient rains. Further north, in Makran, there are large streams such as the Kech and Dasht, which have substantial water in them at certain times of the year. Along these streams fairly extensive agriculture and fruit farming has been carried out since times immemorial. The produce of these activities has been exported, not only to the coast, but also to the Gulf. Thus these farmers with their stronger clan organizations came to politically dominate the coastal belt and appointed *nazims* to govern it. Tradition has it that the original fishermen were Kalmatis, who lived around the Kalmat basin. Today, however, people of all tribes participate in fishing activities.

The Makran coast has had constant contacts with the Persian Gulf, and through the Muscat-Oman maritime empire, with Africa. A sizeable part of the population is of African descent. These factors made it difficult for the Baloch tribal system to fulfil its traditional functions on the coast. From the eighteenth century onwards these factors were supplemented by central control of the coast from either the Sultanate of Oman or the Baloch Confederacy at Kalat. Another factor which has contributed to the changes that have taken place is employment in the Gulf. It is estimated that between 1960 and 1985 about one thousand persons from the district were recruited as soldiers and policemen by the Gulf governments every year.[1] The money they remitted home increased wages, changed the nature of houses people lived in, resulted in a big decline of agriculture as cheap labour for it was no longer available, introduced consumer goods, expanded the services sector, especially transportation and made social and economic mobility possible. It also resulted in the import of food from Karachi, especially wheat, since local agriculture declined. These changes have created a society in which, as an old Pasni resident put it, all are now free. And he is right, for the *sardari* system or the rule of clan elders simply does not function in Gwadar's coastal areas. However, there is a down side to these positive developments. Due to Gulf money, the cost of living in Gwadar and of skills that people require in their daily lives, is much higher than in the rest of Balochistan or even Karachi for that matter. For the poorer sections of the population, who do not have family members in the Gulf, this is a big problem.

Makran's wealth in fisheries is enormous. Its exploitation really began with the introduction, by the FAO for demonstration purposes, of mechanized boats and out-board motors. By 1985, the whole picture had changed with sail-boats declining in number from 1639 to 327, and mechanized boats and gill netters increasing from 846 to 2,206 and from 21 to 159 respectively, all in a period of five years.[2] Along with this development, *seths* emerged on the same pattern as the *bayparis* in Lasbela and ice factories sprung up as ice was required to protect the fish from rotting during its long journey to Karachi. The demand for diesel, spare parts for engines, timber for the increasing number of under-construction boats, and mechanics for repairs, increased with all this activity. For the most part this demand is now met by imports, by road, from Karachi. As the road to Karachi is bad, organizing this activity requires considerable managerial skills. At Pasni three to four trucks arrive from Karachi every day. They bring diesel, fodder, vegetables, kerosene and other necessities. They take back sharks, tuna, prawns, lobsters and pomfret, all in ice boxes. All this activity has changed the Makran coast and its social economy.

Although figures for migration to the Gulf are available, there is no data regarding migration from the district to the other areas of Pakistan or within the district itself. Conversations with people in Gwadar, Pasni and Sur show that there is no major movement of this nature except to Karachi, where seasonally 5 per cent of male adults seek jobs in the fisheries, something that was unknown before the commercialization of fishing. People in small numbers from the Quetta and Pishin areas of the province do come and work as *tandoor* operators, agricultural and construction labour and in trade related jobs.

LIVELIHOODS

It is estimated by the residents of the settlements visited that 50 per cent of the coastal families are *khalasis*. Many of these *khalasis* also have small boats of 6 to 10 feet which do not go into the open sea, and hence they cannot survive on incomes from them. *Khalasis* on the Makran coast earn more than their Lasbela counterparts. However, given the high cost of living on the Makran coast this does not mean much.

Drying of fish is a major activity on the Makran coast. This drying saves the *seth* the cost of ice required to preserve fish during its journey to Karachi. The fisheries department has constructed drying yards which are used by the *seths* on payment of a commission to the government. A number of people work as loaders, unloaders, packers, cleaners of fish and caretakers at these yards. Fishing companies, which bring wheat to Pasni and Gwadar, also employ a large number of loaders and unloaders for their cargo. Since this supply runs into 200,000 to 300,000 bags of wheat a year,[3] and since the ships anchor five or six kilometres from the shore, this is a very major exercise. In addition, all sail-boats are chartered to carry the wheat bags from the ship to the shore. A small number of people also work in the ice factories in Pasni and Gwadar. These sources of employment did not exist before 1960.

Boat-owners, as in the Lasbela district, are in debt to the *seths*. However, in Gwadar district, the relationship between the *seths* and the boat-owners is a far more unequal one than in the other coastal districts. This is because of bad road conditions between Karachi and the district, and hence the greater dependence of the boat-owners on the *seths* for supply of provisions, nets and other necessities for fishing activities.

In coastal settlements, where the *seths* cannot function directly, the *dallal* system operates. *Dallals*, or middlemen, auction the catch of the fishermen to the agents of the *seth* or the fishing company. Five to ten per cent of the value of the catch is taken by the *dallal*. Fishermen agree to this arrangement because at times they have to borrow money from the *dallal* for financing their fishing operations. These loans are paid off in cash on a yearly basis.

Due to logistic problems created by the distance and lack of road facilities to Karachi, *seths* in the district seldom operate as individuals. They register companies, have partnerships and enrol a large number of support staff. Most of them belong to the Ismaili and Khoja communities, who have been traders and shopkeepers on the coast for many generations. Both these communities send their children to Karachi for education. In recent years many of them have moved their entire families to Karachi as they do not feel that conditions on the coast are 'what they used to be'. When Mohammad Ismail, a Gwadar *seth* was asked why he felt that conditions were forcing him to leave for Karachi, he replied, 'There is no *izzat* left for us. People have become ill mannered and as such there is no security for us or our children'. Another trader commented, 'Small people have become big, serfs have become traders and because of their *ghoondaism* they are pushing us out of business. Business is now linked to politics and politics to muscle, and we are no politicians'.

A very large number of boats are made in the Gwadar district. This is because, unlike the Thatta district, it is not possible to build boats in Karachi and float them down. Most of the timber for boat-making comes from Karachi. However, with the establishment of a saw mill in Gwadar, local timber is also being used. There are over 70 to 80 *ostas* in Pasni alone, working as boat-makers. According to Osta Amjad Baloch, about twelve launches of over fifty feet length and eighty of twenty to thirty feet length are manufactured in Pasni each year.

Again, due to the lack of a good communication system with Karachi, boat engines cannot be sent there for repairs or a mechanic asked to come from there to make the repairs. Therefore, to cater to the demand, mechanics have established themselves in the major settlements and import spare parts from Karachi. These mechanics have been trained in the Gulf and in Karachi. The fisheries department operates a maintenance workshop in Pasni. People working there as apprentices will eventually open their independent businesses.

An increasingly large number of people in the district have taken to fishing or have gone abroad. This has created severe labour problems for the agriculture sector. Coupled with a recent cycle of drought, this has led to large scale importation of grain and vegetables from Karachi. As in Lasbela district, most agriculturists planted trees on their lands or along the torrents and sold this timber as firewood to the coastal settlements. This process still continues. Jats, Negwars and Raykhani Baloch bring this timber on camel back. Although these clans are not traditionally fish eaters, they have now started to buy fish from the settlements. Recently urban entrepreneurs have also started to go to the forests to buy timber from the Jats. They transport it to the settlements by truck, thus reducing costs. With the death of a subsistence barter economy it is no longer possible for agriculturists, or the suppliers of timber, to exist on earnings from their traditional work and they have to supplement their incomes from some other source. Almost invariably, this source is fishing.

Due to the fact that the Gwadar district has comparatively large urban populations, considerable capital, and that its road link with its principal market is poor, the services sector in the district is very large. Transportation of fish to Mund, Tomb and Turbat, on the one hand, and to Karachi on the other, provides jobs to people as drivers, cleaners, loaders and unloaders. Donkey-carts, and labourers where the beach is too sandy for the carts to operate, transport catch from the shore to the auction platforms or to the store houses of the *seths*. Similarly, ice has to be loaded, transported, sometimes over long distances, by truck, and unloaded again. Hotels, tea-houses and vendors to cater to this activity have also sprung up. In addition, inter-city transport has also developed. A large number of pick-ups, financed by Gulf earnings, ply between Turbat, Gwadar, Pasni and Ormara.

Due to a lack of good roads in the district and poor links with the rest of the country, prices of consumer goods, including food stuffs, are 30 to 50 per cent higher than Karachi. For the same reasons, fish is acquired by *seths* at less than half its Karachi value.

HOUSING AND INFRASTRUCTURE

Most houses in the coastal settlements are constructed of a *lai* skeleton plastered over with mud. *Timmar*, apart from the Dasht estuary, is not available in any substantial quantity in the district. The roof is pitched and finished with mats made of branches of the *gaz* plant. Mats are also made from the branches of the *peeche* tree and are of two kinds. One is made by men and is called *gorpath*. It is used for the roof and sells at about 2 rupees per square foot. The other is made by women and is called *tagird*. It is used for flooring and sells at 5 rupees per square foot. With jobs increasingly available in the fishing industry the production of both *gorpath* and *tagrid* is fast declining. Abdul Rahman who sells these mats in the bazaar at Sur, says that in a few years they will not be available anymore and he will switch to some fishing related work. Already his son works at the fish drying yard in Pasni.

Often, the houses of the poor just have mat walls instead of *lai* lattice-work with earth infill. All these materials of construction are brought on camel back to the settlements from sparsely forested areas along or near the torrents, by the same people who supply fuel wood. In recent years, structural elements of bamboo have also started to be used. Bamboo is imported from Karachi and costs 50 per cent more than the Karachi price. However, it is still cheaper than *lai* branches of over 10 feet length and is easier to use. Cement in the Gwadar district comes from Karachi and costs 115 rupees in Pasni and 130 rupees in Gwadar. The Karachi price is 79 rupees. Aggregate is available in the torrents and in the hills. Stone in mud mortar is used in the plinths of most traditional construction, and sometimes even in new concrete construction to prevent rising damp.

Previously, affluent people built their homes of sun dried mud brick and date palm rafters. The bricks were used in thick walls and plastered over with mud mixed with straw. The rafters, imported from Turbat, formed the roof structure. They were finished with *gorpath* and eighteen inches of earth. This form of construction does not take place anymore. The thick mud walls have been replaced by six inches concrete blocks and the rafters by bamboo or steel sections. *Gorpath* is still used over this structure, but it is increasingly being replaced by corrugated sheets and reinforced concrete slabs. The new houses of the rich are copies of middle-income housing in Pakistan's larger cities and of government domestic architecture, in the district. They have washrooms, pit-lavatories and sometimes underground water tanks. Most of this new architecture is climatically unsuitable and uncomfortable for the Gwadar district and made of imported materials.

Most coastal settlements are built on Central Board of Revenue (CBR) land. Theoretically speaking, one should be able to get allotment of land from the CBR. However, in practice it is a long and difficult procedure. Consequently, as in the Lasbela district, people occupy land, if their neighbours-to-be have no objection, and then come to some illegal financial settlement with the relevant state officials to prevent eviction or harassment.

Traditional water sources and collection systems in the Gwadar district are identical to those in the Lasbela district's coastal areas, except that since settlements here are larger, the water is in shorter supply, except in the Dasht estuary. This shorter supply of water means that often sea water has to be mixed with fresh water to fulfil requirements.

Generally there is no system of lavatories and waste water disposal in the settlements. People excrete in the open, some distance from their houses, except in large settlements where densities are high. However, a number of affluent families have built latrines. Most of these lavatories are pit-lavatories and follow the UNICEF model promoted by Balochistan Integrated Area Development (BIAD). There is no solid waste management in the settlements either, with the result that, where populations are large, settlements are littered with all forms of garbage. Even in a settlement like Pasni, which has a population of 20,000 and considerable revenues, no waste management programme exists.

PASNI

Pasni has a population of about 20,000. It is situated on the Makran coast, about 500 kilometres west of Karachi and 130 kilometres east of Gwadar.[4] It is on the open sea and so large boats have to anchor for away from the shore, and in the stormy season in summer, they cannot go into the sea. After the under-construction fish harbour is completed, this major problem will be overcome. A seasonal river, Shadi Kaur, flows near the town and has traditionally been the settlement's main source of water.

Pasni is linked by road to the East with Ormara and Karachi, to the West with Gwadar and to the North with Turbat. All these links are through earth roads that get badly affected whenever it rains. The area around the town is barren, hilly and uninhabited. Some agriculture does take place in the bed and on the banks of Shadi Kaur but it cannot even satisfy the needs of those engaged in it. To protect the earth roads from sand drifts, the forest department, in the vicinity of Pasni, has planted *devi* trees on either sides of these approach roads. People protect these plantations since the roads are crucial for their livelihoods.

Pick-ups and buses link Pasni with Karachi, Gwadar, Ormara and Turbat. There are three buses a week to Karachi and the journey takes two days. The Pasni airport links the town to Turbat, Gwadar, Quetta, Panjgur, Karachi and the Gulf. The sea link with Karachi, especially for transportation of cargo would be very beneficial to the coastal population as it would lower transportation costs considerably. However, customs restrictions, and more so, the manner in which they are applied, have so far prevented this mode of transport from developing.

Here there is a conflict between the requirements of the new social economy and an administration that lives by rules and regulations of the past.

Pasni can be divided into four distinct areas. These are: the bazaar and the old settlement; the government area; the government employees' housing colony and the beach. The bazaar consists of two near parallel streets. The larger one is about half a kilometre while the smaller is no more than 250 yards. A number of buildings in the bazaar are old and made of mud brick and thatch. They have *verandas* with arches and round columns in front of them. The new buildings are of cement concrete blocks but with traditional roofing. In the bazaar there are a number of hotels and tea houses; fruit and vegetable vendors and sweetmeat merchants; video hire and sound cassette shops; provision stores; cloth and grain merchants; jewellers and every variety of consumer goods. Yousef Baloch an old shopkeeper of the bazaar says, 'Close down the fisheries and the bazaar will disappear. Not even an eating place will be left.'

Off the bazaar there is an open piece of land where firewood, mats and timber for construction from the countryside are stored and sold. The camels and the men who bring these materials also camp in this space. On three sides of the bazaar are the houses of the population. Most of them are of *lai* lattice-work with earth infill. However, almost all of the under construction ones are of concrete blocks. The offices of the Town Committee and the schools are also in this part of town. Between the government area and the bazaar is the truck *adda* (stand). There are always trucks, buses and pick-ups at the *adda*, with people loading, unloading or cleaning the vehicles. On a hill nearby is the old, and now uninhabited, mud house belonging to the Nawab of Makran.

The government area contains the offices of the revenue, health and education departments; the fisheries; the RHC; the Expanded Programme for Immunization (EPI) office and the under construction fish harbour. All buildings here are of concrete construction, although some of them do have asbestos sheet roofs. These structures are linked to each other and to other parts of the town, with poorly surfaced metalled roads.

Not far from the beach is the housing made for government employees. It is of reinforced concrete, has running water, flush latrines but no roads, paths or pavements, and no storm drainage. It resembles government housing in any district of the country.

Along the beach there are two government owned fish drying yards, an ice factory, store houses of the *seths* and *dallals*, boat-makers' yards, mechanics' establishments and weighing platforms for fish. Pick-ups that carry the catch to Karachi, are constantly being loaded and sent off. Along the beach, on the shore, stand hundreds of boats, all of them mechanized. The beach is littered with dry or rotting fish, nylon nets, cigarettes and dirt.

A piped water scheme supplies water to the town. It is managed by the PHED. From the stand-posts at surface water tanks, donkey-carts carry water to peoples' houses. A number of houses have their own underground tanks and house connections. Most of such houses belong to traders, shopkeepers or to families whose relatives are working in the Gulf. Water from the piped system is insufficient for Pasni's population and is brackish. In early summer, it becomes undrinkable. According to the local population, this never used to happen before since the population was small and also because a piped water system, which is wasteful, did not exist.

There is no waste water disposal system in Pasni. In places people have dug *nalis*, or open drains, which discharge their contents into depressions, creating large pools of foul smelling stagnant water. A number of houses in the bazaar, and all the houses in the government colony, have latrines connected to soak-pits of some sort or the other. However, the fishermen living off the beach excrete in the open. There is no garbage collection system either. The wind carries garbage and human and animal excreta away after it is dry, and it collects around the *devi* shrubs and whatever other little vegetation there is.

Pasni is a typical case of a settlement where social and economic change has taken place resulting in ad-hoc physical changes. However, there has been no proper planning response to these changes. Also, the crucial link with Karachi is only through a *katcha* road which makes it difficult to fully develop the economic potential of the city and the Makran coast.

Environmental Degradation

Due to the expansion and modernization of the fish industry, major social, economic and physical changes have taken place. In social terms, the nuclear family is in the process of becoming independent of the extended family and clan; there is considerable social mobility; groups engaged in agriculture and forestry are taking to fishing and dependence on and involvement with state institutions and local bodies is increasing. In economic terms incomes have increased, new jobs have been created and the service sector has expanded. The economic benefits of this are counter-balanced by the high cost of living and the burden of debts that the fishing communities have to bear. Also the gap between the rich and the poor in economic terms is rapidly increasing. In physical terms, settlements have expanded and now need sewerage, water, health and road infrastructure which for the most part are missing. This is creating rapid degradation of the built environment and affecting health adversely. The catching, loading, unloading, packing of fish and the storage of ice, diesel, salt, all create a considerable amount of solid waste, much of it inorganic in nature. In the absence of any garbage collection system, this litters the beaches, and by all accounts is increasing in quantity. Again, in the absence of a seasonal ban on the operation of trawlers, and because of their fishing methods, there are indications that fish life is being depleted.

The increase in urban population and the emergence of a cash economy, have led to greater consumption of firewood. In addition, forestry and agriculture are being increasingly neglected as people take to fishing and related occupations. The subsistence barter economy, that made these two activities economically viable, is now dead. Another factor is the growing use of local timber in the manufacturing of boats. In a Gwadar saw mill six to seven truck loads of timber are brought in every month and are exclusively used for boat-making. Two years ago the quantity of timber brought to the mill was less than half of what it is today. The owner, Bashir Ahmed, says that a boat made with local timber is half the price of a boat made by timber imported from Karachi. He also feels that as no new trees are being planted, and as tamarisk and *babar* grow very slowly, the sparse Makran and Gwadar forests will soon be extinct.

The piped water schemes are extracting water from the rain-fed acquifer in and around the vicinity of seasonal torrents. This acquifer is of a limited quantity. Traditionally, it also partially fulfilled the needs of agriculture. With the present method of ad-hoc extraction, residents fear that this acquifer, which disappears seasonally, might soon disappear altogether. It seems that existing water sources cannot serve large settlements through piped water schemes, let alone cater to agriculture, forestry and dairy farming as well.

No organizations were encountered which involved cooperative effort of any kind. However, at Gwadar and Sur, fishermen mentioned that attempts to create organizations that could protect fishermen from the exploitation of *seths* and *dallals*, had been made. These attempts failed due to the lack of an acceptable leadership, opposition from the agents of *seths* and *dallals*, and a lack of faith on the part of the members that things could change. In the recent national and provincial elections, all parties, especially the PNP and the BNA, raised issues relevant to the fishing communities. Such issues have been raised in all previous elections as well. However, social relations in the district are far too anarchic to lead to the creation of any joint action unless it is fostered from some external source.

Two environmental issues are well understood by the fishing communities in the Gwadar district. One is the denuding of the coast by Karachi trawlers, and the other the problems arising from over-taxing existing water sources. The communities also understand that a good road link to Karachi will result in their having a more equitable relationship with the *seths* and the Karachi fish companies. However, the communities are not properly organized to struggle against over-taxing of the subsoil acquifer and the trawlers which denude the coast, or for a road link with Karachi.

The above are extracts from the author's field notes and reports prepared for the UN ESCAP sponsored Coastal Environmental Management Plan for Pakistan, 1989.

Postscript 2008

The trends identified for the Gwadar district in 1989 have also continued. A road link with Karachi has been established by the completion of the coastal highway in 2003 due to which Gwadar fishing companies and communities have been able to expand boat building, machinery servicing and transport facilities. Government has also invested in a number of projects since 1989. Gwadar's fish port was completed in 1993 and became accessible to large ships of up to 1,000 tons. The Pasni fisheries harbour was also completed in 1990. Both these facilities boosted production and eased the movement and anchoring of boats which previously had to anchor far away from the shores. The Akra Kaur Dam on the Akra River near Gwadar has also been completed, providing a more reliable source of water for Gwadar town.

The major change that has taken place, however, is the building of the Gwadar deep-sea port and the idea of transforming Gwadar into a major industrial port city. Due to this large scale land transactions have taken place which according to local representatives have adversely affected the fishing communities and made them vulnerable to evictions from their settlements. The initial Gwadar master plan prepared by the government also proposed the shifting of the residents of the old town from the centuries_old neighbourhoods. In addition, the presence of labour, entrepreneurs and middlemen is also resented as the vast majority of them are not locals. It is felt that they will exploit the resources of the area for themselves at the expense of the locals.[5] These issues have been politicized at the Balochistan level and have figured in a big way in the nationalist politics of the province. However, a lot of money has come into Gwadar since local landowners have sold their lands to Karachi based real estate developers. It is felt that these earnings have been used for luxury goods such as four-wheel drive vehicles and as such they will bring no benefits to the district or in the long run to the old land owners themselves.[6]

Gwadar district was already urbanized in 1981 with an urban population of 41.4 per cent. According to the 1998 Census, this figure is now 54 per cent. Literacy which was 6.10 per cent in 1981 increased to 25.47 per cent in 1998 and female literacy increased from 0.9 to 13.81 per cent in the same period.[7] However, health and education facilities have not increased in the same proportion as an increase in population. The use of latrines in the urban areas has gone up considerably but waste water disposal and solid waste management problems have increased due to an increase in populations and commercial and fishing activities.[8]

As in the Lasbela district fishing communities have begun to organize themselves to protect their interests against middlemen and to pressurize the government to adopt policies that support the protection of fish life and the coastal environment against big fishing related businesses, both Pakistani and foreign. These organizations, as in the case of the Lasbela district, are also a part of the PFF which has an office in Gwadar.

NOTES

1. The 1981 Population Census figures show that 6.2 per cent of the urban and 0.06 per cent of the rural population had gone abroad in the intercensus period.
2. Government of Pakistan, *Handbook of Marine Fisheries Department*, Volume 14, Ministry of Food and Agriculture, 1985.
3. Figures provided by the owner of a ship unloading at the jetty.
4. Government of Pakistan, *Population Census Reports 1981*, Population Census Organization, Islamabad.
5. Media reports.
6. Author's conversation with Hafeez Jamali on 11 June 2008, who is working on a Gwadar related PhD at Austin University, Texas, USA.
7. Government of Pakistan, *Population Census Reports 1998*, Population Census Organization, Islamabad.
8. Author's observations based on a visit in November 2004.

15

Rehri Goth: 1993

This chapter is derived from the report 'Evaluation of Community Development Work at Rehri Goth carried out by the IUCN' prepared by the author for the Coastal Ecosystem Unit of the IUCN. It was put together through a number of visits to the Goth and through 49 detailed interviews with IUCN staff; local councillors; community elders; government administrative and service delivery departments; smugglers; building contractors; vendors; money lenders; middlemen in the fishing industry; animal herders; boat owners and boat hands; re-manufacturing units; hotel owners; transporters; real estate dealers; residents; numbers of local CBOs and school teachers. These interviews and visits to Rehri took place between April and July 1993.

Rehri village is supposed to be four hundred years old. Its original inhabitants are the Moros, descendants of Moro, the hero of Shah Abdul Latif's Sur Ghatto. The story of the Sur is centred round the creeks of what is today Karachi and its heroes and villains are local fishermen. The Moros are divided into five sub-clans, each sub-clan being a descendant of one of Moro's four sons. The sub-clans are Kasmani or the descendants of Kasim; Musami or the descendants of Musa; Panjwani or the descendants of Panju; Varyani or the descendants of Varial; and Siarani or the descendants of Siar. The Moros live in the area of the village nearest to the creek and each sub-clan has its own neighbourhood. A small percentage of the Khaskheli clan are also old inhabitants of the area. They claim that they helped the Moros in establishing the village. Intermarriage between the various sub-clans of the Moros and between them and the old Khaskhelis is common.

After the commissioning of the Kotri Barrage in 1958 and the commissioning of the Tarbela and Mangla dams, fresh water disappeared from many areas of the Indus delta due to which water for drinking and agricultural purposes was no longer available. A large number of residents of the affected areas migrated. Some of them came and settled on the fringes of Rehri village and for administrative and census purposes are considered as part of the village. The migrants consisted for the most part of Khaskheli, Jat and Dabla clans. Each clan has its own neighbourhood and has tried unsuccessfully to maintain its traditional social and political structure. The migrant Khaskhelis do not live in the same neighbourhood as their older clan members and have their separate neighbourhood. Marriages between the older and more recent residents of Rehri village, or between the different migrant clans themselves, are rare and are discouraged by the clan elders. The Jat tribe especially does not intermarry with others.

The Old Society

Before the advent of the fisheries department and the development of fishing into an 'industry' in the early sixties, the social economy of Rehri and most other fishing villages on the Korangi creek, was a subsistence one. Most extended families owned small non-mechanized boats, seldom ventured into the open seas, and sold their produce directly to retailers at the Karachi fish markets in the old city. Some, after the city expanded, became roving fish vendors. Fish was taken to the markets by camel carts, and after 1962 by the circular railway.

Almost all families also owned animals before 1960. These took care of the milk requirements of the family and their fodder needs were met by mangrove leaves, grazing on the village community lands, and by their owners exchanging fish for fodder with the farmers of the Landhi-Malir oasis. Food for the most part consisted of dairy products, fish and rice. Rice was either purchased from the city markets or came by boat from the agricultural areas of the Indus delta. Very often the evening meal consisted of *sulimani* tea and *roti*. *Ghee*, locally prepared, was used for cooking. Clothes, shoes, tobacco and alcohol were the only items always purchased by cash. The older generation in Rehri feels that because of this austerity a family in the 'old days' used less than half the mangrove timber it uses today as fuel.

Almost all families in the old set up had a uniform social status. A couple of wealthy households did emerge in the fifties as a result of their participation in the smuggling activities of the well-known Baba and Bhit Island smuggling gangs. The more important members of these households have since left the village and their remaining members, because of their comparative affluence, are considered today as the village 'elders'.

All personal and property disputes and matters in the village were settled by the clan *punchayats* whose decisions were binding on all members. Failure to accept or act on the decisions made one an outcast and in some cases he could no longer live in the village. Inter-clan disputes and issues related to the village as a whole, were settled through a consensus of clan elders whose deliberations were helped by the Jamote or the village elder. The Jamote also represented the village in all its dealings with government administrative and development agencies. Jamote literally means a representative of the Jam or overlord and although originally a Jamote was an appointee of the ruler only for a period of time, this title and function became hereditary over time. Thus, for all practical purposes the average Rehri resident had very little control on the factors that shaped his life and almost no possibility of participating in decision making in development related activity.

The village had substantial community lands, over 300 acres according to some estimates. These were used for grazing cattle and according to the older generation they were fairly fertile due to the custom of blocking rainwater run-off by building small stone check dams in the dry stream beds. These dams were also built and maintained by the village communities. This work was organized by the elders of the various clans who also controlled encroachment on the community lands and decided on their utilization.

From well before partition (no one in the village knows exactly when) to the time a piped water main was installed for the village in 1973, water supply for the village came from a large reservoir. This reservoir was created by building a stone and concrete dam in the gorge of a large dry stream in the rocks adjacent to the village. During the rainy season the reservoir was filled with water which lasted throughout the year and was used exclusively for domestic needs and watering animals. In periods of drought the water did run out. When this happened wells were dug in the stream just below the reservoir. The village residents claim that this water was excellent for drinking and was sufficient for their needs. The building of the dams, the operation and maintenance of the system, and the distribution of water were all arranged through *begar* by the clan elders.

There was no sanitation system in the village before the early seventies. All residents, male and female, went out in the bushes to excrete and urinate. Since there was no habitation around the village and the population density in the village was low, this was practicable. Washing of clothes and larger domestic pots and pans, and bathing of children and men was usually done at the controlled outlets to the reservoir. Waste water was disposed off in soak ways in the street which did not overflow due to the small quantities of water involved.

There were no schools or health facilities in Rehri before 1958. A few families did send their children to stay with their relatives in the city to study but by and large the entire village was illiterate. Similarly, there were no health facilities and if one fell seriously ill he/she was taken to a KMC dispensary or the Civil Hospital in the city but according to the older generation, 'seldom came back alive'.

The Change

The subsistence economy and the relationships, as well as the culture and institutions that sustained them, were already under attack because of the demographic and cultural changes Karachi experienced after partition. However, they underwent a rapid transition after 1958 with the building of the Landhi-Korangi industrial and residential estates and the establishment of the Fisheries Department during the same period.

The Landhi-Korangi industrial and residential estates were built between 1959 and 1964. In the initial stages of their construction Rehri residents worked on the building sites as construction labour. Thus for the first time a fairly large number of villagers worked for a long period of time for daily wages. However, their contractors and much of the skilled labour they employed were from the north of the country and soon they started to employ migrants from their own areas as building site labour whom they found to be more punctual and efficient. By the mid-sixties the coastal villagers had been elbowed out of the building sites. The same fate awaited the villagers in other trades. There were four taxi drivers from Rehri who worked in Karachi in 1960. However, the taxi owners were from the north. Soon they were replaced by relatives and fellow villagers of the owners. Obtaining credit for the purchase of taxis did occur to some Rehri residents but such credit again was not available to them as the moneylenders in the transport trade favoured their own communities.

In the early sixties the Fisheries Department was set up with FAO assistance. It established a credit line and technical support for the mechanization of fishing craft and the introduction and use of new varieties of nets. This intervention coincided with the development of the poultry industry in Pakistan in general, and Karachi in particular.

The poultry industry depended heavily on fish feed and the fish feed factory owners also offered loans for mechanization of boats and the purchase of nets. These two factors changed fishing activity from a subsistence to a commercial activity.

THE MIDDLEMEN

Given the relationship of mistrust and hostility between the working classes and the state sector in Pakistan, and the complicated and sophisticated procedures and conditions for acquiring a loan, the credit line established for the fishing industry could not be utilized directly by the fisherman. Middlemen emerged to utilize these loans and facilities, establish marketing systems, and giving loans to small fishermen for the mechanization of their boats, purchase of nets and financing of their fishing trips. In return the fishermen had to sell their produce to the middleman, or the agent appointed by him, at 30 to 60 per cent of its market value. In the process most fishermen have become no more than bonded labour to the middlemen. The same system operates in the fish feed industry where the industrialists give loans to middlemen to disburse and manage.

The development of commercial fishing also resulted in the expansion of the Karachi fish harbour in the sixties and the introduction of trawlers for deep sea fishing. This activity created a large number of jobs of boat hands for the local fishing communities.

In the early sixties a number of Rehri residents went to work at the Karachi fish harbour. A couple of better connected and wealthier residents of Rehri also acquired loans directly from the fisheries department for the purchase of trawlers. However, by the late sixties the Mianwali middlemen came to dominate the Karachi fish harbour and increasingly employed their relatives and fellow villagers at the expense of local fishermen. In the absence of jobs the local fishermen had to depend increasingly on loans from middlemen to survive in the commercial market. By the late seventies no Rehri resident was operating a trawler and almost all Rehri boat owners were in debt.

The seventies also saw the growth of large informal settlements of migrants along the Korangi creek. Many of the migrants (especially those from Bangladesh, Burma and the upper Indus valley) had fishing experience. These were recruited by the middlemen, supplied with nets and boats, given protection from the police where necessary, and made to work for them. Being migrants, they worked longer hours for less wages and their insecurity made them easier to deal with than the locals.

The local middlemen and influentials have also supported the migrant communities at the expense of their fellow villagers, both for economic and political reasons. They feel that if they can keep the local population economically and socially backward they can continue to dominate it politically.

Unlike the parts of the village occupied by the local community the migrant settlements are dynamic. Houses are being built; real estate agencies are actively selling illegally subdivided land; a large number of people work on building sites and as industrial labour; and there are informal small scale industries such as carpet weaving, looms for the manufacture of yarn, and lathe machines related production in their settlements. These activities and their diverse nature will bring about major social and economic improvements in these settlements in the not too distant future; make them more receptive to new ideas and integrate them with the political, social and economic life of Karachi.

In spite of the many disadvantages that the Rehri residents suffer from, the settlement is certainly not stagnating. Participation in four national and provincial elections in the last two decades and in four local body elections have made an impact. The village has acquired a water supply and a sewage system (even if they do not work) and schools and health facilities. In addition, city based NGOs are active in the village. The residents have tried to form social welfare groups and women are acquiring education in spite of opposition from their elders.

The changes that have taken place have had major repercussions on the social, economic and cultural aspects of life in Rehri. With the emergence of middlemen as the major providers of livelihood the old system of *punchayat* and collective action through the power exercised by the clan elders has come to an end. The Jamote system survives inasmuch as he continues to represent the community in most of its dealings with state agencies. However, without support from operational *punchayats* and accepted clan elders he can hardly claim to represent the community. Although clan elders are still approached to settle property and personal matters, their decisions are often rejected by the community which then seeks the intervention of the police and/or legal redress.

The middlemen who have emerged as a major power in the village are interested only in reaping the economic benefits of their activity and their social involvement is limited to financing and organizing collective action for fishing activities. Some of these middlemen are also politically ambitious and contest and win local body elections, usually to the union council. In this position they are able to act as benefactors to the local population.

Due to the political and social disadvantages and the crisis of leadership the Rehri population suffers from, it has withdrawn from competing with the migrant populations and from developing social and economic links with other groups and entrepreneurs in its vicinity or in the city of Karachi. However, the recently educated members of the community are trying to get themselves government jobs and lobby with the district council for benefits for their village.

There have also been cultural changes. Eating habits reflect the influence of city dwellers. Marriage ceremonies also reflect city culture. There are eight mosques, all with local *imams* for a population of 35,000 whereas before 1974 there was only one mosque. The people, especially the younger generation, are far more religious than they were two decades ago. All this is the result of the growing influence of the city's political culture.

There are also attitudinal changes. The younger generation, especially the educated lot, wish to free themselves from the political and economic control of middlemen and the Jamote. The primary school teachers in the village are in the forefront of this effort which so far is limited to voicing their concerns. In addition, the community wants piped water supply and sewage systems and education and health facilities.

The number of animals in the village has declined and milk produced by the village is no longer sufficient for its need. This is partly due to the increase in population and partly due to the lack of cash available with the villagers for the purchase of animals. A fairly large quantity of milk is imported from the neighbouring Bhainse Colony or sold by locals who have an excess of it to their neighbours.

Due to a change of eating habits and an increase of population, the quantity of mangrove timber used as fuel has increased considerably. The long trips that fishermen now undertake at sea in their mechanized boats makes it easier for them to bring back mangrove timber.

The most important change, however, that has taken place is the emergence of a few educated women. This is leading to a desire in the younger generation of women to acquire education and will help in the establishment and staffing of government and private schools. This in turn will have a major impact on the sociology of the village. At present there is only one local female teacher in the government school and the entire female medical and paramedical staff working in Rehri is non local.

The linking of the village by road with Karachi and the plying of public transport recently will also have an impact. Already about 1,500 persons leave the village every day for Karachi as compared to 200 a year ago, before the transport services commenced. In addition, a few women have started working as domestic help in Karachi as a result of the transport system.

SOCIO-ECONOMIC CONDITIONS

Different clans in Rehri have a different level of development. The Moros are only involved in fishing and related activity. Very few of them are educated or have an interest in education. However, because of their long residence near Karachi their awareness levels are higher than those of the Dablas and Jats who have migrated from the Indus delta. Being older residents, they also feel more secure than most of the other clans.

The Dablas are the most backward of the clans in Rehri. Even in the Thatta district, from where they have migrated, they are considered 'low caste'. They belong to a culture of poverty and deprivation and do not aspire to improving their economic status by seeking employment in other sectors. According to the Dablas interviewed, their community is almost entirely illiterate and only 15 per cent own boats.

The Khaskhelis and the Sheikhs have links with their clan organizations outside Rehri. Members of their clan are engaged in commerce, trade and agriculture in many urban and rural areas of Sindh. This gives them a bigger vision, better and more sophisticated organizational links outside of the village and more ambitious aspirations. Thus, much of the limited commercial activity in the village is run by them and they are by far the most educated members of the village. Almost all the school teachers and the educated women belong to these clans. The pressure for change as such also comes from the Khaskheli youth.

Almost all families who own boats in Rehri are in debt to middlemen and almost all *Khalasis* are in debt to boat-owners. The debt of the boat-owners varies from 15,000 rupees to 600,000 rupees and of the *Khalasi* to the boat-owners from 2,000 rupees to 10,000 rupees. *Khalasis* borrow this money for use in periods when fishing activity is banned or is slack. They do not seek other employment during such periods. Because of the loan they take they have to work at lower wages for the boat-owners. In addition, there are a few boat-owners who do not have a debt on their boats but borrow money from middlemen so as to finance their fishing trips and meet their domestic and personal expenses during the period when fishing activity is suspended. Such loans vary between 15,000 rupees to 20,000 rupees for the operation of larger mechanized boats.

Although there are no figures available for the number of boats in Rehri, there is general consensus among the village residents that 30 per cent of the residents own boats. The largest number of boats are 20 to 30 feet long and are known as *tikri jaal* boats. Residents feel that 4 to 6 per cent of the total number of boats are free of credit and no more than 1 to 2 per cent of the mechanized boats are free of credit. There are about 15 middlemen in Rehri. All these middlemen are really sub-contractors to bigger middlemen in Ibrahim Hyderi and to Sabu Khan of Lad Basti and are in debt to them. In collaboration with the main middleman they seek to control the local bodies (district and union councils) and put up their candidates for elections. They also participate in the settlement process in the new informal settlements along the coast and help settle Bengali and Burmese migrants seasonally in the mangrove marshes and in the process prevent the locals from fishing in certain key locations. Thus they act against the interests of the village population even though they represent it politically.

Many of the persons interviewed were not bothered that they were in debt and happily accepted that they would have to borrow more. Ismail Dabla, who owes Seth Niko of Ibrahim Hyderi 175,000 rupees said that he will leave this debt to his son and he will deal with it after he dies.

The services sector in Rehri is almost entirely managed by outsiders. The small contractors and building component manufacturing yards in the village are owned by Pathans. The masons and unskilled labour employed by them are also non-locals. In addition, there are forty to fifty vegetable and fruit vendors who serve the village. They are also from the north of the country and live in the informal settlements that have sprung up in the Landhi-Korangi area. The provisions and general stores and chemists' shops are owned by Hindu *Banyas* from the Badin and Tharparkar districts. One of these shops has been there since before partition. These provision and general stores also give people provision on credit and recover their dues with interest. Similarly, tailors and cobblers (except for one tailor) are not from the village.

However, boat making is done by the village residents themselves and so is the mechanical maintenance of the boat engines. It is estimated that 20 per cent of the families in the village have *wados* or boat makers in them. These boat makers produce about 15 to 20 boats per year and when they are unemployed they work as *khalasis* for boat-owners. However, they do not use their carpentry skills for furniture making or other related work. In addition, there are a number of Rehri families (mostly Khaskhelis) who are involved in producing, collecting and or selling milk to individual households and tea shops. Most of this activity is managed by women and every neighbourhood has four to five women who are engaged in this. The Rehri population keeps cows, not buffaloes. They feel that buffaloes require too much care, fodder and fresh water. A number of tea shops in Rehri are owned by outsiders and these use buffalo milk which they import from Bhainse Colony and in this transaction the local population is not involved in anyway. About twenty members of the local population are involved in the transportation, wholesaling and distribution of ice but there is no ice factory in Rehri. Ice is imported from the Landhi industrial area.

Another activity in which the local population is involved is transportation. There are about twenty Suzukis and pick ups in the village. Most of them are owned by members of the Khaskheli and Baloch clans. These vehicles have been purchased through loans from Pathan money-lenders in Landhi. They are used to transport fish and prawns to the fisheries in Karachi and Ibrahim Hyderi. They used to carry fish to the intermediate Sindh cities but for the last few years this activity has declined due to civic strife in the province. In addition, they are also hired by the local population for going to Karachi, Ibrahim Hyderi and other localities. This, however, is now less common since the mini-bus services began a few months back. The mini-buses are not owned by the locals and the pick up owners complain that since the mini-buses started plying they have lost a lot of business.

COMMUNITY ORGANIZATION

As mentioned earlier, the village has extensive community lands. Till recently, with the permission of the clan elders, a local or a non-local could acquire a piece of the village community land for building his house. However, this has now become more difficult. Under the

Goth-Abad-Scheme of the government of Sindh, titles are registered for those in possession of homes or vacant land. The villagers claim that clandestinely the Jamotes and councillors have had most of the vacant community lands registered in their names. The Mahigeer Samaji Sangat (MSS) has filed complaints with the *mukhtarkar* regarding this illegal occupation. In addition, the MSS has made a colony of 300 plots on community land so as to save it from the Jamote and councillors. This land has been given to village residents who are living in high density areas in the settlement. However, the scheme has not been officially approved (the MSS says that this is because of an understanding between the Jamote, councillors and the *mukhtarkar*) and the allottees do not have the money to build on their plots. All this points to the need for developing strong community based organizations whose members can then context and win local body elections to break the power of powerful vested interests. The MSS seems to be the beginning of such a community organization.

A few attempts have been made by the local population for setting up community based organizations. The Jat clan of the *Khalifa Para* has established the Anjuman-e-Falah-o-Bahbood (AFB). The organization has not grown beyond financing marriage and death ceremonies, trying to pressurize the UC for civil amenities and helping send a few children to school. In addition, there is the Anjuman Samaji Behbood (ASB) of the Malkai community. It is now inactive and has limited its activities to supporting marriage and death ceremonies. Both these organizations were run by the elders of their community and were imbibed with the spirit of charity.

The MSS was founded in 1990, and unlike the other organizations its founder members were young school teachers working in the local government run educational institutions. They belonged to the Khaskheli and Sheikh clans but wanted the organization to be a village based and not a clan based organization. Educated girls of the village also became members of the organization. The membership of the organization is seventy-five of which about one-third are educated women. The emphasis of the MSS has been on education, especially of women, and the development of political and social awareness among the young. MSS has collaborated with various NGOs who have been active in Rehri in the recent past. These NGOs include BUSTI, the IUCN and Ghaffar Biloo's Mother and Child (MCH) Clinic. The motivation for the formation of the organization came from Ghaffar Biloo's team which has been working in Rehri for the last five to six years.

EDUCATION AND HEALTHCARE

Out of a population of 30,000 there are only 20 matriculates in Rehri. Four of these are women. In addition, about 600 boys and 200 girls attend school; that is, less than 5 per cent of the school going age population.[1] There are three government primary schools for boys and one lower middle school. The education system and its administration are extremely poor and since there is no pressure from the local population for their improvement, they continue to deteriorate. Parents complain that in addition to school fees and expenses on books, the headmasters frequently ask children for money. Parents also complain that the school hours are inappropriate since they need their children to help them in their work in those hours. In addition, when boys become older they go for long fishing trips with their male relatives and as such cannot attend school regularly. They feel that some sort of education should be provided to boys during the two to three months period when fishing activity is suspended. In addition to the government schools there are also NGO operated home schools and adult education centres. These are discussed later in the text.

Although there is a union council dispensary and a district council rural health centre, families complain that their members suffer routinely from dysentery, respiratory problems, eczema and malaria. Typhoid is not uncommon. All these diseases are related to poor quality of water, which is also insufficient for people's needs, and the absence of sanitation. In addition, the creek water with which the residents constantly come in touch is now heavily polluted with sewage and industrial effluents. There is no solid waste collection system either and fishing and related activity generates a considerable amount of waste, both organic and inorganic. This increases the incidence of disease.

On the basis of the interviews carried out at Rehri it is estimated that an average household in the village spends about 200 rupees per month on water; 150 rupees on fuel; 300 to 400 rupees on milk; and 150 rupees on medicines. In addition, the principal working member in a household loses at an average about four working days in a month due to illness. These costs, along with two and a half months of unemployment due to the suspension of fishing activities, are a major cause for the population being in debt, apart from the fact that they cannot sell their catch at market prices due to their being in debt. It is thus a vicious circle.

Camel breeding, an important source of livelihood, is carried out by the Faqirani clan in the Rehri-Chashma Goth area. According to the Jats interviewed, the camel population is increasing. They claim that the only income from camel breeding comes from the sale of two to three male camels per year. Each male camel fetches a price of 1,200 rupees to 1,500 rupees. The camel breeders pay the forest department staff gratification amounting to one-third of their earnings to permit them to graze the camels in the mangroves. In addition, the Jats have to carry water in boats to the camels every day while they are grazing in the marshes. This water has to be purchased from tankers. The Jats claim that they would willingly give up their profession provided an alternative source of income could be made available to them. The sale of camel's milk could be a possible source of income for them. However, in their tradition the sale of camel's milk is supposed to bring bad luck.

Drugs (*hashish* and heroin) are common in Rehri. Almost all the persons interviewed have claimed that the drug peddlers are the employees of the middlemen and that the councillors are involved in this business. They further claim that the drug trade in Rehri has the protection of the police. Much of the money generated by this trade goes into the financing of middlemen credit activity.

ADMINISTRATIVE STRUCTURE

Rehri village is part of the Ibrahim Hyderi UC which is one of the eleven councils in the area that constitutes the Karachi District Council (DC) which represents the rural areas of the city. The Ibrahim Hyderi UC has thirty-eight members, six of them from Rehri village. It is important to note that one of the councillors of the Ibrahim Hyderi UC is a Burmese. The annual budget of the UC is around 20 million rupees and is generated from octroi (mainly on fish) and from the Thermal Power Station.

The UC budgets have not been utilized for development work in Rehri for the last four years. However, councillors have handed out 500 rupees per month, or on an ad hoc basis to 'sick and needy' residents of the village, most of whom it is claimed are their relatives and friends. The people who have been interviewed do not trust their councillors and have only voted for them as there was really not much to choose between them and others who had stood for election.

The District Council of Karachi is an extremely wealthy organization. Its total revenue, including capital income, has increased from 40 million rupees in 1986–87 to about 67 million rupees in 1990–91. About 30 per cent of its expenditures are on administration and operation and maintenance and the rest on development. Its development schemes are badly conceived, of very poor quality and excessively high cost, and are built without adequate engineering and supervisory inputs. Most of them consist of dispensaries, school buildings, sewage and water schemes that do not function due to bad design and construction or are sometimes not even commissioned, and road pavings. However, through its work some roads in Rehri have been paved and a number of neighbourhoods have acquired underground water tanks where they can store water for domestic use. Both the UC and the DC are controlled by middlemen and by the Jamotes.

In addition to the UC and DC involvement in development related works, the PHED, Sindh, is responsible for developing water supply and sanitation for the rural areas of Karachi. The PHED is a sophisticated engineering department and does not work in collaboration with communities or with the UCs and DCs. However, its schemes, after a two-year period, are handed over to the DC or UC for maintenance and operation. The PHED has developed water and sewage system for Rehri and these are described below.

INFRASTRUCTURE

In 1973 the Karachi Development Authority (KDA) provided Rehri village with a water main. People collected water from the main and the few stand posts that were linked to it. As a result of this supply the Rehri residents abandoned their old water source. Between 1973 and 1977 the supply was adequate after which the line was taken over by the Export Promotion Zone (EPZ), through which it passed, and the people of Rehri faced major water problems. In the mid-eighties a water supply system was developed for Rehri by the PHED under Prime Minister Junejo's Five Point Programme. This system consisted of a new line for the village from the Bhainse Colony pumping station. In addition, two storage tanks, each of 250 thousand gallons were constructed on the high ground near the village and a gravity fed distribution network was developed for the settlement. This network served about 60 per cent of the village.

The system has not worked because the water meant for Rehri is illegally tapped by the cattle yards and residents of Bhainse Colony with the result that the Rehri residents do not get more than 80,000 gallons per week from the system. This is far from adequate. In addition, the distribution network leaks and the water does not reach certain areas of the settlement at all such as the Dabla *para*. To make up for the shortfall individuals purchase water tankers and share this cost with their neighbours, or sell water to them at one rupee per canister. Usually the purchased water is stored in the neighbourhood underground tanks built by the DC.

In 1979 water started to pour out of the rock formations in the north east part of the village. The water of this 'spring' is constantly increasing in volume and the discharge at present is 1750 gallons per hour. This water is unfit for human consumption and is chemically very hard. However, it can be consumed by animals and can be used for growing certain varieties of plants. The only way that it can be made potable is through osmosis. The source of this spring is perhaps the leakages of the sewerage and water pipelines in Bhainse Colony and or the effluents from Sindh Alkalais a neighbouring industrial complex.

This spring water is used only by residents who live next to the spring, for no other purpose but washing, bathing and watering animals. Most residents do not like using this water because of its hardness and brackishness. Many women interviewed said that they would not pay even 25 paisas per canister for it.

Fifty per cent of the homes in Rehri were provided with an underground sewage system under the Prime Minister's Five Point Programme in the mid eighties. However, very few houses have constructed sanitary latrines to link themselves to the sewage line. The sewage lines run parallel to each other and discharge raw sewage directly into the sea. During high tides they are inundated by sea water. Because of a shortage of water for flushing most of the lines are now choked. Only the ones which have the spring water flushing them seem to work. In addition to these problems, people are reclaiming land from the creek with the result that the sewage outlets are either being blocked or discharging into unpaved open nullahs which are increasing in length.

In the areas where sanitation facilities do not work or do not exist, people still excrete in the open or build simple latrines in areas which are subject to flooding at high tide, so that the excreta can be washed away.

Waste water generated by cooking and washing activities is usually disposed off in a ditch in the house itself or is thrown out on the street by the women of the house. This water is considerable as an average family in Rehri uses a minimum of ten to fifteen canisters of water per day.

Seven out of ten neighbourhoods in Rehri have electricity. However, not more than 30 per cent of the residents of these neighbourhoods have a direct electric connection. Most households purchase electricity from their neighbours who have a connection and pay 100 rupees per month for lighting two 40 watt bulbs. This is an exorbitant cost. The reason why people do not have their own meters is that they cannot afford the KESC connection charges.

Almost all households use mangrove timber as cooking fuel because it is easily and cheaply available and because they say that it burns longer and better than *tali* or *kekar* and the food cooked on it tastes better. The residents and housewives interviewed had a preference for gas and would be happy to pay for it even if it costs 10 to 15 per cent more that what they spend on fuel today. However, gas cylinders are not easily available and even if they were, the vast majority of Rehri households would not be able to afford to pay the initial deposit required for the purchase of the cylinder.

The residents were asked about the benefits of the Korangi fish harbour to them. They feel that only those fishermen who can sell their produce in the open market and are not bound to middlemen will benefit from the harbour as they will no longer have to go to Ibrahim Hyderi, which is far away, to sell their catch. Since almost all fishermen are in debt to middlemen, residents feel that the fish harbour will not be beneficial.

Fishermen are also of the opinion that the large boats that will operate from the fish harbour will not employ them since they will be owned by non-locals who will prefer to employ people from their own areas. In addition, the fishermen also feel that the local entrepreneurs, if they do decide to use the fish harbour facilities, will prefer to employ Bengali and Burmese fishermen and boat-hands rather than Rehri residents.

A few roads and streets in the older neighbourhoods of the village have been paved either by the DC as part of its ADP or the PHED under the Prime Minister's Five Point Programme. In most of the settlements, however, access ways and streets are *katcha*. There are no parks and playgrounds in the neighbourhoods either and the existing open spaces are used as garbage dumps. However, the settlement is connected to Ibrahim Hyderi, Landhi-Korangi and the city of Karachi by motorable roads.

MARGINALIZATION

The majority of the clans in Rehri are being marginalized out of the lucrative fishing activity. In addition, they are not becoming involved in other economic activities that are available in the city. They do not possess the means or the skills to develop alternative sources of income and their culture and traditional social organization do not help them in developing aspirations for education and commerce. Collectively these factors make them an easy target for exploitation. This also weakens their position in all lobbying efforts with the government and in their relationships with the political power structure. The burden of debt makes matters worse. Many such marginalized communities exist in Karachi and mostly consist of the original inhabitants of the old *goths*. These *goths* are now surrounded by large informal settlements of recent origin. Examples of this marginalization can be found in Orangi, Baldia, Mauripur and Drigh Colony. In these cases the marginalized communities (except for Mauripur) are agricultural societies.

The more enterprising clans, who have wider links, such as the Khaskheli and Sheikhs, will acquire education. Most of their educated members will seek government jobs, initially as school teachers and later as clerical staff in the district and provincial administration. The first generation of the educated youth will try to work for the betterment of the village community as a whole and will struggle and organize themselves for it. However, when their children start growing up, many of them will give up this activity and some of them will leave the settlement and go and settle in middle class areas. With the second generation of educated persons, class differences between them and the village residents will be consolidated and the better educated members of the more developed clans will stop identifying themselves with Rehri and its inhabitants.

Unless and until support systems for the development of skills and entrepreneurship are created, almost all trade, commerce and small scale industrial activity related to fishing and or development as a whole, will pass into the hands of the migrant communities in the neighbouring informal settlements.

These conditions will guarantee that the political representatives of the village will continue to be from among the middlemen. It is possible that some of the educated young men may be elected as councillors during some major political movement. However, they will in time be co-opted by their more powerful colleagues.

In the conditions described above effective collective action will not be possible, and if the nature and scale of NGO intervention remains what it is today, it will not change the situation appreciably. In the absence of effective collective action and an equitable relationship with political power, it is also unlikely that UC and DC civic and social sector schemes will improve in quality or in their maintenance and operation.

It is likely that women from Rehri village will start working as domestic help in the richer areas of the city or for the better off residents of the neighbouring settlements. This is a common activity of women in old *goths* where the marginalization process has taken place.

Visits to the migrant settlements along the coast such as Irkanabad, Ittehad Colony, Ali Akber Shah, demonstrate that they are growing at a phenomenal rate. Real estate agents and the Sindh Katchi Abadi Authority (SKAA), estimate the growth at 8 to 9 per cent per year. If this is true, then in a ten year period the entire Korangi coastal belt will become urbanized. These settlements will differ from Rehri inasmuch as they will contain a large number of white collar workers, skilled workmen, shop-keepers and entrepreneurs. As such they will have considerable political power due to which they will be able to pressurize the administration to provide them with water and other civic amenities. However, it is unlikely that a sewage system for these settlements will be developed and in the absence of a sewage system and treatment plants for it, increasingly large quantities of untreated sewage will flow into the Korangi creek. This will pollute the creek and create major environmental problems for the residents living along it and for the marine life that lives and breeds in it. It is also unlikely that an effective solid waste collection and management system will be developed for this area and unless industrial pollution can be controlled, it will add to the environmental problems of the creek and the coastal population.

In the coming decade a number of sewage farms, using raw sewage, will develop in and around the coastal belt, especially after the development of an increased water supply system. The development of these farms in the vicinity of large settlements will create a number of environmental and health hazards in addition to producing vegetables and fruits that will, for health reasons, be inedible. Such farms for example Hyder Baloch's farm, have already started to take shape just adjacent to Rehri.

With the development of increased water supply and the absence of sanitation and sewage treatment plants, the water front at Rehri will be polluted and will have a foul odour, especially at low tide. People will continue to reclaim land from the sea by using solid waste as infill. This will further pollute the atmosphere. The acidity of the sewage will attack the timber of boats in the creek and damage them. This process has already begun in those areas where boats are kept near the existing sewage outlets.

The wealthier Rehri residents will improve their homes and the community lands will be sold to outsiders. This sale will either be made to developers or to individual purchasers. In either case, the real beneficiaries will be the political leaders and middlemen of Rehri village who will organize these transactions.

NOTE

1. Figures provided by the local CBO.

PART SIX: THE CITY

Pakistan has urbanized. In 1951 17.80 per cent of its population lived in urban settlements. In 1998, the figure had increased to 32.51. This figure has been contested by some planners. According to them, the urban population is much higher since only those settlements are considered urban for the purposes of the census which have an urban system of governance. Also, many towns have expanded way beyond their municipal limits. Yet, this expansion has not been considered urban. It is believed that if the definition is changed to what it was before 1981 and if municipal limits are redefined, Pakistan's urban population would be nearer to 50 per cent of the country's total population.*

Urbanization in Pakistan is unplanned. The expansion of almost all urban centres has been through the development of *katchi abadis* on state land; through the informal subdivision of agricultural land; or through the densification of the inner cities. The majority of the urban population lives in these settlements and the densified inner cities. Government agencies have failed to service the physical and social needs of these settlements. As a result, communities have organized to manage certain aspects of development and the informal sector has supported them in the provision of water, jobs, solid waste management and health and education services. The effectiveness of this sector and nature of its relationship with communities, NGOs and state agencies, varies from town to town. In Karachi it is by far the most developed and in many of the smaller towns it is non-existent. Chapter 16 describes the functioning of this informal sector. As this text was prepared in August 1989, a postscript has been added since the relationships between the informal sector, communities and state agencies have undergone considerable changes since then.

The state has not only failed to provide housing and related physical and social infrastructure, it has also failed to cater to the infrastructure needs of increasing trade, industrial activity, wholesaling and related transport and warehousing requirements. As a result, much of these activities which took place on a small scale in the inner cities of Pakistan, have expanded to engulf almost the entire inner cities. These inner cities also house much of Pakistan's historical and cultural built heritage which has been severely damaged due this expansion and is in danger of being eliminated altogether. Chapter 17 deals with this issue.

In the past decade, major social and demographic changes have taken place in Karachi in general and its younger generation in particular. These changes conflict with the culture of the state and as a result, there is a feeling of alienation among an increasing number of younger Karachiites. Chapters 18 and 19 deal with these changes and their repercussions. Structural adjustment, globalization, the media and IT revolution, have also affected the culture of Karachi and changed the nature of its informal sector and its formal planning processes. These changes are discussed in Chapters 20, 21, and 22.

The trends identified in this section of this book for Karachi, are also visible, though to a lesser extent, in other major towns of Pakistan.

* Reza Ali, *How Urban is Pakistan*, November 1999 and Iffat Ara and Arshad Zaman, *Asian Urbanization in the New Millennium: Pakistan Chapter*, unpublished paper written for a publication of the Asian Urban Information Centre for Kobe, August 2002.

16

The Informal Sector in Urban Development 1989

This chapter is a synopsis of a study done for the Swiss Development Cooperation on 'Community Development Groups in Pakistan' in 1989. The cities which were studied were Karachi, Hyderabad, Faisalabad, Lahore and Peshawar. A postscript has been added to update the reader with changes that have taken place since 1989.

Government policies for the urban poor in Pakistan have failed to provide them with: land for housing at an affordable price, credit and technical assistance for house building, a service infrastructure, education and health facilities, and credit and assistance for income generation. However, an informal sector, dominated by middlemen, has developed which caters to the needs of the urban poor.

In the absence of access to regularized raw or serviced land, the urban poor have to depend on various methods and sources for acquiring land. Most of Lahore, Hyderabad and the earlier Faisalabad and Karachi *katchi abadis* developed through unorganized invasions. Migrants came in groups and occupied vacant land in the city centre or near their places of work. These settlements have no regular plan or open spaces for schools or playgrounds. Plot sizes vary from 12 metre square to over 200, and the streets are narrow and winding because of which a large number of households in them get displaced due to the provincial government's upgrading process. In these early *abadis* people maintained their clan structure and as such neighbourhoods in them are not only ethnically but also socially homogeneous. Houses in these settlements were constructed on the rural pattern and improved over a long period of time. Basic services, such as water, were acquired as a result of considerable lobbying by the people with state officials and politicians.

INFORMAL SUBDIVISIONS

In the 1960s there was considerable bulldozing of informal settlements in Karachi which made the development of unorganized invasions settlements impossible. As a result the system of informal subdivision (ISD) of state land on the city fringe was commenced. This process also caught on in Faisalabad and Hyderabad, where, like Karachi, considerable state land was available. The key actor in the informal subdivision drama is the middleman or *dallal*. He occupies government land by involving relevant state officials in an informal business deal. He subdivides the land and sells the plots to the urban poor at prices they can afford. He arranges water for them through bowzers (where subsoil water is brackish) and the residents organize the distribution. Protection from eviction is guaranteed by him and for this the residents pay a small sum to the police and local government officials until the settlement is large enough to feel secure from eviction.

Over the years this system has been institutionalized. The *dallal* forms a welfare society of all the residents and gets it registered. Through the society he lobbies for electricity, gas and transport facilities. As he sets aside over thirty per cent of the plots for speculation, and as government servants of relevant departments and politicians own most of them, he, the government functionaries and the politicians have a direct interest in the development of the area. For protecting their interests and projecting the problems of their settlements, *dallals* in Karachi are known to retain lawyers and journalists on a permanent basis.

The planning of these ISD's is done, as far as possible, according to the regulations of the development authority, complete with spaces for mosques and commercial areas. As such these settlements require very little adjustments when being upgraded.

Speculation on the plots sold to the poor is controlled by forcing the owner to build a house on his land and move in within a week of the sale. If he does not do it, the plot is sold to someone else and the money of the original buyer is confiscated by the *dallal*.

Value of land in older, well planned ISD settlements in all five cities (Karachi, Hyderabad, Faisalabad, Lahore, Peshawar) that were visited, is almost as high as that in regularized lower-middle-income areas. As a result, the urban poor have to seek land in the newer settlements which are increasingly located far from their places of work. This is

The Informal Subdivisions of Yakoobabad

Yakoobabad is an informal subdivision settlement of about 2,000 houses in Orangi Township. Before 1977, it was vacant land belonging to the CBR. The CBR had given it on a renewable one year lease as pasture land to an elder of the Rind tribe (henceforth referred to as X).

Mr Y is one of a number of informal developers who have illegally developed more than 200,000 plots on government land in West Karachi alone, over the last 30 years. Like other developers he has close links with officials in the CBR, KMC, police and other departments relevant to his work.

In February 1977, Y moved onto X's land with 100 'destitute' families. These families were transported in trucks along with bamboo posts and mats (supplied by Y) for the construction of shacks. Y had identified these families through his contacts in the settlements he had created earlier. As soon as the families started putting up their shacks, members of the Rind tribe arrived in jeeps carrying guns and tried to eject them. A scuffle followed and a number of Y's people were injured. It was decided between the two parties that no houses would be put up but the 'destitutes' could stay on the land until matters were settled.

The next day X hired a lawyer and made a case in a court of law against the occupation of his land. The case was admitted. Y on the other hand, filed a complaint with the local police saying that the Rind tribe had caused 'bodily harm' to his clients. After this the local *thana* (police station) arranged negotiations between the two parties. As a result, it was decided that the Rind tribe would receive Rs500 for every plot that was developed by Y. The plots being given to the 100 'destitutes' were exempt from this payment and Y also did not receive any payments for them. It was further agreed that Y would pay Rs200 per plot to the KMC officials from the sale proceeds and that the police would recover Rs200 or more directly from the owners when they converted their shacks into concrete wall constructions. After the negotiations were completed, the Rind tribe withdrew its case against Y.

Y then laid out Yakoobabad on a gridiron plan. His apprentices (he was also an apprentice once) helped him in this work. The roads were levelled by informally hiring tractors and a bulldozer at a nominal cost from Karachi Metropolitan Corporation (KMC) staff in West Karachi. Space for a mosque and a school were set aside and plots on the main road were allocated for shops and businesses. At this stage negotiations were entered into with representatives and touts of government officials who could be of help in the future development of the settlements. 30 per cent of all plots were set aside for these officials for speculation purposes. Whoever purchased a plot in the settlement (except for the ones reserved for officials) had to construct a house in a month's time and move in, failing which he would lose his plot and the money he had paid for it. Thus Y prevented speculation and saw to it that the settlement would expand fast.

X appointed a *chowkidar* (care taker) to keep track of the number of plots that were developed so that Y may not cheat him. In the same manner, the KMC officials also had their informal representatives visiting the site regularly. Accounts were settled between the parties every week.

Y engaged donkey cart owners to supply water to the settlement. These suppliers acquired water illegally from the KMC water mains in Orangi. The payment of the first supply of water was made by Y, after which the people dealt with the water suppliers directly. A few weeks after the first shacks were built, a contractor, Nawab Ali, established a building component manufacturing yard, or *thalla*, in the settlement. He started supplying concrete blocks and tin roof sheets for the construction of houses along with technical advice and small credit. As such, he became the architect and the HBFC to the residents of Yakoobabad. He also constructed a water tank for curing purposes and this tank became a source of water supply for which the residents paid. In the initial ten year period, 92 per cent families had built their homes with support from Nawab Ali and 62 per cent had made use of the credit offered by him. At the same time as Nawab Ali, another entrepreneur, Faiz Mohammad Baloch, moved into the area. He set up a generator and started supplying electricity to the residents at the rate of Rs30 per tube light or a 40 watt bulb. This sum was to be paid in advance and an advance non-payment for the next month would lead to a disconnection. Later, Faiz Muhammad Baloch opened a video hall where three films per day were advertised and illegally exhibited to an audience of about 20 to 50 people per show. The local *thana* permitted this and received *bhatta* (illegal gratification) for their support.

Y has formed a welfare association of all the households who have ever purchased a plot from him. This association is a legal organisation registered under the Societies Act. The Yakoobabad families became members of this association and through it Y and the Yakoobabad leadership have lobbied for infrastructure and improvements in the settlement. In this they have been helped by officials and politicians, who hold plots in Yakoobabad, since all improvements increase the value of property.

Most of the early residents of Yakoobabad were people who owned no homes or who could not afford to pay rent. Later residents came to Yakoobabad to escape from degraded physical, social and environmental conditions in the inner city. By 1989, Yakoobabad had become a 'proper' settlement and even lower middle income families started to shift here and as a result, the physical and social environment of Yakoobabad underwent a major improvement.

Today, 60 per cent of Yakoobabad has electric connections (acquired through the bribe market) and the rest of the 40 per cent either buy electricity from their neighbours or illegally tap the Karachi Electric Supply Corporation (KESC) mains by paying the KESC staff. There is still no piped water although water mains and trunk sewers under an ADB financed project have been laid. However, water now comes through tankers and not by donkey carts. The area has 10 primary schools, 2 secondary schools, 6 clinics and many roads have been paved by the councillors. The education and health facilities are all in the private sector. Transport through mini buses and Suzuki pickups is available. In addition, 401 micro enterprise units provide employment to over 2,600 persons in the settlement. Most of the units are engaged in garment stitching and *zari* (golden work on cloth) work and employ women. Nawab Ali has shifted his *thalla* to a newer settlement and Faiz Mohammad Baloch has become a video shop owner. A plot that was sold for Rs900 in 1978 now fetches a price of over Rs30,000.

The people of Yakoobabad have paid far more through bribes and extortion for their land and its development than they would have for a government developed housing scheme. But, they have paid for this incrementally over time and in sums that were affordable to them. In addition, this struggle to improve their conditions has transformed them into a community.

There are over 700 settlements like Yakoobabad in Karachi, housing more than 50 per cent of the city's population. They grow at a rate of 9 per cent per year against an annual urban growth rate of less than 4 per cent. It is they, and not the state agencies, that are determining the future physical, social and political structure of the city.

Source: Arif Hasan; *Understanding Karachi*; City Press, Karachi, 1999.

resulting in the development of renters and the densification of the older settlements.

Since land is sold on the open market, the neighbourhoods in most ISDs are not ethnically homogeneous. Similarly, as regularized land is rapidly becoming unaffordable for the lower-middle-classes as well, the ISDs contain a number of households which cannot be characterized as 'poor'.

In Lahore and Peshawar, and currently in Faisalabad, government land is not as easily available as in Karachi and Hyderabad. Nor is undeveloped desert land available as in these two cities. Consequently, the newer settlements are developing through the informal subdivision of agricultural land on the outskirts of the city. In Peshawar, almost all low-income settlements have been developed in this manner, and in Lahore the majority of the urban poor live in such settlements.

Normally, the owner of the agricultural land, hands it over to a *dallal*, who subdivides it, sells it, arranges for the necessary transfer of title, and collects a commission from the owner and the buyer. In some cases, developers purchase the land directly from the owner and subdivide it after laying some basic infrastructure, in which case they charge higher rates and increase their profit margins. Such developers cater mostly to the lower-middle classes. In none of the settlements visited has the owner of the land carried out the subdivision or sale of land himself. However, both he and the subdivider, hold on to a number of prize plots for speculative purposes.

Prices of agricultural land are very high, up to 200,000 rupees per acre in Lahore, Peshawar and Faisalabad. Thus, the subdivider when catering to lower-income groups, makes the subdivisions as small and the lanes and access roads as narrow as possible. As land values are increasing, the size of the plots is becoming smaller so as to be affordable for the poor. Recently created settlements have plot sizes as small as 16 to 20 square metres, with lanes as narrow as 2 metres and with no open spaces at all. To make the schemes more affordable to the poor, development is often carried out on cheaper unproductive land, such as abandoned quarries and low-lying areas. These create problems for storm water and sewerage disposal.

The ad hoc subdivision of agricultural land is depleting valuable productive land, most of which in the case of all five cities except Karachi is irrigated. This is especially unfortunate as all five cities have a considerable amount of vacant land within their municipal limits which can be developed.

Also, in all the five cities, old villages have become a part of the urban fabric. In all such villages visited, the *shamlaat* or community land had been subdivided and sold by the village elders and the profits shared between them. Old houses have been demolished to make room for smaller sized plots, and the nature of construction in the case of the poorer residents has changed from *katcha* to *pucca*. The number of residents have increased, mainly through the influx of outsiders. In

The Informal Developers of Faisalabad

Chaudhary Ghulam Rasool Cheema is a Faisalabad informal developer. He began this business because his salary as a WAPDA storekeeper was not enough to support his big family. To begin his business he sold a piece of land that he had in his village which is about 20 kilometres from Faisalabad. He chose to work along the Jaranwala Road because the people of the area knew him. He planned his first housing scheme in 1990 but work on it started in 1994. Up till now he has completed five small schemes each having 70 to 150 plots. The size of the plots is usually 5 *marla* and the measurements are 30 feet front into 45 feet depth. The streets are 20 to 28 feet wide. He raises the streets 2 feet above the road level. If the streets are not raised then people do not buy the plots because they are afraid that the settlement will get flooded. The earth-work for the streets is done by the Afghanis who have trolleys and jack machines for this job. Local people do not do this work since they have no experience in it and no machinery. For running his business he employs two persons as office staff. However, he hires a number of 'field workers' as well. These field workers contact prospective clients, prepare layout on site and supervise earth filling. When a project begins he usually has about 20 field workers who provide forms to the clients at 10 rupees each. If they sell ten forms in a day they earn 100 rupees. For the advertisement of a scheme a pamphlet is prepared and is given in newspapers inviting young middle or metric educated boys to come and work as field staff. These boys go to the areas which are congested or where people do not have their own houses. They brief them about the scheme and try to convince them that they should buy a plot. Most of the boys who respond to Mr Cheema's ad, already have experience in this field. They are given a further incentive of a commission for each plot that they sell. The planning of the scheme is done by Mr Cheema himself after which the sketches are provided to a draftsman for further development. The draftsmen who work for him are FDA employees and are hired by him on a per job basis. The most important criteria for the purchase of land for the scheme is availability of transport, which means access to the main inter-city road, and electricity. If the land is more than 2 kilometres from the inter-city road, the scheme does not sell. There is no attempt to develop corner plots or commercial plots. It is simply a five *marla* subdivision. In the smaller schemes Mr Cheema provides no services such as water, sewage or electricity. People acquire water by hand pumps, which they later convert to piston pumps, sewage through self-help (it invariably disposes into a canal) and electricity through lobbying with WAPDA. The developer does not keep any plot for speculation but thirty per cent of the plots normally remain unsold for a period of three to four years. There is a written agreement with the person who purchases the plot and proper records of receipts of instalments paid is maintained. People invariably pay regularly by coming themselves to Mr Cheema's office. For the transfer of land from the land owner to Mr Cheema, both the parties visit the divisional headquarters where land records are kept. Here they pay the legal as well as 'the other' charges. In the revenue department ledger, land remains as agricultural and streets and roads are recorded as amenities. The cost of transfer of land to the developer is borne by the purchaser.

Mr Cheema is also developing a small scheme on 2.75 acres. The name of the scheme is Al-Farooq. It has seventy plots of 5 *marlas* each and all of them have been sold but no house has been constructed so far. He purchased this land at 400,000 rupees per acre and is selling it in instalments at 48,000 rupees per plot. He is providing no services.

When Mr Cheema started his business in 1990, he had to look out for people who wanted to sell their agricultural land. Now that people know that he is in business and has an office where plans are displayed, land owners come to him themselves. Also, wherever he develops a scheme, he puts up a board on which the name, plan and details of the scheme are given. Mr Cheema says that the success of these schemes lies in the fact that the developers have understood what a poor man can afford to pay and they act accordingly. He also says that if the government could support this activity

> and provide the developers some loan, then in two to three years time there would be no one left in Faisalabad who was homeless.
>
> Source: *The Work of the Anjuman Samaji Behbood and the Larger Faisalabad Context;* unpublished report by Salim Alimuddin, Arif Hasan and Asiya Sadiq, December 1999.

Karachi, the villages have expanded onto neighbouring state lands and almost all such expansion has been declared as *katchi abadi*.

The inner cities of Lahore, Peshawar, Hyderabad and Karachi were the residential areas of the elite and merchant classes and contained retail markets that catered to them. Their architecture is of considerable cultural and historic importance. On the periphery of the walled cities, wholesale markets developed. These markets have expanded over the years to cater to increased populations and trade and commerce. At the same time, the merchant classes and the affluent sections of the population have moved out to new housing societies in the suburbs. These societies, unlike the narrow lanes of the walled cities, can accommodate the automobile. As a result of the shifting of the rich and the expansion of the markets, much of these residential areas have been turned into warehousing, storage facilities, manufacturing units and for use by the services sector to transportation that is closely related to the wholesaling process. This is causing immense environmental degradation in these historic areas. It is also resulting in the demolition of beautiful old buildings and their replacement by utilitarian structures that can serve the present functions of these old cities. Lower-income groups, especially without families, are increasingly becoming residents of these degraded areas. In Hyderabad, the open areas in the old city became the site of major *katchi abadis* at the time of partition. Some of them have already caused immense damage to the fortification walls of the Hyderabad Fort. This damage is likely to increase with time. Similarly, the old Lyari-Lea Market area of Karachi is now one enormous slum. Its more affluent residents have left and a large number of its new residents are migrant day labourers without families. Their number is increasing.

HOUSING AND INFRASTRUCTURE

The vast majority of residents (about 70 per cent) of the informal settlements described above, finance the construction of their houses from their savings. About 20 per cent take loans from friends or get money from other sources, such as the *bisee* committee. A small percentage also borrow money from a money lender at 10 to 12 per cent interest per month. In Karachi, building component manufacturing yards, known as *thallas*, that operate in most *katchi abadis*, also give materials on credit, and sometimes cash credit as well. A survey revealed that almost eighty per cent of house owners had taken material on credit from the *thalla* at sometime during the course of construction. The *thalla* owner does not rely on coercion for recovery of loans but on social pressure.

Initially most residents build only a compound wall, one room and a toilet. In Karachi, this construction is of cement concrete blocks and galvanized iron sheets. In the other four cities, it is usually of bad quality brick with a thatch roof. Over a period of time it is added to and after five to ten years it may have four or more rooms, concrete or T-iron and brick tile roof, plastered walls and paved floors. Door and windows are invariably of steel in Karachi and Hyderabad and increasingly so in Lahore and Faisalabad. In Peshawar, timber is still used.

For the initial construction of the house, the owner employs a mason for raising the walls and the family provides unskilled labour and also lays the galvanized iron sheet or thatch roof. However, as the house expands, the role of the mason becomes important as he advises on the design of the expansion, the costs involved, the materials and technology to be used and the structural details. Neighbours, who have already constructed their homes, are also called in for advice.

Masons working in low-income areas are those who because of their lack of skill, cannot get work in the more affluent areas. Their advice and work is faulty and as such houses in lower-income settlements are badly ventilated and lit, and suffer from technically weak details. This results in cracks in the walls; leakage through the roofs; sinking of floors; bad insulation and an unnecessarily high cost of construction.

In all the settlements visited, sewerage was the most neglected of all services. In Karachi and Hyderabad, it flows through open unpaved channels into the nearest *nulla* or natural drain. In Peshawar, Lahore and Faisalabad, such drains are not always available and thus the effluent is allowed to flow into a *jhor* or depression, in the settlement. Garbage, now dominated by polythene bags, also finds its way into the *jhor*. These *jhors* have been diminishing in size over time, as the owners of the land are reclaiming them for construction. In some cases people pay these owners an ad-hoc fee for permitting the *jhor* to stay. In

Peshawar, some settlements discharge their effluent into canals which are also a source of drinking water for the nearby residents.

Most houses in the settlements visited had either bucket or sanitary latrines which discharged onto paved open drains constructed by the councillor. In a small number of cases soak pits have also been constructed. However, these soak pits are of an unnecessarily elaborate design and far too expensive for the majority of the population to afford. In Faisalabad, Peshawar and Lahore, a number of settlements have open fields near them. As such a large number of residents here excrete in the open. As fields are also disappearing, the residents are feeling the need for constructing some form of sanitation system.

In areas where piped water is not available, most residents use hand pumps in Hyderabad, Lahore and Faisalabad. In Karachi where subsoil water is brackish, water is supplied by municipal bowzers or through donkey-carts from the nearest water source. In many areas in Faisalabad subsoil water is also brackish, and women walk over 2 kilometres to a municipal water point to get water. In certain other settlements water is available, but the majority of the population cannot afford to pay the connection fee or bear the cost of materials required for making the connection.

Electricity exists in most of the settlements visited. However, certain settlements had very few connections. In such cases people purchased power from those who had connections at rates varying from 30 to 45 rupees per month for a 40 watt tube light. In many settlements there are no banks and people find it very difficult to make payments for their electrical bills. In addition, there were a number of cases where residents had acquired an illegal direct connection from the electricity distribution system by making an informal arrangement with the Water and Power Development Authority (WAPDA) or KESC lineman. In Faisalabad and Karachi certain settlements which had no electricity were visited. Here a number of entrepreneurs run diesel generators commercially and sell electricity to a sizeable minority of residents. In all the informal systems described above, payments are made monthly in advance and as such the question of a default in payment does not arise.

In the absence of a gas connection people have a preference for LPG cylinders as opposed to timber because they are cheaper and easier to use. A cylinder costs 50 to 65 rupees and lasts a month for a household of six persons. This is much cheaper than timber, whose cost for the same number of people would be 120 rupees per month. However, the majority of people continue to use timber because they cannot afford to pay 1,100 rupees as a deposit for the refill bottle.

SOCIAL SERVICES

Over 80 per cent of the population of informal and *katchi abadis* visited use private health care facilities. Most of these clinics are run by non-qualified doctors and paramedics, who rely entirely on patent medicines for treatment. Many of them get date barred medicines from chemists at cheaper prices and sell them to their patients for a profit. Injections of unspecified drugs and glucose drips are commonly used as they add a serious note to the treatment. ORS was not available at the clinics that were visited, although dehydration among children in the settlements is common.

Most of the children in the informal settlements are educated in private schools. The majority of these schools are run on a purely commercial basis keeping the economics of the residents of the *katchi abadis* in mind. This means the school buildings are badly constructed, with insufficient light and ventilation; furniture is non-existent and teachers are untrained and paid less than one-third the standard salary for government teachers. Most of the teachers are women who work at these low wages so as to supplement their family incomes. As a rule they are not paid salaries for the period that the schools are closed. These conditions make it possible for these schools to charge very low fees, sometimes as low as 15 rupees per student. However, there are also schools run by dedicated teachers. They also face the problem of catering to the economics of the lower-income groups and they do not have access to organizations which can help them in raising their standards by imparting training or directions to their staff.

Both in Faisalabad and Karachi, a very large number of women work as stitchers and packers in garment factories. In Faisalabad, it was discovered that the majority of them are contract labour and are paid 16 rupees for 12 hours of work per day. In addition, a larger number of women do 'piece work' at home for contractors.

Middlemen finance a lot of income generation activities in the informal settlements and *katchi abadis*. In many Lahore settlements contractors provide a computerized knitting machine to a woman who knows how to use it, along with raw material. Half of what she produces belongs to the contractor after deducting the cost of raw material and the instalment on the machine. Training for operating the machine is provided by a vocational centre. Similarly, orders for embroidery work and stitching of garments are also placed by contractors on the same conditions.

Many residents of informal settlements and *katchi abadis* in all the five cities keep buffaloes and cows. These are purchased with a loan from middlemen. The owner feeds the animal, looks after it and milks it. The milk is acquired by the middleman at half its market value and sold. Any offspring of the animal is the property of the middleman.

In certain *abadis* visited in Karachi and Faisalabad, women make date fibre mats, nylon ropes and brooms. Raw material is supplied by the middleman and he is also in-charge of marketing the manufactured product. The value of half the produce, after deducting the cost of raw material, goes to the middleman.

Soles and bodies of shoes are manufactured for shoe companies in many Faisalabad *katchi abadis*. Again raw material is supplied by the middleman who picks up the manufactured produce at half the market cost. Shoe manufacturers visited insist that there is a great demand for their produce and if their production could be mechanized, and if they could get loans for raw materials, they could employ many more people and increase production. Similarly, a number of families in Faisalabad and Karachi manufacture cardboard packing boxes for the garment industry. Mechanization of this manufacturing process would double incomes and generate employment.

Garbage picking for recycling is a big business in the lower-income areas. Metal and glass containers and plastics are normally sold by the residents directly to persons who collect them from the homes. These are then sold to dealers in the settlements who in turn sell them to the recycling industry. A large amount of material is sent from the Peshawar settlements to the Punjab cities to be recycled. Paper, cardboard, rags, polythene bags, however, are all collected from the garbage by boys employed by middlemen. These boys are paid according to the weight of material they bring back each day. In the Lahore and Faisalabad settlements, where traditional occupational structures have not yet broken down, this work is done by the hereditary scavengers. The recycling industry is a boon for the urban centres of Pakistan. Without it inorganic solid waste could not have been disposed off causing immense environmental problems.

To conclude, the informal sector provides land at an affordable cost to the poor with immediate possession and with no paper work. It arranges for curtailing speculation and adjusts its standards according to the paying capacity of its client, something state agencies have failed to do. Although technical advice for house building provided by the sector is substandard, without it housing conditions in low-income settlements would be much worse. Though the informal sector fails to acquire sewerage and drainage systems, it does manage to provide water where subsoil water is not available. Again, though its education system is poor, the informal sector is responsible for the growing rate of literacy in the low-income areas, and though its health care system is unsound and exploitative, it does accurately diagnose malaria, typhoid and dengue. The middleman economy is excessively exploitative. However, it provides credit and possesses managerial and marketing skills without which a very large section of the lower-income households would be unemployed.

The main reason for the achievements of the informal sector is that its response to the needs of lower-income groups is compatible with the sociology and economics of the urban poor. This is because the operators of the system are either from the same class as some of the urban poor, or they have strong commercial links with low-income settlements. In addition, they do not have to rely on grants and subsidies for financing their operations.

The informal sector is operated entirely by entrepreneurs who are motivated commercially. They do not deal with issues through which they cannot make money, like sewerage disposal or street paving. In addition, for many sectors they operate in, such as health, education, housing and income generation, they have no access to qualified professionals and social and technical research. Suppose they did? Life in the poor settlements would be so much better!

Extracts from Community Development Groups in the Urban Fields in Pakistan, prepared for the Swiss Development Cooperation, Islamabad, August 1989

POSTSCRIPT 2008

Since 1989, when the above report was written, things have changed. A number of NGOs and CBOs have developed to support the residents and businesses of informal settlements with technical and managerial advise, credit and development activities. In addition, major social and physical changes have also taken place in those settlements which have survived the bulldozing of the sixties and eighties. For an informal settlement to develop there are two basic requirements. One, security of tenure (de-jure or de-facto), and two, infrastructure, especially water and electricity. To acquire these communities have had to organize themselves and form associations. Giving a formal shape to the organization is necessary so that it can be taken seriously. As such, many organizations are legal persons and have elections, audits and rules and regulations. This brings about a major cultural change in poor communities and establishes a more equitable relationship with state and formal sector organizations.

Over the years communities have also learnt that they cannot acquire infrastructure and tenure security simply by lobbying politicians. Where a level of de facto security is available, they invest large sums of money in building their own infrastructure and improving their homes over time as they feel these investments increase their tenure security in addition to providing a better environment. Their struggle for tenure security brings them in conflict with a powerful developer's lobby supported by bureaucrats and politicians that wish to evict them and build on their land. It also brings them in conflict with a lobby of consultants, contractors and government planners who promote insensitive projects which seek to displace them. Therefore, increasingly, residents of informal settlements opt for taking the matter to court or seeking the support of the press. These actions again create a new type of leadership in these settlements and bring the informal settlement closer to the formal processes. A number of important judgements have been given by the courts in this process which are considered 'pro-poor' and are important precedents for future court actions.

It has been observed that in the processes described above, those settlements which have external support have a greater chance of success. For example, where indigenously developed NGOs and professionals have given technical support to communities, infrastructure quality has been much better and its cost has been cheaper. Insensitive government projects that displace people have also been abandoned or altered if communities have been able to present estimates of damage that the projects would cause along with viable alternatives. Again, such estimates and alternatives have invariably been prepared by concerned professionals and NGOs. However, without communities organizing themselves and taking control of their destinies, the support from NGOs and professionals is usually ineffective.

However, the most important change that had taken place in informal settlements was that trade, commerce, manufacturing and education had developed in them. This, along with the struggle against the various lobbies that operate against them, had produced a large number of leaders and activists who were constantly in touch with formal sector agencies and service providers. However, with structural adjustment, globalization and the WTO regime, these developments have received a setback since cheap Chinese goods have adversely affected informal sector manufacturing and commerce. Also, with the increased role of the corporate sector in decision making regarding governance and development issues, the effectiveness of the link between local leadership and the state agencies has weakened. However, what is important is that local leadership and its activists belong to the second generation of informal settlement residents. Unlike their parents or grandparents they are not pioneers. They have a claim on the city and have an urban culture. Hence, it is not in their nature to accept marginalization quietly, and much of the violence and conflict that cities face today is the result of the marginalization of the second generation of informal settlement dwellers. Structural adjustment, the WTO regime and the culture of globalization has increased this marginalization.

As a result, in the planning process the representatives of the informal settlements and the informal sector service providers are almost never involved. Their point of view and their interests are not considered and the immense knowledge that they have on how the city really functions is not made use of. Consequently, most urban planning, physical, social or economic, is based on wrong assumptions, most of which are drawn from the First World planning experience and by and large benefit international and local consultants, contractors and real estate speculators and their partners.

17

The Changing Face of
Karachi's Inner City

With its chaotic traffic, the cacophony of power horns, the smog and
the grime, Karachi's once elegant and sophisticated centre has changed
beyond recognition over the years. Where there were once magnificent
sandstone structures, there are now commercial plazas, warehouses and
distinct signs of dereliction. It is difficult to imagine that the area once
housed numerous dance halls, billiard rooms, bars, theatres and was the
venue for cultural activities such as the May ball.

The Saddar quarter began as Saddar Bazaar in 1839. It was established
as a shopping centre to serve the British military camp which was
located between the bazaar and the walled city. After the British
annexed Karachi in 1843, the camp was dismantled and the residents
moved to more permanent accommodation in the north and east of the
bazaar. Saddar went on to develop as a commercial area where
European officers and their wives could shop in a not too unfamiliar
environment and where the latest fashions and products from 'home'
were available.

After the failure of the 1857 rebellion against British rule, the growth
of Saddar gathered speed. It owed this development not only to the
British policy of promoting trade and commerce in the city, but also to
the pioneering spirit of the Hindu, Goan, Parsi, and much later, the
Muslim business communities which established businesses in the
bazaar. They took an active interest in the area's civic life and established
most of its lasting institutions. The Parsi and Goan residential areas
were located in the bazaar itself, and the European quarters were
situated on its periphery.

At the time of independence, a large number of important
institutions, most of them connected to the Church or to the Goan and
Parsi communities, were located in Saddar. Schools, some established
as early as 1848, community halls, libraries, *gymkhanas* with lovely cast

iron or timber pavilions, dramatic clubs and churches existed in the area. Bars and billiard rooms, Irani cafes for the 'natives' and posh tea rooms for the *gora sahibs* flourished.

Saddar remained an area distinct from the hustle and bustle of the walled city, although a horse drawn tramway did link it up with the native quarter in 1885. Pir Ali Mohammad Rashdi, the celebrated Sindhi writer, describing the Saddar of his youth, maintained that no badly dressed man dared enter the bazaar even as late as the 1930s. He speaks of it as 'a place of intellectual assembly and sophisticated English style shops.'

After independence, 600,000 refugees moved into Karachi and the city was made the capital of Pakistan. Most refugees to the new capital settled in the cantonment area adjacent to Sadder. While the government servants occupied the old army barracks, the poorer refugees settled in the open spaces between them. The new population included poets, artists, performers and intellectuals. Meanwhile, barracks to accommodate the offices of the new government were also constructed adjacent to the bazaar. With these new developments, although the population of the Sadder quarter and its adjacent areas increased by over 400 per cent, distances remained small and people walked or cycled to work. Those working at the port made use of the tramway, and although there were only eight buses in Karachi at the time, transportation did not pose a problem.

The refugee influx enriched the social and intellectual life of Saddar. The local population expanded to include bureaucrats, diplomats, writers, artists and politicians. Bookshops, billiard rooms, bars, libraries, cinemas and eating places mushroomed in the area. Karachi's old colleges were already located on Saddar's periphery and, after independence, a new university was set up at walking distance from the bazaar. The student community made free use of Saddar's facilities and institutions, interacting with the rest of the population.

By 1965, in less than one square kilometre, Saddar Bazaar housed thirty 'respectable' eating places, nine bars, eleven billiard rooms, eighteen bookshops, seven auditoriums, four discotheques and thirteen cinemas. Seminars were held by professional institutions, students organized their debates and variety programmes and the government its conferences in the auditoriums and halls of Saddar. And the participants strolled to one of the neighbouring eating places for their meals.

At the centre of this activity stood the Empress Market. It was flanked by small gardens and in the open spaces before its three entrances, stood beautiful stone troughs for watering transport animals. The residents of Sadder and the bureaucrats and diplomats living in the neighbouring cantonment areas regularly shopped here, while young people flocked to the market 'for fun'.

Saddar's fortunes started to rise or decline, depending on how one perceives the changes that took place, in the late fifties and early sixties. New housing societies were created for government servants situated outside the old municipal limits of the city, and these officers soon moved out of Saddar. The men of letters, artists and journalists who frequented the cafes and bookshops also drifted to the suburbs. During the same period, the university was shifted to its present location, miles away from the city centre, and Karachi ceased to be the capital of the country.

Between 1958 and 1962, the government moved the refugee population to two townships about fifteen miles to the east of Karachi. Most of these refugees worked in the old city, at the Sindh Industrial and Trading Estate (SITE), which lies west of Saddar, and at the port. In those days, the only route to these three places of work was through Saddar. Thus, by 1965 over 80,000 persons per day were moving through Saddar en route to their places of work, and Empress Market had become a major transport junction.

Soon after the establishment of the refugee townships, commercial activity to serve this daily transit movement started to develop in Saddar. Workshops to serve the transport industry, public baths and eating places and the number of hawkers multiplied as the transit population grew. Almost all the new activity was conducted on the pavements or within the open spaces in the bazaar, promoting the process of degradation.

In the late sixties, the more affluent residents of the area started to move out, unable to live in the new environment of their quarter. During the same period, the four and five star hotel culture came to Karachi. Social, academic and artistic functions, even of the communities living in Saddar, were held at what is now the Pearl Continental Hotel, Hotel Metropole or at one of the foreign cultural centres which had been established in the city. One of the major reasons for this change was that the physical and social environment in Saddar was no longer regarded as being conducive to holding these events there.

The final stage of Saddar's degradation came in the seventies. The suburbs started to develop their own commercial centres and recreational institutions and the residents no longer travelled to Saddar to shop. Old shops, which had become institutions after over a century of use, closed down or shifted to the suburbs. An economic boom, fired by Gulf money, increased trade and commerce and a consumer culture engulfed the city. Warehouses, wholesale markets and distribution outlets were needed to support this development. In the absence of new estates to house these facilities and because of its comparatively better road network, infrastructure and changing landuse, Saddar was seen as the ideal place to establish these facilities. In the western and northern part of Saddar warehouses and markets replaced bookshops, eating places and institutional buildings. In the southern part, hotels catering to the new consumer trade replaced old residential apartment houses. The KDA Master Plan 1974–85, by increasing plot ratios in the area and permitting high-rise construction, facilitated this process.

In 1977, prohibition was enforced and the bars closed down. A few years later, unable to keep alive without bars, the billiard rooms also started to shut down. By the mid 1980s, many cinemas had been replaced by plazas and most of Saddar's old residential areas had been reduced to a transit camp by day and graveyards at night which were inhabited after dark by large numbers of social outcasts and drug addicts. The city's cultural and recreational centre was dead and nothing had replaced it!

The processes at work that wreaked havoc on Saddar were also at work in other older parts of the city. However, the factors that put pressures on areas such as the Napier and Sarai quarters were different. Unlike Saddar, these quarters are in close proximity to the old town quarter or the walled city and to the port.

The walled city of Karachi was built in 1729 by Hindu merchants from Karak Bunder after that port had silted up and become inoperative due to heavy floods. The city had two gates: the one facing the sea was called Kharadar or salt gate, and the other facing the seasonal Lyari River to the north, was known as Mithadar or sweet gate. The neighbourhoods where these gates once stood are still known by these names although the wall and gates were demolished by the British in 1849. Kharadar was connected to the port by a road known as Rah-i-Bunder which became a part of the Bunder Road developed by the British in the 1860s. It is now known as M.A. Jinnah Road. The road divides the Sarai Quarter from the older quarters to its north.

Karachi was built specifically for trading purposes and prospered due to the development of the Central Asian trade in the late eighteenth and early nineteenth century. After its conquest by the Talpurs in 1794, a sense of security pervaded the fortified town which soon expanded outside its walls. Textile and tanning industries were also set up in the suburbs of the city. One of these suburbs was Lyari, to the north of the old town, where the city's proletariat, boat hands and port labourers lived. It was also here that most of the tanning works, emitting a foul stench, were located. Between Lyari and Mithadar an open vegetable and fruit market developed in the 1820s. The homes of those who served the market were also located here. After the British conquest of Sindh in 1843, this area was the first to be developed by them. It came to be known as the Napier quarter, after Sir Charles Napier the conqueror of Sindh. The open market also expanded until Lea Market was constructed on its site in 1927.

By 1947, when Pakistan was created, the Napier and Sarai quarters had become major commercial areas, housing in addition to the above mentioned facilities—a number of wholesale markets and related warehousing facilities. The old town itself was predominantly residential, except for textile wholesaling, and housed most of the *mandirs* and *dargahs* around which the cultural and religious activity of the town and the neighbouring quarters was organized.

The old town and its neighbouring quarters were a far cry from Europeanized Saddar. Away from the main arteries, the streets were winding and narrow. Buying and selling in the markets and shops was carried on in the 'native' style. Although tea houses, bars and billiard rooms were found in these quarters as well, the ambience and the people who frequented them, were very different and far less formal. There were no May Balls, dramas, police bands and Easter parties here. Instead, *diwali, milads, urs* of saints and Muharram were celebrated with fervour.

TRADE AND INDUSTRY

There are a number of factors that have led to the degradation of the old city and its neighbouring districts. The most important factor, however, is related to the development of trade and industry and the resulting increase in port activity with its own requirements.

According to press reports, the Karachi port in 1951 handled 2.8 million tons of cargo. The storage facilities for this cargo were available at the port or at the railway marshalling yards. Except for the transportation of goods to the wholesale markets in the city, almost all cargo was handled by the railways. However, in 1991, mainly as a result of industrialization and the introduction of green revolution technologies, over 26 million tons of cargo was being handled. Despite this increase, however, storage facilities at the port and marshalling yards did not develop proportionately. To add to the situation, the railway's capacity to service the needs of the port have actually declined since 1951. Meanwhile, keeping pace with the increase in port activity and with a huge growth in the city's population since 1945, the volume of trade in the wholesale markets within the inner city has also increased manifold. However, space for the expansion of warehousing, transport related and wholesale activity, have not been provided.

As a result of these factors, large areas of the old town and almost all areas of the Napier, Sarai and Lyari have been converted into warehouses that serve the needs of the port and the wholesale markets. The old stone residential buildings, usually two to three storeys in height, have been pulled down and replaced by six storey buildings of more or less standard design. The design usually comprises stores on the ground floor, small flats or individual rooms for port or transport related day-wage labourers on the floors above, and perhaps a large apartment for the original owner of the building. This building activity has been promoted by developers who have developed a number of financial and design packages, with which they approach the building owners.

All byelaws in the area have been flouted and the new buildings are not only inadequately lit and badly ventilated, but have defective plumbing and electrification. Many of the original residents have sold their properties and shifted to squatter settlements in North and West Karachi, claiming that both social and physical conditions are much better in the informal settlements in those areas than in the inner city.

The port, the expanded wholesale markets, and the storage facilities which developed in the old town and adjoining quarters are today serviced by mechanized vehicles, as is the very busy link between the port and SITE, Karachi's major industrial area. This entire movement of men and goods, along with the various linkages between the port and Karachi's hinterland and other industrial areas, takes place through the arteries of the Lyari, Napier and Sarai quarters.

The development of mechanized transport also resulted in the setting up of at least two large trucking stations and a major services sector comprising not only workshops, eating places, hotels and spare part manufacturing, but also prostitution dens, and entertainment and drug venues. Much of this activity is carried on through encroachments on public spaces. Rates for the promotion of such encroachments have been institutionalized. In fact, at an informal level, the city administration, the property owners and the encroachers themselves all participate in the process and benefit from it.

The process of change described above, except for a few small protected pockets, has worked major social changes in Karachi's 'inner city'. For one, it has killed most traditional cultural activity as the vast majority of the new population consists of migrant workers living without their families. This fact helps determine the nature of entertainment, food, shops and attitudes of the area residents. Transporters and the drug mafia are a major economic power in the area and hence, a political force as well. Anti-drug movements, organized by residents of the area have been suppressed by the police and other parties. In the not too distant past, anti-drug activists have even been murdered. Anti-encroachment drives, moves for collection of user charges, and implementation of traffic rules and regulations have met with a similar fate.

The social changes described above apply only to certain parts of the historic quarters. Physical changes also differ in the different parts of this quarter. In the area adjoining McLeod Road and parts of Bunder Road, high-rise office buildings rather than warehouses are being constructed, while in the eastern part of the quarter the old residential areas are still very much intact. However, the main arteries of the quarter do serve as a major conduit for the movement of people and cargo to and from the port. In fact, many wholesale markets are situated on these roads.

CONSERVATION PLANS

Social economic and environmental conditions are all hostile to the operation of an effective area conservation plan for the old quarters. Conservation plans can be realized only if some of the larger issues dealt with above are also tackled alongside. Also, living conditions in these areas are clearly unsatisfactory. Investigations reveal that the majority of people who live and work in these areas on a permanent basis are unhappy with the physical and social environment around them. And they have specific demands to bring about a change.

In the Saddar area, most respondents felt that if the traffic through Saddar was eliminated, the area could be rehabilitated. It was also felt that the old institutions of the area were not irretrievably lost and could be revived if environmental conditions permitted.

One proposal was to build a ring road around Saddar. A pedestrian spine from St. Patrick's Cathedral to the Sindh High Court, so as to redirect all through traffic passing through Saddar, was another suggestion. Adequate space for the development and expansion of wholesale markets and warehouses in attractive locations outside the city, backed by the necessary infrastructure and easily accessible from the port and highways, should also be provided alongside. The rest could be taken care of by a conservation plan.

In the old town and adjoining areas, a number of residents, transporters and traders were interviewed and each group had its own particular complaints and offered a number of solutions. The transporters too were clearly unhappy with working in the inner city. The area is too congested, movement slow and energy consumption high. The traders also complained about the storage facilities, especially of the difficulty in serving them through mechanized transport.

The Karachi Master Plan 1974–85 proposed two bypasses from the port, one each to the two highways that link Karachi with the rest of Pakistan. Karachi's main industrial areas also lie near these highways. The building of these bypasses would reduce traffic pressures in the inner city considerably. In fact, if well planned storage facilities and supporting infrastructure including telephone, telex and banking facilities could be provided along these bypasses as well, a large number of inner city traders would be willing to move out to these areas even without other incentives. With this movement, a sizeable number of residents who are renters and work for the traders and the inner city wholesale markets and transport, would also move out. The release of this pressure would make it possible for the presently besieged inner city communities to breathe once again and rehabilitate what is left of the *purana shehar*. However, although the bypasses were proposed in the old Master Plan, the development of wholesale markets, warehousing and related residential and services sector developments on them were not envisaged.

LOBBIES OF POWER

Planning in Karachi, as in all other Pakistani cities, is the domain of bureaucrats. The people themselves or their neighbourhood or city level representatives have little or no say in the matter. However, powerful lobbies with major economic and political interests are seen operating in the city. These lobbies not only influence the planning process but also ensure that any aspects of the plan detrimental or not beneficial to their interests remain unimplemented.

One major lobby operating in Karachi consists of the formal sector developers. Their main aim is to keep land and property values high in the city centres since many of them own land and property here. They also influence policies related to land-use and housing finance. It lies in their interest to oppose most conservation plans for Saddar and the inner city and a release of pressure on these areas. They have also lobbied for changes in building byelaws and for the increase of covered areas on inner city properties, creating increased congestion.

Informal land developers, very often backed by formal developers and officials in government agencies, are another lobby. They are informed of development plans well before they are made public and develop their strategies accordingly. For instance, when the northern and southern bypasses were planned they made arrangements to eventually occupy the vantage areas on or near them.

The transporters are yet another powerful lobby. They have been known to dictate routes, stops and fares to the public agencies. They have prevented the plying of government transport on certain lucrative routes and made a mockery of traffic laws and of attempts at traffic management by public sector agencies.

Similarly, trade and shopkeepers associations also have a vested interest in city plans. They have in the past successfully prevented certain streets from being declared as one way streets and certain others from being no parking streets. In addition, they have engineered changes in the last traffic management plan for Saddar, and these changes were far from being in the public interests.

Lobbying aside, the manner of Karachi's urbanization also poses a number of problems. Development precedes planning and because of the plan's social inappropriateness as well as the implementing agency's inability, implementation is not carried out. Informal processes then take over, promoting anarchy, administrative helplessness and corruption.

The interests of the various commercial groups in Karachi are protected by their organizations. But there is no 'citizen's lobby' in Karachi to protect the interests of the city as a whole and pressurize government to plan in the larger interest of the city. The need for such a lobby is keenly felt by a large number of Karachiites who have formed various NGOs. Using the organization as a platform they try for a dialogue with the powers that be. But again, these NGOs, except for a few are the domain of the upper middle class, having little or no interaction with the public at large. Further, they depend on whimsical donor funding, often foreign, and find it difficult to relate to the various public sector agencies involved in Karachi's planning and conservancy.

These NGOs and interest groups can only be effective if their lobbying is supported by action research and through constant dialogue with interest groups so that such groups can become a part of their lobbying process. It is only through a process supported by research and dialogue that viable alternatives to government proposals can be formulated and promoted.

POSTSCRIPT 2008

This article was published in 1993. Since then environmental degradation has increased both in Saddar and in the old city. Entire neighbourhoods which in 1993 were considered 'liveable' by their residents have now become 'slums' both in physical and social terms. After considerable push from NGOs, professionals and concerned citizens, the Northern Bypass Project was undertaken and is now nearly complete. However, the inner city wholesale markets, storage and warehousing have not been shifted to it and nor are there any concrete plans for doing so in the near future although the Karachi Strategic Development Plan 2020, approved by the city government in 2008, recommends this.

The city government since it came in existence in 2001 has undertaken a large number of road and drainage projects and the building of parks and flyovers. However, the old city and Saddar have not yet been the beneficiaries of investments which could help in improving social and environmental conditions.

The Sindh Cultural Preservation Act was approved by the Sindh Assembly in 1994. A committee in the Culture Department of the government of Sindh has been set up to oversee the implementation of the Act. As a result, a large number of old buildings in the old town and the inner city have now been listed and are to be conserved. The implementation of the Act has generated a major debate and resulted in the filing of numerous court cases, seeking delisting, by the owners, whose buildings have been declared heritage. Due to this a considerable awareness of conservation related issues has surfaced in NGOs, academic institutions, professional organizations and the media. However, for the long term success of this process, the larger city level planning issues identified in the article above, need to be addressed.

18

Karachi 2000: Social and Demographic Change

Major changes took place in Karachi between 1947 and 1951. Six hundred thousand inhabitants were added to its population; the Hindu population decreased from 51 to 2 per cent while the Muslim population increased to 96 per cent. Similarly, the Sindhi speaking population decreased from 61.2 to 8.6 per cent while the Urdu–Hindi speaking population increased from 6.3 to 50 per cent. However, these changes did not substantially increase the physical size of the city. From a low density city, divided into ethnic and class quarters, it became a high density multi class city. Its centre, Saddar Bazaar was easily accessible to all its inhabitants. A university, government offices, most major educational, community and religious facilities, and embassies were within walking distance to it and new intellectuals, artists and artisans were added to the old as a result of these demographic changes. All this enriched intellectual and cultural life, especially of the centre, even if it degraded the city physically.

However, all this changed. The MRV Plan of 1952 took the university away in 1958 from the centre and a year later Ayub Khan decided to take the capital away to Islamabad. Doxiadis's Greater Karachi Resettlement Plan created satellite cities for the poorer Karachiites, far away from the city in Landhi-Korangi and New Karachi, and the better off or more influential were given plots in the housing societies nearer to the centre. The division between the rich and poor was complete and the transport problems for the poor multiplied since they had to commute from distant homes to the city centre which over the years has degenerated into an unplanned bus terminal, devoid of its former status of a space for multi-class entertainment, intellectual life and community and political activities. One can safely say that the Doxiadis Plan led to the fragmentation of the city, the death of its centre, and is to a large measure responsible for the city's social and political turmoil.

However, the physical and social changes that have taken place in Karachi between 1981 and 1998 (the period between the two last censuses) are far more dramatic than the ones that took place between 1947 and 1951. The population of the city in this period has increased from 5.4 to 10 million. The physical needs of this increase, in the absence of adequate planning, have been met through densification and consolidation of the parameters developed by the Doxiadis Plan; informal development and the helplessness of government agencies leading to corruption and mismanagement. All this has created powerful interest lobbies and community organizations. These developments have been accompanied by the communications revolution; political turmoil; return of families from the Middle East with new ideas, lifestyles and money; decline in formal sector economic growth; an increase (in real terms) in the aging population; and above all, the coming of age of a second and third generation of Karachi born Karachiites who have no other identity and who, because of the factors mentioned above, are completely different from their parents and grandparents. They constitute the vast majority of the population of the city today. We will be able to say a lot more about them in statistical terms, once the 1998 census results are published. All one can say from the data available so far is that the male-female literacy gap has narrowed substantially, the rate of divorce and the age at which one gets married have increased considerably, and so has the male-female sex ratio. In addition, the percentage of nuclear families has also increased and natural growth rate has declined sharply. Observation, press reports and surveys establish that senior citizens now look for jobs as their families, unlike previously, cannot cater to their changed needs. Government agencies recognize this problem and have recently started employing them at pedestrian crossings for helping children to cross the roads. All these trends are indications of urban values and culture.

The enormous spatial expansion of the city has also fragmented it. Time and struggle taken in travelling, the distances involved, law and order problems and large scale environmental degradation, have made the neighbourhood and its environment more important and helped in the death of the city centre. Thus neighbourhoods are increasingly developing the facilities required for urban life and the physical, and hence social and ethnic divisions are increasing, even while a large Karachi identity is asserting itself.

Karachi: What the Census Tells Us

Literacy has increased considerably and the male-female literacy gap has decreased substantially, especially in the younger generation. In 1972, 51.18 per cent and in 1981, 55.04 per cent of Karachiites were literate. In 1998, the figure was 67.42 per cent. In 1972, 45.02 and in 1981, 48.84 per cent of women were literate as compared to 62.88 per cent in 1998. The differences are far more dramatic in the age group of 10 to 14 years. In 1972, 55.59 per cent and in 1981, 55.24 per cent of this age group was literate. In 1998, this figure had increased to 74.71 per cent. In this age group 55.38 per cent of females were literate in 1981. In 1998 this increased to 74.16 per cent, almost closing the male-female literacy gap. These trends point to the importance given to education and to its availability in spite of the failures of the government in this sector and to the fact that a more equitable gender relationship is being created. Besides other repercussions, these developments are a source of stress and strain in a society which is dominated by a retrogressive state culture.

Marital status and related matters have also changed. Total married population of 15 and above has decreased from 62.08 per cent in 1981 (in 1972 this figure was 66.22) to 56.29 per cent in 1998. Between the age group of 15 and 24 these changes are even more marked. The number of married people in this age group has fallen from 24.37 per cent to 18.58 per cent in the inter-census years. For women the fall is even greater (from 37.92 per cent in 1981 to 28.54 per cent in 1998). The divorce rate has also gone up by more than 100 per cent between 1981 and 1998. It has increased most in the age group of between 25 and 49 (by 226 per cent) and between 50 and 59 (by 323 per cent). These figures are important as they point to the erosion of feudal values, weakening of the joint family system and the assertion of individual decision making.

Karachiites are living in dramatically better environmental conditions at the micro level in spite of increasingly bad conditions at the macro level. The number of one room houses has fallen from 44.94 per cent to 30.09 per cent of the total stock and the number of three room houses has increased from 13.96 per cent to 21.12 per cent. The number of houses with electric connections has increased from 65.78 per cent in 1980 to 93.79 per cent in 1998 and the number of homes with pipe water connections has increased from 44.45 per cent to 74.38 per cent during the same period. The number of homes with reinforced concrete roofs has increased from 42.54 per cent to 56.04 per cent during the inter-housing census years.

The reality on the ground and what a comparison between the two census figures tell us is that we are living in a society and state full of contradictions. Statistics tell us that we are definitely a post feudal society, but state culture promotes irrationality, obscurantism and dogmatism. We are becoming an increasingly cosmopolitan city but our politics is dominated by ethnicity. Statistics tell us that at the micro level physical conditions are improving but even a dimwit can see that at the macro level they are rapidly deteriorating. The census tells us that there are major differences between the districts and common sense tells us that in the absence of representative local government (which we have not had for about a decade) they can only increase and with serious political repercussions. The above contradictions can only be overcome through relating the changes in Karachi to those taking place in the rest of Pakistan in general and in Sindh in particular, and by the operation of a coercion-free political process out of which a badly needed broad political consensus can emerge. However, we have a military government that has banned political activity.

Source: Extracts from an article by Arif Hasan and Mansoor Reza, *What the Census Tells Us*, published in Daily *Dawn*, February 2001.

The rich now live in ghettos, surrounded by armed guards and security systems. They are developing their entertainment, recreational, educational and commercial facilities in their own areas. Old Karachi food, books and other retail outlets have relocated to these posh neighbourhoods, and boutiques selling first world designer goods and international food chains have sprung up. Their children do not visit the national museum or the Karachi Zoo and are more at home in London's Hyde Park than at the Safari Park in Gulshan-i-Iqbal. Their textbooks too teach them nothing of their city, its history, its problems or its culture. The sprawling lower middle income settlements of District Central, the *katchi abadis* of District West, or the chaos of the inner city simply do not exist for them. Thus, Karachi has lost, what is perhaps a city's greatest asset, an interested, informed and enlightened elite and in the absence of such an elite, a decline in civic services and institutions is bound to happen.

The old *katchi abadis*, which were once on the city fringe, have also consolidated since 1981. They have acquired social and physical infrastructure. Private schools and clinics set up by their entrepreneurs or through community effort take care of their education and health needs. Previously, they were totally working class areas, but a sizeable number of the new generation, both men and women, work in white-collar jobs in the city. In these settlements, there are bank managers, college teachers, telephone operators, receptionists, doctors, engineers, information technology professionals and technicians and para-professionals of all descriptions. They are all young. Working women are increasingly becoming a factor in the economy and sociology of these settlements. The small informal artisanal workshops that were set up here three or four decades ago when the settlements began, have also expanded to become formal business enterprises. They are run by a younger generation which is better educated and quite comfortable with dealing with officialdom, banks and export agencies. This is the new leadership which is replacing the old pioneers. The aspirations of the residents of these *abadis* are middle class and in most cases there is little difference between them and the planned lower middle income areas of the city in social, cultural and economic terms. The majority of Karachiites live in these settlements and in the lower middle income planned areas of District Central and the Landhi-Korangi areas. The vocabulary of the young people of these settlements and also of the older university residential areas that still survive, is different from their parents'. *Janab*, *hazoor*, *sain*, *sahib* are out; uncle, aunty and *bhai* are in.

There is no more *niazmandi, sharf hasil hona* or *tabaydari* and no more *mai-bap*; it is *thaik-thak hai, tik-tika* and *chaloo pan*.

The new *katchi abadis*, however, are different. They have yet to consolidate and acquire facilities. Their leadership still consists of land grabbers and middlemen, income levels are low and social cohesion is missing. Most of the population here is first generation migrant and the female population is very small as compared to the male. In many of the inner city settlements too, conditions have changed in the inter-census years. Wholesale markets have expanded along with the services sector to cargo transport activities, families have moved out, day-wage labour has moved in. Much of this labour is also seasonal. As a result of these changes, large areas have become slums in sociological terms, societies without structure and cohesion. It is here that most of Karachi's rapidly expanding underclass lives, an underclass whose aspirations are to become like the older *katchi abadis* but the means, except for a small few are simply not there.

All these conflicting fragments of Karachi come together in Gulshan-i-Iqbal and as such its lifestyle is imitated in other settlements (except of the elite) and its young men and women are role models for others. Here *khokas* co-exist with foreign food chain outlets, *katchi abadis* with planned apartment complexes; real estate agencies and car showrooms with supposedly clandestine betting shops and drug outlets; a fast expanding flat culture with old *goths* struggling for survival and succeeding. And all these elements share a common space and vocabulary.

The middle and lower middle income areas of Karachi and the older *katchi abadis* have a number of things in common which are trickling through to other settlements and becoming the most important parts of Karachi culture. One is cable television. It is now universal in these areas. It is in people's homes, in barbershops, in eating places catering to all classes, even in the waiting rooms of private clinics. Indian films and western pop are now a part of family life except for the religious and conservation minority. This minority is also increasing in number though not in percentage terms. It is perhaps because of the cable and all that goes with it that beauty parlours, run by women for women, have cropped up in a big way all over these middle and lower middle income settlements. The beautification items on the menu sometimes contain the names of Indian film actresses. In an increasing number of parlours, a waiting room for men is being provided! The cable TV is also changing lifestyles. Cooking classes have opened up where the preparation of Chinese and Thai dishes is taught to women and also small schools for interior and flower decoration for women are increasing. Eating out, especially non-Pakistani food, is something to look forward to and restaurants are full to capacity, many with young couples and families, especially in the first week of the month after salaries have been paid. The number of women managed and operated retail outlets are also increasing. All this is a major social revolution and what its effects on family life and values, and hence on society are, and are going to be, needs to be studied, analyzed and catered to by the planning agencies in the city.

The other most important change is related to information technology. All the lower middle income settlements and older *katchi abadis* have a large number of computer training centres, many dealing with programming as well. Karachiites have understood the economic and job potential of information technology and as such these centres are full of young men and women students. Another important factor is the mushrooming of private schools and tuition centres advertising the teaching of English and the fact that almost all of them are co-educational.

The above directions point to the fact that the new Karachiites are fiercely upwardly mobile and are anxious to become a part of the international global culture. Their dress patterns and bearing have changed over the last decade and a half to reflect these new aspirations and they have also become addicted to FM 100 which represents their culture. However, their incomes are low as compared to their aspirations and that is because they live in an economy plagued with recession and inflation. To overcome this problem, it has become necessary for women to work and hence the need for their education and acquisition of skills. Families now look for educated and or skilled women as wives for their sons and it is not a coincidence that the University of Karachi today has more female than male students. Then most lower middle income employed males, and also working class ones, do an extra job or a business of some sort. After office hours, they work in an estate agency, as life insurance salesmen, give tuitions, run a small business or a taxi. In the lower income areas, homes are being turned into workshops and businesses. Garment stitching, flower making, fruit packaging, cardboard box making, gas kit manufacturing, are some of the things that families do collectively to beat inflation and recession, educate their children, and acquire the new electronic gadgets that have become a necessity for them.

In spite of this extra work and family businesses, the economic and lifestyle aspirations of the young Karachiites cannot be met. This is because of a clash between their aspirations and the conservative and puritanical aspects of our state culture. The other reason is corruption and nepotism. This upwardly mobile population of young people has to pay a bribe or have connections to get a job, a commission, or contract. They have no access to the corridors of power and no capital. Thus, the city is full of young people trying desperately to go abroad (at any cost) or to attach themselves to 'progressive' political groups that can give them access to the means for fulfilling their aspirations. Unfortunately, these are perhaps the brightest of the younger generation and definitely with the most initiative. Under different circumstances, they would be an asset to their society, role models for promoting progress and social justice.

Entertainment and recreation are an essential part of the nature of urban society described in the preceding paragraphs. At the city and larger suburban level, cinemas catered to this requirement for entire families. However, in Karachi the age of the cinemas is dead and most of them have ceased to exist. What is more important today is recreation at the neighbourhood level. In the lower and lower middle income settlements, people play drafts and cards on the crossroads under street lights and often pay the police *bhatta* so that they are not harassed. There are carom and snooker clubs and illegal video halls that people frequent, and social welfare organizations that exist in almost every Karachi neighbourhood (and are always run by younger people) often operate reading rooms and lending libraries. Sports clubs also exist at the neighbourhood level and cricket and football matches between different teams and neighbourhoods, are common. However, most of this activity is for men only. Women do participate sometime as spectators in sports and also as participants, in *mushairas*, religious functions and in rare cases where society permits (this is increasing) in musical performances. Many youth organizations have tried to initiate theatre and music groups but this has met with limited success in the absence of state support, difficulties in being permitted by the establishment to perform at a public place, and due to being frowned upon by the elders in the neighbourhood. But what will happen in the next ten years when part of this generation becomes the elders and the state?

However, one thing that Karachi families and young groups do, is to go out. On Sundays, the beaches in and around the city, as far as Gadani, are full of families and groups from the lower and lower middle income areas of the city. They get to these beaches and to other picturesque locations such as Kalri and Haleji Lakes, on hired Suzukis. They picnic and listen to loud Indian film songs, (many dance as well) and enjoy themselves (they also leave behind an enormous amount of solid waste!). They invade the parks and in certain locations, such as the Hill Park in PECHS, the Pakhtoons perform the Khattak every Sunday and have wrestling competitions. On occasions such as Eid, Bakra Eid, and long weekends whenever they happen, places like Alladin Park and Clifton Funland are full to capacity. A large number of families, men and women, also get together to visit *Mazars* in Karachi and the Sindh interior for the *Urs* of *Pirs*. This is both a religious event and an outing.

The importance of the neighbourhood, inadequate planning and facilities, and land grabbing have led to the formation of neighbourhood groups that struggle to protect parks and playgrounds from encroachment, lobby for and even finance and build infrastructure, and invest in the development of social facilities. These groups are becoming an important factor in the development of the city and their leadership consists of young men and in a few cases of young women as well.

The younger generation (fifteen to twenty-four years) of the middle and lower middle income class Karachiites and those that imitate them constitute the single largest group in the city, apart from those below fifteen. This generation is suave, worldly, upwardly mobile and quick to seize any opportunity. They are in love with anything new and contemporary and not burdened with the ethical values of their parents. These qualities are both their strengths and weakness. What is important for the future of the city is not so much the present social profile of this group but the trends within it. What handicaps this generation (and as such Karachi as a whole) is a retrogressive state culture, difficulties in fulfilling their desires because of nepotism and corruption, and the terrible physical and administrative state of urban services and civic agencies. If the state could address these issues and be supportive of the trends, this generation would make Karachi blossom, with or without an interested elite. But the state is afraid of change and so it refuses to support the agents of change and suppress the culture that they aspire to.

19

Interviews on the Beach: 2001

During the last decade, the nature and type of people who visit the various recreational areas of Karachi like the Manora Beach, Sea View, Hill Park and various locations outside of Karachi such as Kalri and Haleji Lakes, has changed. Earlier, the vast majority of the visitors consisted of large families with women trailing behind the men and lots of young children being shouted at and bullied by the elders. Music playing was rare and dancing was non-existent. Slowly all this has changed. Families still come but a very large number of the visitors are now young couples. A vast majority of them are married and an increasing number are not. Many of the couples have young children (seldom more than two) whom they pamper and cater to. Both the men and the women (even the ones that wear the *hijab* and many do) are well groomed and have a confidence, that the previous visitors did not. In addition to the couples, there are segregated groups of young boys and girls (sometimes mixed groups as well) that are seen talking to each other and listening to loud Indian music, often issuing out of the Suzuki vans and pick-ups which they have hired or borrowed to come to these recreational spots. This is especially true of locations outside Karachi such as the Kalri Lake, where large groups visit every Sunday. The young people often dress in jeans, the men with T-shirts over them and the women with long *kurtas*. Both sexes wear caps over their heads and often groups of men are seen dancing while women watch and clap to the rhythm of the music.

Who are these young people? Why are they so different from their parents? What are their aspirations and problems? In an attempt to answer these questions thirty young couples visiting the Sea Wall were approached for interviews between 25 February and 28 April 2001. However, only seventeen were willing to talk about their personal lives and the environment in which they lived. Almost all of those who were willing to be interviewed belonged to the lower middle or working class. The upper middle income English speaking couples were the most reluctant to have a dialogue. Sociologists can draw their own conclusions from this fact. Parts of four of these seventeen interviews are given below. These four interviews are the ones that are most representative of the seventeen interviews.

INTERVIEW—ONE

Two women were sitting together, one with a *dupatta* wrapped round her neck like a rope, and the other with a *hijab*. A man was standing next to them sharing a pair of binoculars. By the time I got to them, the man had moved away and taken the binoculars with him. The two women had no problem discussing their lives. On speaking with them I discovered that the man with the binoculars was not with them. They had simply requested him to let them see the distant ships through his binoculars.

The name of the woman without the *hijab* is Safia and the one with the *hijab* is called Izzet. Both are dolled up. Safia's father was a clerk in a government department. Her mother had done her matriculation. Izzet's father still worked in a junior position in the District Courts in Hyderabad. The two women live together with Safia's mother in a small apartment in Gulistan-e-Jauhar. Safia works in a travel agency and Izzet is a telephone operator at the Gateway Exchange. Parts of the conversation I had with them are given below.

Author Do you come here often?
Safia Almost every week.
Author Why do you come here?
Safia To get away. We work all week and we live in a suffocating environment. No air. No light. Almost no privacy. Living in the flat in which we live is like living in a bird cage. So we come here. We look at people. We relax.
Author How do you come here?
Safia We come with Asad Bhai. He has a car.
Author Is he your elder brother?
Safia No. He is more than a brother. He lives just below us. His wife died and his children more or less grew up in our house. Sometimes they come with us.
Author And you? Are you married?
Safia I was but my husband left me and took our child away.
        (Safia opens her bag takes out a cigarette and lights it)

Author Why did he leave you?

Izzet He wanted to have a modern wife. Safia was not modern enough.

Author But Safia is modern. She smokes.

Safia (Blows smoke out of her nose) Doing bad things does not make one modern. Non-modern women also do bad things all the time. Being modern is style. Style like Madhuri.

Izzet Madhuri is now old fashioned.

Author What other recreation do you have?

Safia Sometimes I cook a meal. We get a film and eat and watch it together.

Author Who is 'we'?

Safia Some neighbours, Asad Bhai, his children and ourselves.

Author What do you cook?

Safia Anything. Sometimes *desi* and sometimes Chinese.

Author Where did you learn to cook Chinese?

Safia From TV programmes.

Author Do you have cable?

Safia One cannot live without cable these days. What else is there to do in this city. Watch TV and come to Sea View. Everything else is far too expensive. If only there were nice places to sit and nice things to see like they have in other countries. Asad Bhai has been abroad. He has told us many things and shown us photographs as well.

Author And Izzet? How about you? Are you married?

Izzet No, I am not. My parents live in Hyderabad and they want me back. They keep trying to get me married off. Of course I want to get married but to someone I know or at least have seen and spoken to. I must judge for myself.

Author Do you have anyone in mind?

Izzet That is a big '*raaz*' (secret).

Safia It is *raaz* that the whole world knows about (Safia laughs). (Izzet looks away into the distance with a smug expression on her face)

INTERVIEW—TWO

Shahid and Humaira were married six years ago. Shahid is an engineer and works in a small firm. Humaira teaches at a school near their place of residence. Shahid's father was a teacher in a government high school.

He is now retired. His mother and father are first cousins. His mother did not receive a formal education but she can read and write. Humaira's father is an accountant in a large hardware retail outlet and Humaira's mother is educated up to middle school. Neither Shahid's nor Humaira's mother have ever worked or contributed financially to household expenses. Humaira however, has graduated, and even before her marriage she was teaching at a junior school in her neighbourhood.

Humaira's brother and Shahid were class fellows. Shahid met Humaira a few times when he went to visit his friend. He liked her and asked her if she would agree to marry him and she said that she would if her parents had no objection. Shahid's father proposed formally and after much discussion and time, the proposal was accepted in spite of the fact that Humaira's father did not want his daughter to be married outside his community and Shahid's family was certainly outside it. Humaira moved in with Shahid's family who lived in a small flat near New Challi. She had to give up her job since the school where she taught was too far away from their place of residence. It was cramped in the flat although they had a small space to themselves. Finally, Humaira found a job in a nearby school and as a result the couple could afford to hire an apartment next to that of Shahid's parents. Shahid's and Humaira's fathers both contributed a loan to the young couple to help them pay a year's advance for their apartment. Two years after their marriage, Humaira had a son who is now four years old and studies at the school in which she teaches. Parts of the conversation I had with the couple are given below.

Author   Could you have managed to get a flat without help from your parents?

Shahid   It would not have been possible. We tried all options before asking our parents. In this country only rich people can own homes. This is a big problem. It worries us for the future.

Author   Do you come here often?

Shahid   Yes, every Sunday. It is important for us and for our son.

Author   Why is it important?

Humaira Sunday is important for us. All the other six days we work. I look after the house. Cook. Clean. There are always little problems like no water, blocked drains, shopping to do since we do not have a fridge. These little things are very energy consuming. Then waiting for Shahid. When he is late I get worried. Travelling by motorbike is dangerous and there is so much violence in Karachi.

Author   What does Sunday have to do with this?

Humaira On Sunday I do not cook or clean. Shahid gets *halwa puri* for breakfast and we bring food with us and eat it at the Sea Wall on Sundays. Zahid (their son) enjoys the outing as well. We look forward to Sunday.

Author   What else do you do for entertainment?

Shahid   Nothing much. Sometimes we eat out or watch TV. Sometimes we get the VCR from my friend and watch an Indian film.

Author   Where do you eat out?

Shahid   McDonald's is what we prefer and Zahid enjoys it as well. We have also visited Alladin Park and a couple of times we have taken him to the zoo.

Humaira McDonald's and Alladin Park are far too expensive but then everything is. To have a good life in Karachi you need money and by working for others you seldom earn enough.

Author   What do you need money for?

Shahid   Well. We need a house. Nothing big. A small flat that we can call our own. I need a car. Right now I have a motorcycle and all three ride on it. But we intend to have one more child so we will need a car. We need a fridge and a VCR. The smaller things we will be able to get with time but the bigger things? No way. It is not possible. And then we would like our children to be educated. Good education is far too expensive.

Author   What would you like to see in your city that could overcome your problems?

Shahid   Credit for buying a place to live, a clean environment, cheap education and a good transport system. Like in other countries. Environment is important. We live in dirt, broken roads full of sewage and our apartments are also full of sewage and garbage. We live like animals. Even this place is dirty. This beach could be so much better but no one is concerned. There should be places like museums (as in other countries) where children can learn. These things are important.

Humaira Also what is important is respect. We need to be respected. Wherever you go, like the post office, the bank to pay your bills, you are insulted. Every government servant insults you.

They are bad mannered and the police is the worst. Often they trouble us when we are together on the motorbike. This is no way to live.

Author   You mention other countries. Have you ever considered going abroad?

Shahid   Many times. But we do not have the means. Also, we do not wish to leave our parents. They are getting old. But going abroad would solve some problems and would guarantee a better life for our kids. Sometimes we think that that better life without a sense of belonging would perhaps not be better. We are undecided.

INTERVIEW—THREE

Muhammad Ali works as a message carrier for a local firm. He delivers their mail on a motorbike. In the evenings he drives a taxi which he owns. He bought it under the Yellow Cab Scheme. His parents come from the Pushto speaking area of Hazara district but he was born in Karachi. His father was a driver and eventually became a taxi owner. Muhammad Ali studied till F.A. The family finally settled in Shireen Jinnah Colony where Muhammad Ali was married to Sakina. Sakina's father is a *bajjri* contractor and owns two trucks. The marriage was arranged by their parents but Muhammad Ali laid down one condition. He wanted to marry an educated girl and Sakina was one of the few girls in the community who had done her matric. After marriage a separate room was built in the family home of Muhammad Ali for the young couple. After four years of marriage, the couple could not have any children. There was pressure on Muhammad Ali to take another wife since children are considered as the purpose for getting married. Muhammad Ali resisted this pressure but life became very difficult for Sakina. Finally, Muhammad Ali decided to move from Shireen Jinnah Colony to Dehli Colony. Sakina's mother decided to move with the young couple since Sakina's father had got married again. It was not easy to get a house in Dehli Colony since Muhammad Ali was a Pukhtoon but as he says 'money can get you almost everything but happiness'. After living two years in Dehli Colony, Sakina gave birth to a girl child. The child is not with them on the Sea Wall. She is at home with her grandmother. Sakina is dressed in a white *shalwar*, a long blue *kurta* and a white *dupatta* which covers the back part of her brown hair.

Author   Why did you not agree to get married again when your elders pressurized you?

Mohd. Ali   Sakina has been a good wife to me. She and I have shared a lot of things which only educated people can share. I did not wish to destroy the peace of my house and complicate her life for no fault of hers. I am thankful that God has given me a daughter.

Author   But do you not want a son?

Mohd. Ali   Of course I do but if I do not have one then my daughter's sons will be my sons. After she was born we could not believe that it had happened. We just looked at her in amazement and kept thanking God. She has given us happiness.

Author   What do you wish for her?

Mohd. Ali   I want her to be educated. To become a doctor. To live in a decent place and marry a good man.

Author   Will you marry her within your community?

Mohd. Ali   I would prefer to. But in my community there are not many educated people. She will be educated so she should marry someone who respects her education and allows her to work as a doctor. So I would even consider marrying her to someone from another community if he is a good man.

Author   What about her wishes? What if she does not wish to become a doctor or marry someone you choose?

Mohd. Ali   Times are changing. People are deciding things for themselves. This is both good and bad. I will respect her sentiments—I think so. God knows how things will be 10 to 15 years from now when she is grown up.

Author   Can I ask your wife a few questions?

Mohd. Ali   Why not. You are her elder.

Author   Was there opposition to your receiving an education?

Sakina   Yes, everyone objected but my mother fought it out. It is because of her that I was able to study. Also, she told me to always read the newspapers whenever we could get hold of one. Our system is quite difficult. There are so many jealousies that prevent people from having good and peaceful lives. I have suffered due to this and now because we live separately we are happy but the jealousies have

increased as a result. We can ignore them now but only to
an extent.

Author   Why do you come to the Sea Wall?

Sakina   He (Mohd. Ali) works from 9 in the morning to 12 at night
every day so that we can have a good life. On Sunday he
does not work and we spend it together as a family. We do
not only come here but go to other places as well. It is a
break and when our daughter is older we will have to take
her out also. We cannot wait for that day.

Author   Do you visit your village at all?

Sakina   I have never been but 'he' has visited it a few times.

Author   Do you like going there?

Mohd. Ali   I do not feel at home there but one has to when someone
dies or gets married. I doubt if the generation after me will
ever go there. It is a different society from Karachi.

Author   What would you like to see in Karachi that could improve
your lives?

Mohd. Ali   The roads are terrible. Always full of dirty water. The shock
absorbers of my taxi are ruined within no time. Also, the
police causes problems. This should stop. Then there are
the usual problems: expensive petrol, no electricity, no
water. This should change. The rest is OK but some places
for recreation like this one are required. They are too few
so they are over-crowded like this place. Where there is too
much congestion you cannot enjoy things. This is becoming
the problem. Then Karachi is not safe. Anything can
happen to a taxi driver. I have been robbed at gun point
and lost my day's earnings three times. My wife does not
rest in peace till I return home. This problem is the most
serious.

Author   Do you watch TV? And what do you watch?

Mohd. Ali   We watch a lot of channels. News, films, science also. We
learn a lot of things. But the TV has bad things in it also.

Author   (to Sakina) Do you think your daughter will face the same
problems as you did?

Sakina   No. Times have changed. But problems will always be there.
They will be different but she will not be tormented by her
elders as we were.

Interview—Four

Rafiq and Fozia got married two years ago. Rafiq works in a junior position in a packaging firm. He has done his B. Com. Fozia does not work. She has also done her graduation and taken a course in teacher's training. Rafiq's father is a stationary supply contractor and Fozia'a father is a partner in an electrical appliances business. The marriage was arranged by the parents and after marriage Fozia moved in with Rafiq's family.

Fozia has a friend, Sara. They grew up together in the same neighbourhood. Sara's father is a 'decoration' contractor. Sara is friendly with Mushtaq. Mushtaq and Sara both work in the same firm as sales representatives. Although they worked together they really got to know and like each other only when the staff of the firm went for a picnic to Haleji Lake. Since then they have met after office hours. Sometimes Sara and Mushtaq come to Sea View with Rafiq and Fozia. Sara is able to come because she tells her parents that she is going out with Fozia. If they knew that she was going out with Mushtaq, they would never permit it. The mothers of both the couples have never worked outside the home although Fozia's mother did do a lot of stitching work at one time.

Author   (to Rafiq) How often do you come here?
Rafiq   Almost every week.
Author   Why do you come here?
Rafiq   To relax. Get away from the environment where I live.
Fozia   We come here to quarrel (she looks defiant).
Author   What do you mean?
Fozia   We live in a very cramped apartment. We are eight people in three rooms. We have been married for almost two years and have hardly any space for ourselves. We cannot even quarrel which all couples do.
Author   Why do you not move out of your parent's home?
Fozia   We have no money. I could work but his parents do not wish me to. We will have to move out at some stage. It is difficult to continue like this.
Rafiq   In Pakistan you need connections to get anywhere or you need money or both. We do not have these connections. Everything is rotten over here. Everything is breaking down, roads, electricity, sewage, buildings. I had to go to the law

courts for some work a few days ago. It was like going to an archeological site (*aasar-e-qadima*). It was full of filth. But we are trying to go abroad and then hopefully all our problems will be solved.

Author What will you get by going abroad that you cannot get here?

Rafiq A good job, enough money to have a house and a car, education for our children and above all respect for the work we do. Also, the possibility of leading a decent life without pressure from our family members.

Author But you will be second class citizens in another country.

Rafiq That is better than here. Here we are third class citizens.

Fozia It is not easy to go abroad. It takes a lot of money. I do not know where we will get it from. Also, it is not a matter of first class or second class citizen. In this country you cannot do what you wish to. You are always being judged. You are always under surveillance. You are always afraid. I have hardly any life outside the home and the home is not mine.

Author (to Mushtaq) Do you share Rafiq's views?

Mushtaq To a great extent. Sara and I wish to get married. There are so many problems that our families have created for us. They cannot accept that people can decide things by themselves. This is wrong. In the city we cannot even meet openly. We do not meet to do anything bad but just to talk and discuss. You know, share things.

Author So how and where do you meet?

Mushtaq Before, after work we used to go to a tea shop where they have cabins but then we stopped doing it.

Author Why?

Sara It did not seem right. The waiters were insolent. We were vulnerable although a lot of couples do go to such places.

Author So you meet here?

Mushtaq Yes. Sara has an excuse to come out to see Fozia. We come together. I borrow my brother's car.

Author What else do you do as recreation or entertainment?

Mushtaq There is nothing much you can do here. There is no place to go to. We do not even have cinemas with good films. The Pakistani films are terrible. We hear and read about concerts usually at the Bahria Auditorium. But they are far too expensive. There is nothing one can do. Sometime we go to

Manora. The boat ride is enjoyable. We watch people and pass comments. So the time passes. People from the office arrange to get together, but that is very rare.

Author	What happens at these get togethers?

Sara	They are boring. Everybody sits around and someone is asked to sing a song or recite a poem or something. Then we eat. Sometimes they get a singer to sing *ghazals* or Indian songs. But it is better than nothing. It provides the possibility of an outing.

Author	Will you manage to get married?

Sara	Yes. It will happen. My parents are anxious to get me married off. They have not succeeded. I will see to it that Mushtaq remains the only option.

Author	How will you do that?

Mushtaq	She is very clever. She will manage it. (Sara smiles proudly)

Author	There must be hundreds of couples who face the same problems as you do in meeting each other and getting married.

Sara	Not hundreds. More likely *lakhs*. Karachi is full of people who have the same problem as us.

An analysis of the seventeen interviews points to four important inter-related issues that need to be addressed if the increasing marginalization of Karachi's educated young population is to be arrested. One, the social values of the younger generation are different from that of their parents. They wish to live as nuclear families and want to have the freedom of choice in the way they live and in whom they marry. There is a questioning of tradition and concern for the future of their children. Fifteen of the seventeen women interviewed referred to their husbands and or their friends by their first name. A big change from their mother's tradition! Two, there is a big gap between the economic reality of the young couples and their aspirations. They feel that this gap can only be overcome by going abroad or through *heyra pherey*. Owning a house and a means of transport are the first priorities. Three, young couples want entertainment for themselves and their children. They want this entertainment to be cheap and in a clean and friendly environment. They feel that the environment is not only unfriendly in physical terms but also unfriendly in social terms and behaviour patterns. And four, that they deal with a non-caring and medieval establishment whereas they are a generation that belongs to the contemporary world and to a global culture. Any plan for the development of Karachi cannot succeed unless it takes into consideration these four important and inter-related issues. And such a plan cannot be initiated and implemented unless the younger generation becomes the dominant power in the politics of the city.

POSTSCRIPT 2008

As mentioned in the text, the above interviews were carried out between 25 February and 28 April 2001 at Sea View, Karachi. I have continued this process of interviews both at the beach and increasingly at the Hill Park. The couples interviewed at the Hill Park are very different from those interviewed at the beach although they are also from the working or lower middle classes. Almost all of them are unmarried and most of the women work in offices, many in the neighbouring Shahrah-e-Faisal area. Also, unlike the couples at the beach, they show a lot of affection for each other publicly, sitting very close to each other, embracing and/ or lying in each other's laps. This behaviour is surprisingly tolerated by the other visitors (even bearded ones) to the park and has led to the segregation of spaces between families, male visitors and couples. As one waiter at Hill Park put it, 'there is nothing you can do about this. You cannot quarrel with the *zamana*.'

So far, 100 couples have been interviewed or have responded to structured questions. Of these 28 couples were married. Of the 100 women 68 wore the *hijab* or a black or grey *abaya*. Only 18 couples were interested in politics and/or read political news in the newspapers. Eighty three were interested in migrating to another country of and for which seven married couples and 16 unmarried men have taken some steps. The reasons for wanting to migrate were in order of importance; one, there was no justice in Pakistan; two, they would never be able to own a place to live or to rent a proper home; three, married couples were afraid that they would not be able to educate their children properly; four, there was no affordable entertainment and recreation; five, there were too many family disputes often related to behaviour patterns of the young which they considered hypocritical; and six, they lived, worked and travelled in terrible environmental conditions. The parents of five unmarried couples knew of their relationship but due to social considerations they could not meet each other in the *mohallas* or the building complexes in which they lived. In the case of 14 couples the male and female were of different ethnic backgrounds. These couples certainly do not constitute the majority of young people in lower and lower middle income settlements in Karachi but they are definitely trend setters as their numbers are rapidly increasing.

In order to know more I discussed the changes that I have noticed with older residents and the more upwardly mobile community members of low income settlements and with the staff of the URC. There was general agreement that the major change that has taken place is the break-up of the extended or joint family and this has played a big role in a change of values and behaviour patterns. Among the reasons given for the break-up of the joint family is that previously there was one earning member and others were dependents. Today there are many earning members and hence the patriarchal structure cannot survive. Money from abroad was also cited as a reason for the break-up of the family since it created jealousy in the extended family, and the nuclear family of the person sending it broke away from the rest. In addition, the presence of working women has also adversely affected the joint family system for it has led to quarrels and disputes around family honour and traditional values. A survey of people sleeping in the streets revealed that the majority of them consisted of young men who had run away from home and old men who had been abandoned by their families.[1]

During one of the discussions it was also mentioned that people were not conscious of the changes that have taken place and as a result are a bit confused. For instance, one person reported how after much heart burning and violence, he agreed to let his daughter marry out of his caste and how he was terrified of what the reaction of his clan would be. However, there was no reaction except for a few elders being sarcastic—his peers did not particularly care. 'The traditions are gone but we do not know it for out of fear we do not discuss these things' was his conclusion.

Older residents agreed that an increasing number of youth are 'undisciplined' and violent gangs are emerging in their localities. One of the reasons given for this is that parents have become more liberal because of a 'change in the times'. Other reasons given are unemployment and the terrible state of public education and its uselessness. An increasing number of young people are doing their matric and intermediate and after that they are not willing to do manual labour. Meanwhile, jobs that are available in the market require technical skills and more and more of them require formal 'sanads' and not just experience with an *ustad*. These jobs are mostly in the textile, medical and construction industry. However, there are no educational centres where one can be trained for these jobs and those that are, are too few and far too expensive. For example, there is a great demand for male nurses but there are only five institutions that one can apply to. Admission fee to these institutions is between Rs30 to 40,000 and the monthly fee is between Rs2 to 3,000.

An important factor that has emerged in the interviews at the beach and the Hill Park is related to the effect of congestion and stress on family relations. Many interviewed women said that they hardly saw their fathers since they left the house early in the morning and returned home very late and very tired at night. Also, they lived six to eight siblings in two or three rooms and so staying away from the house was accepted by the elders. Earnings of women had also given them considerable independence in staying out.

The above observations are from an ongoing research of the author on 'Youth and the City'.

NOTE

1. Mansoor Raza, *Interviews of homeless individuals,* ongoing unpublished research.

20

The New Urban Development
Paradigm and Civil Society Responses
in Karachi

The Asian Coalition for Housing Rights (ACHR) is an Asia-Pacific Network of professionals, NGOs and community organizations. Its headquarters are in Bangkok. The decision to create the ACHR was taken in 1987 and was formalized in 1989. Its founding members were professionals and NGO and community projects working on housing and urban issues related to poor communities. Since then, through an orientation and exchange programme between innovative projects and interested communities and professionals, the Network has expanded throughout South, South-East and East Asia. Links have also been created with Central Asia and Africa through the savings, credit and housing programmes of the Shack Dwellers International.

The ACHR senior members have been very conscious that conditions at the local and international level today are very different from what they were in 1989 when the ACHR was created. They are also conscious that these conditions are affecting the shape and form of our urban settlements and the living conditions of the poorer sections of society. As a result of this consciousness, the ACHR in 2003 decided to carry out a research on a number of Asian cities to identify the process of socio-economic, physical and institutional change that has taken place since the ACHR was founded; the actors involved in this change; and the effect of this change on disadvantaged communities and interest groups. Eight Asian cities, along with researchers, were identified for the purpose of this research.[1]

The objectives of the research were: (i) To understand the process of socio-economic, physical and institutional change in Asian cities, the actors involved in it and its effect on disadvantaged communities and interest groups; (ii) to identify/understand civil society and/or community movements and their role in the process of change; (iii) to help the NGO, CBO, ACHR partners/ACHR in taking a position on national and international forums on housing rights and development issues; and (iv) to support in eight cities a group that monitors the city/continuous learning. The researchers were advised to identify demographic and socio-economic trends on the basis of an analysis of the data of the past three censuses; develop poverty profile and evaluate anti-poverty programmes; discuss the institutional governance structure of the city; develop physical growth maps, landuse trends and important projects being implemented; details of housing policies and changes over time; identify and analyze civil society organizations; and assess the impact of globalization and structural adjustment on the city. All researchers did not strictly follow the terms of reference. However, an enormous amount of material regarding these cities has been generated and is available with the ACHR Secretariat. The research and logistics related to it have been funded by the German funding agency, Misereor.

A synthesis of the case studies has been prepared by David Satterthwaite, Senior Fellow of the International Institute for Environment and Development (IIED) UK and published by the ACHR under the title 'Understanding Asian Cities'. The cities chosen for the research were: Beijing (China); Pune (India); Chiang Mai (Thailand); Phnom Penh (Cambodia); Karachi (Pakistan); Muntinlupa (Manila, Philippines); Hanoi (Vietnam); and Surabaya (Indonesia).

FINDINGS OF THE RESEARCH

The research has identified many differences between the eight cities. However, there are a number of strong similarities which are the result not only of how these cities have evolved historically but also of the major changes that have taken place in the world since the late eighties. It has been identified that these changes are the result of structural adjustment, the WTO regime and the dominance of the culture and institutions of globalization in the development policies (or lack of them) at the national level.

The most important finding of the report is that 'urban development in Asia is largely driven by the concentration of local, national and increasingly, international profit-seeking enterprises in and around particular urban centres'; and that 'cities may concentrate wealth both in terms of new investment and of high-income residents but there is no automatic process by which this contributes to the costs of needed infrastructure and services.'[2]

The case studies have identified that globalization has led to direct foreign investment in Asian cities along with the development of a more aggressive business sector at the national level. This has resulted in the establishment of corporate sector industries, increased tourism, building of elite townships with foreign investment, gentrification of the historic core of many cities and a rapid increase in the middle classes. Consequently, there is a demand for strategically located land for industrial, commercial, tourism and middle class residential purposes. As a result, poor communities are being evicted from land that they occupy in or near the city centres, often without compensation, or are being relocated formally or informally to land on the city fringes far away from their places of work, education, recreation and from better health facilities.[3] This process has also meant an increase in land prices due to which the lower middle income groups have also been adversely affected and can no longer afford to purchase or rent a house in the formal land and housing market.

Due to relocation, transport costs and travel time to and from work has increased considerably. This has resulted in economic stress and social disintegration as earning members have less time to interact with the family. Incomes have been adversely affected since women can no longer find work in the relocation areas and children can no longer go to school.[4] In addition, due to an absence of alternatives for housing, old informal settlements have become congested and as such living conditions in them have deteriorated, in spite of the fact that many of them have acquired water supply and road paving and have better social indicators such as higher literacy and lower infant mortality rates.[5]

Local governments in all the research cities have evolved an 'image' for their cities. This image is all about catering to the automobile, high-rise construction and gentrification of poor areas. For this they are seeking foreign investment for building automobile related infrastructure and elite townships. Much of this is being implemented through the BOT process which is two to three times more expensive than the normal local process of implementation. Foreign investment has also introduced foreign fast food outlets, stores for household provisions, and expensive theme parks and golf courses. Much of this development has pushed small businesses out of elite and middle income areas and occupied public parks and natural assets of these cities for elite and middle-middle class entertainment and recreation at the expense of poor and lower middle income communities.

In the last decade, an increase in the number of automobiles in Asian cities has created severe traffic problems and this in turn has resulted in increased travelling time, stress, and environment related diseases. Much of the financing of automobiles is being done by loans from banks and leasing companies.[6] New transport systems (such as light rail) that have been or are being implemented do not serve the vast majority of the commuting public and in most cases are far too expensive for the poor to afford.[7]

As a result of the culture of globalization and structural adjustment conditionalities, there are proposals for the privatization of public sector utilities and land assets. In some cities the process has already taken place. There are indications that this process is detrimental to the interests of the poor and disadvantaged groups and there is civil society pressure to prevent privatization and to reverse it where it has taken place[8]. An important issue that has surfaced is, how the interests of the poor can be protected in the implementation of the privatization process.

However, the most serious repercussions of the new policies dictated by international capital and IFI conditionalities are related to the removal or curtailing of government subsidies for the social sectors. This has directly affected poor communities who have to pay more for education and health. In addition, the private sector in education, both at school and university levels, has expanded, creating two systems of education: one for the rich and the other for the poor. This is a major change from the pre-1990s era and is having serious political and social consequences as it is further fragmenting society into rich and poor sections.

As a result of the changes described above, there has been an enormous increase in real estate development. This has led to the strengthening of the nexus between politicians-bureaucrats and developers due to which building by-laws and zoning regulations have become easier to violate and due to which the natural and cultural heritage assets of Asian cities are in danger or in the process of being wiped out.

In all cities but two, governments that are already heavily in debt are seeking loans from IFIs. Development through these loans is exorbitantly expensive, loan conditionalities are detrimental to the development of in-country technical and entrepreneurial expertise and to the evolution of effective municipal institutions.[9]

However, the city case studies also bring out a number of positive changes and trends that have taken or are taking place. The most important change is that over the last two decades urban poor organizations have emerged in most Asian cities. These organizations are backed by professionals and/or NGOs. Where they are powerful, governments are forced to negotiate with them. Their involvement in the planning and decision-making process is increasing. In addition, civil society organizations have successfully come together in a number of cities so as to put pressure on governments for the development of more equitable development policies and/or to oppose insensitive government projects. There are now also a number of government-NGO-community projects and programmes. It is true that the lessons from these programmes have yet to become policies in most countries but the lessons learnt from them have been understood and appreciated by politicians and city planners whose attitudes to the disadvantaged sections have changed considerably since 1987 when the ACHR was conceived. However, the speed at which the marginalization of the more vulnerable sections of the population is taking place, is not matched by the positive involvement of the NGO-government collaboration projects.

Another important change is that in all the case study cities, there has been a process of decentralization. This has opened up new opportunities for decision-making at the local level and for the involvement of local communities and interest groups in the decision-making process. In some cases, this has also meant a weakening of the community process in the face of formal institutions at the local level. In this regard the synthesis paper asks two important questions, 'Does decentralization give city governments more power and resources and thus capacity to act?' and 'If the city government does get more capacity to act, does this actually bring benefits to urban poor groups?' The answer in both cases is 'not necessarily'.

The Current Karachi Context

Karachi is Pakistan's largest city and its industrial and services sector hub. It also contains the two major ports of the country through which over 90 per cent of sea borne trade is carried out. It has a population of about 13 million of which about 50 per cent lives in informal settlements known as *katchi abadis*.[10] About 75 per cent of the population works in the informal sector, 65 per cent belongs to the lower income group and about 60 per cent are below the age of 25.[11] Thus, the problems of the poor and the young have to be addressed if a just and conflict free city is to be created. These problems are related to housing, employment, transport, recreation and larger environmental issues related to physical planning and the social sector. The Karachi Master Plan 1975–85 gave priority to these problems and to the less privileged citizens of the city. The Karachi Development Plan 2000 sought to create a monitoring system related to these issues. It is true that none of the two plans were able to achieve their objectives but the planning process gave priority to social issues and their physical requirements.

However, in the last decade, the whole approach to planning has undergone a change in Karachi and this change is reflected in the new under-preparation Master Plan. The local government is obsessed by making Karachi 'beautiful' to visitors and investors and is desirous of making it a 'world class city'. What this actually means has never been explained but it is one of the objectives of the Karachi Master Plan 2020.[12] This author in his work and meetings with government officials, planners and NGOs in other Asian cities has observed that the same term is being used for the objectives of their development plans as well. In addition to being a 'world class' city, Karachi has to develop 'investment friendly infrastructure'. Again, what this means has not been clearly defined. However, it seems from the programmes of the local government that this means building flyovers and elevated expressways as opposed to traffic management and planning; high-rise apartments as opposed to upgraded settlements; malls as opposed to traditional markets (which are being removed); removing poverty from the centre of the city to the periphery to improve the image of the city so as to promote direct foreign investment; catering to tourism rather than supporting local commerce; seeking the support of the international corporate sector (developers, banks, suppliers of technologies and the IFIs) for the above.

The above agenda is an expensive one. For this, sizeable loans have been negotiated with the IFIs on a scale unthinkable before.[13] Projects designed and funded through previous loans for Karachi have all been failures.[14] Given this fact and the fact that local government institutions are much weaker in technical terms than they were in previous decades,[15] it is unlikely that the new projects will be successful. Also, it is quite clear from the nature of projects being funded that they are not a part of a larger planning exercise. In addition, they are increasingly being floated on a BOT process. It is quite obvious that projects have replaced planning and that the shape of the city is being determined increasingly by foreign capital and its promoters and supporters and much of the capital generated through the BOT process will be transferred from Pakistan to more lucrative locations. This project based 'planning' process is also anti-people and has resulted in increased evictions both of settlements and hawkers and the creation of conditions which make it difficult for working class people to access previously accessible public space. As a result, multi-class public space for entertainment and recreation is rapidly disappearing in Karachi.

The power of the national and international corporate sector has strengthened the already existing nexus of developers-bureaucrats-politicians, and as such existing legislations and bylaws and zoning regulations are being bypassed far more easily than ever before. In this connection, *Shehri*, a Karachi NGO has put together a document identifying the commercialization of beaches, building of an elevated highway through the city centre and illegal conversion and commercialization of parks and playgrounds. In addition, the commercialization of railway land is also being undertaken in violation of the leasing rules and regulations of the Railways Commercial Manual 1935.[16]

This increasing strength of the nexus, backed by foreign investment, has weakened government institutions and the democratic political process. As a result, negotiations between the decision-makers and community and interest groups are no longer possible. It seems that the government has become deaf to the concerns of the more vulnerable sections of society who form the majority and of the environmental and human rights lobbies. Similar complaints have been made to the author by academics, professionals and NGO representatives of other Asian cities such as Delhi, Bombay, Dhaka and Phnom Penh.

The commercialization of beaches in Karachi is going to have a major physical, social and environmental impact on the city. The city government has built a park along six kilometres of the beach. Though the park is most welcome, its development has removed all hawkers, sea-shell salesmen and performers from this stretch of beach and replaced them by expensive food outlets as a matter of policy. As a result, low income families can no longer enjoy this beach. The planning of the beach park could have accommodated hawkers and other entertainment providers (who have been there for the last 60 years) but there was a conscious effort by the planners and decision makers to 'gentrify' the beach. In addition, an entrance fee to the park of Rs10 has been imposed for every adult and Rs5 for a child.

Another project called Defence Housing Authority Beachfront Development is under construction. It is a 1,500 million US dollar development along 14 kilometres of the beach. It is being carried out by investments from Dubai and Malaysia based companies. Much of this project is on reclaimed land and restricts public access to the beach. Multi-storey office blocks; theme parks and expo centres (experience in Karachi shows that such parks are too expensive for the poor and expo centres are not used by them); railway tracks along the water's edge (NED University students research shows that the fare will be Rs90 per trip and as such unaffordable by poor and lower middle income families); condominiums and exclusive clubs (which will certainly be cordoned off for security reasons); expensive water sport facilities and most surprisingly, multi-storey car parks on the water's edge, have been planned. An existing and potential multi-class recreational and entertainment asset, visited by the more than 300 thousand Karachiites every weekend, is being usurped for the exclusive use of the rich and powerful.[17]

Similar plans are being developed for another 8 kilometres of beach which is frequented by Karachiites in a big way over the weekend. Over here, Sugarland City (an American franchise), is building an elite township which is going to displace four old villages, a wildlife sanctuary (run by the World Wildlife Fund) and over 300 weekend residences along the beach. No consultations have been held regarding this project and nor have any detailed plans been made available to the public.[18]

In another move the government has sold two islands on the outlet of the Korangi Creek, an abandoned bed of the Indus River and a protected IUCN site, to a Dubai based company for US$43 billion for similar developments. These islands have been used by fishermen from time immemorial for fishing related and cultural activities. The mangroves adjacent to them are nurseries for fish, prawn and shrimp and migratory birds such as flamingos, pelicans and crane visit the waters around the islands in the winter season. The islands are ideal for the development of echo-tourism which could have integrated the biodiversity and the fishing communities and their activities into a development plan—but that did not happen.[19]

The developments described above are bound to have serious ecological repercussions. They are being built by destroying the mangrove ecosystems and through land reclamation tampering with the coast line of a region that is subject to violent cyclones. They are adding to sewage and solid waste problems of an ecologically sensitive area. They are also adding over 80,000 vehicle trips per day to an already congested coastal road network. In addition, these developments are adversely affecting the biodiversity of the region and the possibility of developing ecotourism for the citizens of Karachi. However, the most serious repercussion is social. Karachi's lower, lower middle and middle-middle income communities are being denied access to the beaches of the city. This, coupled with evictions of formal and informal low income settlements due to the construction of mega-projects[20] and the clearing of low income housing on 'valuable' land is further dividing the city into rich and poor areas both physically and socially. Already the rich have ghettoized themselves and have built their health, education, entertainment and recreation facilities in their own areas. Because of insecurity they have also surrounded themselves by armed guards and security systems. The long term repercussions of this divide, which the present development paradigm is promoting, will lead to Karachi becoming like Rio, Johannesburg, Mexico City and many other urban areas where there are serious rich and poor conflicts leading to the exclusion of the poor from civic life.

The 'investment friendly' infrastructure that is being developed is 'signal-free' roads. These are being created on existing corridors by building flyovers and underpasses at important junctions and closing all other entry and access to these corridors. Although this has facilitated movement, especially during non-rush hours, it has created enormous problems for pedestrians wishing to cross the roads. In addition, public transport cannot stop on these flyovers and underpasses and has to use the old routes below the flyovers which have become increasingly congested as a result of not being made a part of the 'signal-free' roads schemes. As such, the commuters and the pedestrians have not benefited from this enormous expense. Karachiites believe that the 'signal-free' roads are only meant to facilitate VIP movements.

It is not possible to prevent the onslaught of global capital. However, it is possible to develop some basic principles for urban planning as a result of which a level of social equity can be achieved and ecological damage can be contained. For this to be achieved, it is recommended that for all urban planning in Karachi four basic principles should be adhered to. These are: one, planning should respect the ecology and the natural environment of the region in which Karachi is located; two, landuse should be determined on the basis of social and environmental considerations and not on the basis of land value or potential land value alone; three, planning should give priority to the needs of the majority population which in the case of Karachi belongs to the lower income and lower middle income classes, the majority of whom are pedestrians, commuters, informal settlement dwellers and workers in the informal sector; and four, planning should respect the tangible and intangible cultural heritage of Karachi and of the communities living in it.

These principles do not suit international and local capital, greedy developers and politicians and professionals driven by megalomania. However, an organized civil society consisting of professional institutions, concerned citizens and community organizations can push for this planning agenda and succeed, if it is properly organized and if its advocacy is supported by solid research. Civil society and concerned citizens in Karachi are coming together to challenge this new agenda.

CIVIL SOCIETY REACTION TO THE NEW PLANNING AGENDA

Civil society organizations and concerned citizens have come together to oppose and/or propose modifications to the projects being implemented in Karachi. The author has been associated with three of these organizations. These are the OPP, the URC and the recently formed Citizens Coalition.

The OPP promotes the upgrading of informal settlements through community mobilization, finance and management by providing technical advice and managerial guidance to communities. It establishes partnerships with government agencies whereby they develop the off-site infrastructure and the communities finance, develop, manage and maintain the on-site infrastructure and runs an education programme which encourages educated young women and men to open informal schools in low income settlements which become formal schools through a process of teachers' training and upgradation. In addition, it operates a savings and credit programme for establishing rural and urban cooperatives and reaches out to over two million people in Pakistan.

The objectives of the OPP were not to propose alternatives to overall development planning but due to the adverse effects of the new paradigm on poor communities, OPP's recent work has focussed on trying to mitigate the effects of this paradigm and to support the URC's advocacy work.[21]

The URC on the other hand is an organization set up in 1989 by teachers of architecture and planning, NGO activists and community leaders. The community organizations and networks developed by the OPP have become an integral part of it. The basic objective of the URC is to influence the planning and implementation process in Karachi and to make it more environment and poor friendly by involving communities and interest groups in this process. To further its objectives the URC collects information regarding the city and its plans and disseminates it to the media, NGOs, CBOs, concerned citizens and formal and informal interest groups. It analyses local and federal government plans for the city from the point of view of communities (especially poor ones), interest groups, academia and NGOs. This analysis is done with the involvement of interest groups and CBOs. On the basis of these analyses the URC holds forums in which all interest groups are present so that a broad consensus may be arrived at. In addition, it seeks to identify and promote research and documentation on major issues in Karachi and to monitor developments and processes related to them. It also monitors and documents evictions, identifies vulnerable communities and informs them of possible threats to them and publishes on eviction issues which in turn get taken up by the print and the electronic media.

As a result of the URC's process, issues related to transport, evictions, hawkers' rehabilitation and integration into planning, inner city environmental and degradation problems have all become important media and civil society issues. As a result of the URC's work, there is very little difference of opinion left between the URC's point of view, the point of view of the print and electronic media and of different citizens' groups and environmental lobbies. On many issues there is also an understanding between the URC and a number of government professionals and bureaucrats. Also, a number of actors such as transporters' associations, informal solid waste recycling industries and the scavenging activities related to them, CBOs of informal settlements, academic institutions and concerned citizens have come together.

Due to the research, informed questioning, involvement of interest groups and preparation of alternatives and modifications to government plans, the URC process has managed to bring about fundamental changes in the thinking of government agencies with regard to mass transit, sewage disposal and certain aspects of housing. It has also resulted in the cancellation of a US$70 million ADB loan for a sewage project and its replacement by a cheaper project which does not require a loan, the pushing of the abandoned Northern Bypass project (now under-construction) and the proposal for revitalizing the Karachi Circular Railway (KCR). The URC was also involved in the public hearings that led to the cancellation of the privatization proposal for the Karachi Water and Sewerage Board (KWSB). Recently, it collected 4,655 signatures from 73 organizations and from 89 low income settlements of Karachi against the Defence Housing Authority's (DHA's) Beach Project. It has also initiated a Secure Housing Initiative (SHI) whereby settlements under threat are documenting their history, government and community investments in their infrastructure, issues related to land title, and details regarding the families living in them. This information will be used for lobbying against evictions and for developing support for the SHI.

The Citizen's Coalition is a very different initiative from the OPP or the URC. It was created by 22 prominent citizens (including two ex-judges of the Supreme Court) who were very concerned at the ecological damage and social fragmentation that was being caused by the Beach Development Projects. This association was then joined by a large number of professionals, businessmen, media personalities, journalists and even executives of the corporate sector. The organization is new and has already held protest marches on the Beach and is preparing to bring out a one-page advertisement in the most important newspaper in Pakistan expressing their concerns.

It is clear that for these movements to succeed, a network of different NGOs, elite professionals, prominent citizens and CBOs will have to come together. In addition, democratic processes will have to be strengthened and the courts will have to become more active. An important factor is that the legal profession has to learn about international covenants that the Government of Pakistan has committed itself to and to make these covenants a part of the judicial system. Once these proposals become reality, a process of negotiations and consultations, leading to modifications in the existing urban development paradigm will become a necessity. This will lead to a more pro-environment and pro-people development process.

From the paper prepared by the author for the International Society of City and Regional Planners (ISoCaRP) Review No. 3, The Hague, The Netherlands.

Notes

1. The names of researchers and the titles of their reports are: (i) Beijing: Alexander Andre, Yutaka Hirako, Lundrup Dorje and Pimpim de Azevado (2004), *Beijing Historic Case Study*; (ii) Pune: Bapat Meera (2004), *Understanding Asian Cities: The Case of Pune*; (iii) Chiang Mai: Charoenmuang, Duongchan, Apavatjurt Tanet Charoenmuang, Wilairat Siampakdee, Siriporn Wangwanapat and Nattawoot Pimsawan (2004), *Understanding Asian Cities: The Case of Chiang Mai*; (iv) Phnom Penh: Crosbie, David (2004), *Understanding Asian Cities: Phnom Penh, Cambodia*; (v) Karachi: Hasan Arif and Asiya Sadiq (2004), *Understanding Asian Cities: The Case of Karachi*; (vi) Muntinlupa: Karaos, Anna Marie and Charito Tordecilla (2004), *Understanding Asian Cities: The Case of Manila, Philippines*; (vii) Hanoi: Thi Thu Huong, Nguyen (2004), *Understanding Asian Cities: The Case of Quynh Mai Ward, Hai Ba Trung District, Hanoi, Vietnam*; (viii) Surabaya: Johan Silas, Andon, Hasian and Wahyu, the Laboratory for Housing and Human Settlements, ITS, Surabaya (2004), *Surabaya and People's Role*.

2. David Satterthwaite; *Understanding Asian Cities*, ACHR, October 2005.

3. ACHR Monitoring of Evictions in seven Asian countries (Bangladesh, China, India, Indonesia, Japan, Malaysia, Philippines) shows that evictions are increasing dramatically. Between January to June 2004, 334,593 people were evicted in the urban areas of these countries. In January to June 2005, 2,084,388 people were evicted. The major reason for these evictions was the beautification of the city. In the majority of cases, people did not receive any compensation for the losses they incurred and where resettlement did take place it was 25 to 60 kilometres from the city centre. (Ken Fernandes, *Some Trends in Evictions in Asia*; ACHR, March 2006).

4. In Karachi, due to the relocation of over 14,000 households for the building of the Lyari Expressway, the schooling of more than 26,000 children has been disrupted (*Lyari Expressway: Citizens' Concerns and Community Opposition*, Urban Resource Centre, Karachi, 2005). In the Philippines, they have decided that evictions will only take place after the final exams have taken place in schools.

5. In Pune (India), in the settlements surveyed for the report, densities in the last 25 years have increased by over 300 per cent without any major improvement in infrastructure and housing resulting in massive environmental degradation and deterioration in living conditions.

6. For example, 502 vehicles have been added to Karachi per day during the last financial year. It is estimated that about 50 per cent of these have been financed through loans from banks and leasing companies who have never had as much liquidity as they have today. This means that loans worth US$1.8 billion were issued for this investment which could easily has been utilized for improving public transport systems.

7. Cities such as Bangkok, Manila, Calcutta have made major investments in light rail and metro systems. Other Asian cities are following their example. However, these systems are far too expensive to be developed on a large enough scale to make a difference. Manila's light rail caters to only 8 per cent of trips and Bangkok's sky train and metro to only 3 per cent of trips and Calcutta's metro to even less. The light rail and metro fares are 3 to 4 times more expensive than bus fares. As a result, the vast majority of commuters travel by run down bus system (for details, see Geetam Tiwari, *Urban Transport for Growing Cities*, Macmillan India Ltd., 2002 and Arif Hasan, *Understanding Karachi's Traffic Problems*, Daily Dawn, 29 January 2004).

8. The privatization of Manila's Water Supply System has benefited the rich and upper middle income areas and has had an adverse effect on lower middle income and lower income areas. The privatization of the Karachi Electric Supply Corporation has created immense problems of power distribution and there is now public pressure to de-privatize it.

9. According to research carried out by the Orangi Pilot Project in Karachi, the government develops infrastructure at 4 to 6 times the cost of labour and material involved. When loans are taken from IFIs the cost goes up by 30 to 50 per cent due to foreign consultants and related purchase conditionalities. Where an international tender is also a condititionality the cost can go up by an additional 200 to 300 per cent. Thus something whose cost is US$ 1 in material and labour terms is delivered at a cost of US$20 to 30. According to a paper by the Cambodia Development Resource Institute titled 'Technical Assistance and Capacity Development in an Aid-Dependent Economy, Working Paper 15, Year 2000', in 1992, 19 per cent of all aid money was spent on technical assistance. In 1998, it had increased to 57 per cent.

10. Karachi Housing Study (draft): Karachi Master Plan 2020; City District Government Karachi, September 2006.

11. Worked out by the author from the data in Karachi Master Plan 2020 draft and the projection of the 1998 Population Census Reports of the Government of Pakistan.

12. This is part of the Mission Statement of the Karachi Master Plan 2020 draft.

13. Between 1976 and 1993, the Sindh province in which Karachi is located borrowed US$799.64 million for urban development. Almost all of this was for Karachi. Recently, the government has arranged to borrow US$800 million for the Karachi Mega City Project. Of this, US$5.33 million is being spent on technical assistance being provided by foreign consultants.

14. ADB-793 PAK: *Evaluation of KUDP and Peshawar Projects*; 1996.

15. Budgets of government planning institutions have increased considerably in the last decade. However, good professionals are no longer attracted to government jobs because of better opportunities in the private corporate sector, NGOs and international agencies. In addition, there is a major migration of professionals to the First World.

16. The elevated highway is being built on BOT basis by a Malaysian Company in spite of community, NGO, academia and interest group objections. At a public hearing these objections demolished the positive Environment Impact Assessment that consultants have made for the project. For details of this and a listing of illegal land conversions, see Shehri website www.shehri.org.

17. For details, see URC website www.urckarachi.org.

18. For details, see Karachi Waterfront website http://www.youtube.com/watch?v=8n1mN21pahA.

19. For details, see Pakistan Fisherfolk Forum website www.pff.org.pk.

20. The Lyari Expressway, considered by planners and academics as unnecessary, is being constructed. It is displacing 25,000 families, over 8,000 businesses and adversely affecting the education of about 26,000 children. For details see Arif Hasan, *The Political and Institutional Blockages to Good Governance: The Case of the Lyari Expressway in Karachi*, Environment & Urbanization Volume 17, No. 2, October 2005.

21. For details, see OPP-RTI website www.oppinstitutions.org.

21

The Impact of Globalization on the Informal Sector in Karachi

This paper is not the result of a scientific research on the effects of liberalization on the informal sectors and settlements of Karachi. It is more the result of observation and dialogue with informal sector operators and residents of informal settlements. This interaction between the actors in the informal sector drama and myself has been made possible by my association with the OPP-Research & Training Institute (RTI), its replication in seven Pakistani cities, and the work of the URC in Karachi. The OPP-RTI is a community financed and managed settlement upgrading project and operates from Orangi Township in Karachi. The Township has a population of 1.2 million (about 12 per cent of the city) and is the largest informal settlement in Pakistan. Settlement in Orangi began in 1965. The Township is also the hub of much of informal sector activity in the city and was created by middlemen through the illegal subdivision and sale of state land. The URC on the other hand analyzes government plans from the point of view of various community organizations, informal service providers and interest groups operating in Karachi. Its forums, supported by research, have created a space for interaction between interest lobbies and communities on the one hand and politicians and bureaucrats on the other. Statistics in this paper are given as footnotes and most of them are derived from the research work of these two organizations.

The informal sector in Karachi, as in other Pakistani cities, has served the physical and social infrastructure needs of low and lower middle income communities and settlements. In the last decade new needs have surfaced and they have been accompanied by major changes in the global and hence in the local economy. For the vast majority of Karachiites the formal sector cannot service these needs as its products are unaffordable to them and its organizational culture far removed from theirs. In addition, these changes have redefined the relationship between the various actors in the informal sector drama. This paper is an attempt to understand these changes and to identify the directions they are likely to take. However, before attempting this, it is important to understand the causes for the emergence of the informal sector in Karachi and its scale and manner of operation.

The regions that constitute Pakistan today became independent in 1947 after just over a hundred years of British rule. The elites, who took over from the British, were educated in Britain and their view on development, as in other matters, reflected that of their colonial masters. As such, the new state adopted the British post-war 'welfare state model' as its model for development. According to this model, the state was responsible for providing subsidized housing, health and education and jobs to its citizens. In addition, it was to determine the parameters within which private enterprise was to function and industrialization was to take place. The model was not successful in the Pakistani context for a variety of reasons. The necessary institutional framework for its planning and implementation did not exist. Revenues to subsidize the planned social and physical infrastructure could not be generated. The organizational culture of the post-colonial establishment was one of controlling through the coercive force of the state rather than of dialogue, discussion and interaction with urban interest groups. It can even be argued effectively that such interest groups did not even exist in an organized form till the late seventies.

The failure of the state to provide was accompanied by an urban population explosion. For this there were three reasons. One, the migration from India at the time of partition of the sub-continent in 1947 more than doubled the population of a large number of towns in the Sindh and Punjab provinces[1]. Two, the eradication of malaria, small pox and cholera and the promotion of immunization programmes decreased infant and child mortality in a big way. And three, green revolution technologies and mechanization forced landless labour and small peasants to migrate to the cities. Thus, the demand-supply gaps in housing, transport, health, education and jobs increased and with it the state's inability to service this demand. By the late seventies most state initiatives in these fields had declined and those that remained operative were being run at an increasing subsidy which the state was unable to provide. Helplessness of the administration to provide and hence administer, fuelled corruption.

Traditionally middlemen have always existed in Pakistani society and they have provided, at a considerable price, lower income groups with finances in difficult times and with access to the corridors of power and hence to patronage. Historically their activities had been small in scale as compared to the larger social and economic context. Initially, it was these middlemen who came forward to bridge the housing and employment demand-supply gap in Karachi. Since the gap was considerable, they employed apprentices from various communities, and these in turn became the new informal sector entrepreneurs. Today, it is the third generation of these entrepreneurs that are active in informal sector activities in Karachi. The relationship that their predecessors established with government officials and agencies for support has long since been institutionalized. The amount of under the table payments to be made to different government functionaries, through whom and at what time, have also been formalized.

The vast majority of Karachiites live in informal settlements[2]. These have been developed on government land, illegally occupied by developers with the support of government servants and protected through bribes to the police. Almost all these settlements have residents' organizations (created by the developers), who constantly lobby with the government agencies for infrastructure and security of tenure. The developers hire journalists to write about the 'terrible conditions' in their settlements and engage lawyers to help regularize tenure. Many of Karachi's important link roads and commercial areas have been developed by these informal developers. Loans, material and advice for construction of homes are provided by small neighbourhood contractors who become the architects, housing banks and engineers to low income households.[3] Similarly, over 72 per cent of Karachiites travel in individually owned mini-buses which have been purchased by informal loans on large interest rates from moneylenders. Since these buses have no terminals, depots or workshops, they use the roads for these purposes and informally pay the police and the local administration for permission to do so.[4] Another important sector is related to the recycling of solid waste. Instead of taking solid waste to land fill sites, municipal waste collectors, in defiance of rules and regulations, take the solid waste to informal recycling factories spread all over the city. In the process even organic waste, which cannot be recycled, does not reach the land fill sites. Here again large sums of money exchange hands illegally.[5]

As settlements consolidate, private schools are established in them. They far outnumber government schools and are affordable to the residents because educated women from the neighbourhood teach in them at low salaries.[6] Most of these schools begin as one classroom in somebody's home and some of them expand to become large institutions. They are established by entrepreneurs, public-spirited individuals and/ or neighbourhood community organizations and remain unregistered and unrecognized till attempts at their registration are made long after their establishment. Private medical practitioners (qualified, unqualified or traditional), establish health clinics in the informal settlements and are not registered with any government agency or medical council. Entertainment and recreation also develops in informal settlements. Video machines, table football and carom and card game tables are set up by entrepreneurs unofficially. The profits from these activities are shared between the entrepreneurs and the law enforcing agencies.

The most important informal sector activity however is related to generation of employment. Garments, leather goods, carpets are all produced in the informal settlements. Middlemen provide training, materials, equipment and cash for the production of these items. The production takes place in people's homes on a contract basis. The manufactured items are taken to the factories where a label is placed on them before they are packed in alternative packets. In this way, exporters and industrialists are able to reduce production costs and prevent the unionization of labour and the application of labour laws and minimum wage. Various parts for the light engineering and the electronic industry are also produced in a similar manner on lathe and rubber moulding machines in informal settlements. Spare parts for machinery, cars, tractors, and diesel engines are also manufactured in these settlements and their price is about half that of industrially produced products. It is because of these spare parts that the transport and services sector to agricultural machinery is affordable to the operators and hence to primary producers.

The success of the activities of the informal sector in Karachi described above, has a lot to do with the availability of cheap government land, protection to local industry provided by high import duties, the pioneering spirit of the first generation of migrants and entrepreneurs and the helplessness of state institutions in the face of an increasing demand-supply gap in physical and social sector infrastructure. However, with liberalization and other related developments all this has started to change.

Economic liberalization has been accompanied by structural readjustment, the communication revolution and major sociological changes in society and as such its effects cannot be seen in isolation from these developments. Structural adjustment has meant reduction in import duties on all manufactured goods. By the year 2003, these duties will cease to exist. It is already becoming apparent that the Pakistani light engineering industry cannot compete with products from South East Asian countries. Consequently, lathe machine operators in the informal settlements are not receiving sufficient orders or are being asked by the contractors to lower the quality and prices of their products.[7] Structural readjustment has also meant a huge increase in utility charges, especially electricity. As a result, carpet and textile power looms, most of which function through contractor funded orders in informal settlements, are working on reduced profits or closing down.[8] According to a recent newspaper report, illegal electric connections to informal workshops have increased and so has the bribe cost of acquiring these connections.[9]

One of the major objectives of the structural adjustment programme is to help Pakistan service its international debts more effectively. Thus, the devaluation of the Pakistani rupee, so as to increase imports, is an essential part of the structural adjustment plan. The rupee's constant devaluation has caused large-scale inflation and a search among the marginalized and lower income groups for additional employment. It has increased child labour and forced a larger number of women to work and have their incomes considered as more than a 'bonus'. Most working men now do more than one job. Teachers give tuition in the evenings, government servants drive taxis, policemen fleece shopkeepers and motorcyclists and white-collar workers work evening shifts as part-time employees in the services sector in addition to their full time jobs.

Under structural adjustment Pakistan has also undertaken to privatize profitable government institutions and utilities and to sell state assets, mainly related to land, real estate and industries. As a result, land that was not considered valuable has now become an important commodity. It can no longer be easily encroached upon and where it is transferred to private ownership, it is protected. This deprives the informal sector developers of raw land for development at places appropriate for their clients. The government has also undertaken to privatize health and higher education. All this is adversely affecting low income groups, especially those who had an element of upward mobility. Many non-establishment development experts believe that as a result of these issues Pakistan has double digit inflation and recession.[10]

Privatization has also meant employment on merit rather than through political patronage or quota systems. It has also meant the sacking of a large number of government employees. With the privatization of education, merit means those who can afford education and this marginalizes poor communities. An alternative source of education and skill acquisition from what is available, thus becomes necessary for them.

This inflation and recession is taking place at a time when the older squatter colonies have been consolidating and such colonies constitute the majority of informal settlements. These are no longer purely working class settlements. The younger generation in them is overwhelmingly literate.[11] Many of them have become doctors, engineers, college teachers, bank managers and white-collar workers. Many of the small workshops and looms that were established by the first generation of entrepreneurs and artisans through middlemen support, have now developed direct links with the formal sector industries and exporters whom they service. Similarly, schools (begun as informal ones) have developed links with NGO and government support agencies and some health clinics have started to access government facilities in population planning and immunization. Interest groups have organized themselves to present their claims and protect their gains. So there are now vocal transporter's organizations, loom operators' associations, neighbourhood groups, sports and cultural clubs (that manage to access government funds), and hawkers' associations. Almost every sector of informal activity now has an organization registered under the Societies Act. Increasingly these organizations are being led by second or third generation of city dwellers who have broken with their rural culture and background. They are better educated than their parents or grandparents and more comfortable than they in dealing with those in power. Instead of seeking access through middlemen and touts of political parties they approach the establishment through the power of their organizations who increasingly have yearly audits and elections.

Due to the changes mentioned above, there has been a change in lifestyles, supported by the communications revolution. Nuclear families are replacing joint family systems. Clan and tribal organizations, that the migrants had brought with them have ceased to be effective and are being replaced by new community organizations or by a dependence on state institutions. The communications revolution has made the television and video important entertainment tools. The television is the main source of information for the vast majority of Karachi households[12], more than 50 per cent of whom have access to some form of cable. Thus, video shops and cable operators, all too expensive in the formal sector for the lower and lower middle income population, have become a necessity. *Santa Barbara*, *The Bold and The Beautiful*, MTV and all variety of news is now available in homes in all low income settlements of Karachi and in the tea shops and eating places located in them. These have brought about a clash of values and cultural confusion. They have also brought about a generation gap which seems unbridgeable and is one of the major reasons for an increase in honour killings of women in first generation urban families. Vocabularies have also changed. Words of respect for elders or for those of a higher class have been substituted by the English words 'uncle' and 'aunty'. The whole feudal vocabulary, which the migrants had brought with them, has simply vanished with the new generation.

The liberalization and the communication revolution has also brought the corporate culture to Karachi. There is a great demand for information technology professionals, operators and technicians not only for the local market but also for employment abroad. The training for these professions is provided both by government and private institutions. In the case of government institutions, this training is affordable to low income groups but is on too small a scale to service the demand. As such, only those who are exceptional students can get into government institutions. Private institutions are far too expensive and only the rich can afford them. Thus, a large gap has been created between demand and formal sector supply.

The corporate culture has introduced a nature of affluence in the city which was unknown before. Golf clubs and various recreational and cultural facilities have been developed and are sponsored by companies for their clients, employees and for advertisement purposes. Unlike previously, these activities are performed in new locations in elite areas or five star hotels and not in municipal or public buildings in the inner city. As a result, the inner city as a space for multi-class entertainment is dead. These corporate sector-promoted activities and the glamour and pomp that surrounds them is in sharp contrast to the physical and social conditions in lower and lower middle income settlements. There is an increasing feeling of insecurity among the promoters of these activities and so they and the corporate sector employees and clients are surrounded by security systems and armed guards. This is in sharp contrast to the Karachi of the pre-liberalization period.

Liberalization has also meant the introduction of fast food chain stores and the popularization of various consumer items. McDonalds, Pizza Hut, and others have opened branches all over the city. Huge advertisements, colourful and well lit dominate the urban landscape and dwarf badly constructed, badly lit, businesses and homes. New postmodern buildings of the corporate sector, with posh interiors, stand in sharp contrast to the sedate government buildings of the previous decades. Since a lot of young people from Karachi's informal settlements work in this environment, ties, white or blue shirts and the 'corporate hair cut' are becoming a common phenomenon and everyone knows what a credit card is and wishes to acquire one.

What has been described above is really the emergence of a First World economy and sociology with a Third World wage and political structure. It is the emergence of new aspirations related to consumerism and the desire for belonging to the 'contemporary' world as portrayed by the media but without the means of achieving these aspirations and desires through formal institutions and processes. Thus the most important role (and it is a new one), that the informal sector is trying to play today, and is likely to continue to play for the foreseeable future, is to help bridge this aspirations-means gap. In Karachi a whole new world has emerged to do just this.

Although the younger generation has new aspirations, state culture and family pressures prevent or hinder them from pursuing their desires. There is a major conflict between the individualism of the young and the conservative social values of the older generation that seek to protect the joint family and clan systems. This, apart from the financial incentive, is one of the major reasons why young Pakistanis wish to migrate abroad.[13] Getting a visa, a job and establishing connections after you migrate to a First World country, is not easy for young Karachiites from low or lower middle income settlements. Middlemen have emerged to cater to this need and help in acquiring genuine and/or forged visas and arranging jobs abroad. Newspaper reports suggest that these operators have contacts in visa sections in the embassies and that large sums of money exchange hands in this trade. For acquiring an American or Japanese visa, young Pakistanis claim to have paid up to Rs200,000 (US$3,333) to middlemen.[14] An entire street in the inner city of Karachi deals with arranging the necessary papers for migration and employment, and from observation one can see that the number of middlemen and clients in it is increasing every day.

All Karachi neighbourhoods, including low income and even marginalized ones, have not one but many video shops. All these shops rent out pirated videos. Video copies of Indian films arrive in Karachi even before those films have been released in India. Similarly, videos of American films arrive well before the films have been released in Karachi. All attempts at curbing piracy have failed. If they were to succeed, the vast majority of Karachiites would not be able to hire video cassettes. The same holds true for the purchase of audio cassettes. More recently, cable television has also made a big appearance in Karachi. Most of the cable companies are illegal and informally use the telephone network for providing home connections. They service all areas of Karachi irrespective of class. The telephone department officials and the police are informally paid by the cable companies to let this happen. The cost of a cable connection varies from Rs450 per month for a connection from a legal company to Rs150 from an illegal one. At a modest estimate there are over 150,000 people involved in video and cable related trade.

All low income settlements (formal or informal) have video halls in them. These are large asbestos roofed shacks which show video films of all varieties. The films are advertised on the notice board outside the hall along with the names of the stars and are screened at regular hours. In the interval tea and chips are available. This is an illegal activity but it provides entertainment to the male only day wage labour that lives around the port and wholesale markets. The video hall operators consider this as a 'joint venture' between them, the police and the excise department officials.

New aspirations and an exposure through the media to a new and glamorous world has led to the opening of a number of 'beauty parlours' and tuition centres for spoken English. Neighbourhood beauty parlours are multiplying in the low income settlements and they advertise various hair styles that are named after Indian film stars. Being well groomed and speaking English has become an added asset for a woman in the marriage 'market' in Karachi's older informal settlements. The pioneering beauticians have been trained informally through existing hairdressers in upper middle income beauty parlours. Now their apprentices, who are multiplying in number, are taking over in the informal settlements. This trade has become so important that popular radio programmes now give regular beauty tips for women and for the trade operators.

The most important informal sector activity today is related to information technology. Training schools, actually no more than tuition centres, have opened up informally in all low and lower middle income areas. These centres require no qualifications for admission and offer no qualifications either. Their trainees are employed after having been tested by the prospective employers. If they are well trained the employers prefer them to qualified persons since they can pay them a much lower salary for the same work. Similarly, there is a whole sector that deals with pirating computer software and marketing it to both informal and formal outlets. All attempts at curbing this activity have also failed and as a result both international companies and the government have simply given up. The cost of such software can be as little as five per cent of its original value. Without this sector information technology would also be unaffordable to the lower or even middle income groups in Karachi.

New lifestyles promoted by the media and the corporate sector have also had an influence on the lifestyles of the poorer sections of the population. They wish to consume 7up, coca-cola and beef-burgers. They are interested in designer shirts and brand name perfumes. However, these are all unaffordable to them. But then fake 7up and coca-cola, in the original bottles costing half the price of the real one, is manufactured in informal factories and marketed in a big way. Fake brand name perfumes and fake designer shirts are also manufactured and marketed. A cheap alternative to the beef burger is available in every Karachi locality.

This new informal sector activity, the result of liberalization and related changes, really tries to serve the better off and the slightly upwardly mobile residents of old consolidated or consolidating informal settlements. At the same time this process also marginalizes a large section of these settlements and deprives them of employment and access to diminishing government subsidies and benefits. This division has increased crime such as armed robberies and car and purse snatching in Karachi. These 'criminal' activities are not easy to carry out in Karachi's affluent areas due to the presence of the police and private sector guards and security systems. However, they continue to happen and grow in the lower income settlements. Hence, residents of many of these settlements are organizing informal neighbourhood policing systems and trying to get approval from the government for operating them. So far such approval has not been forthcoming and these neighbourhood policing systems continue to operate and grow in defiance of state rules and regulations.

Apart from the emergence of these new informal sector activities, the old ones have also undergone a change. Informal developers are now forced to develop their settlements very far from the centre of the city because land in the centre has become an important asset to its owners. The diminishing purchasing power of the new migrants to the city means smaller lots of land, narrower lanes and less open space. Health and education institutions established by the informal sector in the older settlements have come of age and struggle to become formal institutions and try increasingly successfully to access government poverty alleviation funds (also a by-product of structural adjustment policies) and related programmes. However, they find it difficult to establish themselves in the new settlements. This is because these settlements, unlike the older ones when they were established, do not dominate the politics or the economy of the city. They also contain a smaller percentage of the city population and as such politicians are less interested in them. They are also far away from the city and can be ignored more easily by local government and entrepreneurs. Given inflation and recession, their buying power is also limited.

The future of the informal sector in Karachi is difficult to predict. However, some trends are clear. Links of the informal workshops with formal sector industry are slowly being eroded except with those industries (such as garments) which have an export potential. It is feared that even these links will cease to be when formal sector garment factories are set up through local and foreign investment. The process has begun and since these industries have sophisticated machinery, they will be far less labour intensive. This will result in further unemployment.

The informal sector is now moving into producing cheap consumer goods for the poorer sections of the population. This means less profit and marginalization from formal sector processes and economy. At the same time, the state sector is rapidly shrinking, especially in the provision of physical development and social services. This means that politicians will not be able to hand out favours and patronage. And it was through favours and patronage that informal settlements were established and informal entrepreneurs were able to function. Favours and patronage are being replaced by cash payments for protection of activities that are in defiance of state regulations. All this means the marginalization of all those without merit or skills or access to expensive private sector education.

The above trends are creating unemployment and this will increase till such time as formal sector private investment replaces the informal sector job market. This is nowhere in sight and as a result, the rich-poor divide is increasing, leading to violence and crime. The worst affected are those sections of the new generation of consolidated lower and lower middle income settlements whose aspirations to belong to this new world cannot be fulfilled. Also, badly affected are those entrepreneurs and contractors who had established a working relationship with formal sector businesses and industries. It is important to note that these groups are potentially the most powerful in political terms. Their marginalization creates a new situation.

It is therefore understandable that the present situation of inflation, recession and increasing marginalization of these groups, is being blamed on liberalization, WTO, structural adjustment, and World Bank and IMF policies. The press (especially the populist newspapers), politicians of various shades, NGOs and now even transporters and solid waste recyclers' associations, backed by academia, all participate in this debate and issue statements against globalization. Seminars, symposiums and workshops are held on the subject and endorse these views. The anti WTO, World Bank and IMF protests in Seattle, Melbourne, Chang Mai and Prague, electrified the residents of lower middle income settlements in Karachi and various interest groups operating in the city. The informal sector and the frustrated potentially-upwardly-mobile sections of Karachi, look forward to joining this movement against 'the new world order'. How all this will resolve itself is important. So far there has been no proper research into the long term effects of liberalization on the city. There have only been observations and discussions and this paper is yet another such attempt.

'The Changing Nature of the Informal Sector in Karachi due to Global Restructuring and Liberalization', paper read at the Symposium on 'Urban Informality in the Era of Liberalization: A Trans-national Perspective', University of California, Berkeley, 26–27 January 2001), 22 November 2000.

NOTES

1. Karachi's population increased from 450,000 in 1947 to 1.137 million in 1951. According to the 1951 census 48.6 per cent of Pakistan's urban population had originated in India.
2. According to the Sindh Katchi Abadi (squatter settlement) Authority, over 50 per cent of Karachiites live in 716 informal settlements which grow at twice the annual urban growth rate of Karachi.
3. According to the 1987 'Yakoobabad Case Study' by the author, 93 per cent of Yakoobabad residents had taken materials and/or cash on credit from small contractors to build their homes.
4. Of the 13,200 mini-buses in Karachi, 6,000 are unregistered since there is a ban on the registration of mini-buses. In addition, the mini-bus operators pay Rs 780 million (US$ 13 million) a year as bribes to the city administration to use the roads as bus terminals, depots and workshops.
5. According to Urban Resource Centre (URC) figures, the solid waste recycling industry's annual turnover is Rs1.2 billion (US$20 million). It pays about Rs 220 million (US$ 3.6 million) informally every year to various government agencies to permit it to function.
6. In Orangi Township, there are 72 government schools and 682 private schools most of which began as informal, one class affairs (source: OPP: 79th Quarterly Progress Report, September 1999).
7. Salim Alimuddin, Arif Hasan, Asiya Sadiq, 'The Work of the Anjuman Samaji Behbood' (unpublished report), December 1999.
8. Ibid.
9. Daily *Jang*, Karachi, October 2000.
10. Akhtar Hameed Khan: 'The Orangi Pilot Project Programmes', OPP, July 1998.
11. According to the 1998 census results, 74.04 per cent of the Karachi age group of between 10 and 24 is literate as compared to a total Karachi figure of 67.42 per cent. In the 1981 census, 61.10 per cent of the age groups of between 10 and 24 was literate.
12. According to the 1998 Census, 79 per cent of Karachi households said that their main source of information was the television.
13. According to a survey reported in Daily *Dawn*, Karachi (November 2000), 38 per cent of Pakistanis wish to migrate. The figure for Karachi therefore must surely be higher.
14. Author's interviews with persons wishing to migrate (unpublished).

22

The Lyari Expressway: History, Citizen's Concerns and Community Resistance

The Lyari River rises in the foothills of the Kirthar Range. It is a seasonal river and flows only when it rains in its catchment area. Such rains never last for more than ten to twelve days in a year. Four kilometres before reaching the sea, the river used to divide into two. The northern branch entered the sea, as it still does, through the Sandspit backwaters and the southern branch used to enter the sea directly through the China Creek, which is the estuary of the river and Karachi's natural harbour. On the left bank of the southern branch and just on the eastern edge of the natural harbour, the fortified settlement of Karachi (or Kolachi as it was then called) was built in 1729. By the end of the eighteenth century, two working class suburbs developed outside of the walled settlement, on the right bank of the southern branch of the Lyari River. These suburbs were called Lyari and Khadda. Most of their inhabitants were of Makrani origin and had migrated to Karachi due to famine conditions in Makran. Tanneries, salt works (Karachi's main export items at that time apart from textiles) and graveyards were also located within these suburbs. The southern branch of the river was blocked by the British in the 1890s since it was eroding the left bank and endangering the buildings of the old town. Thus, these suburbs were integrated into metropolitan Karachi.

Since the 1730s, Baloch families from Makran were permitted to settle along the right bank of the northern branch of the Lyari River by the Kalhoras. This tradition was continued by the Kalat rulers, the Talpurs and the British. These settlements or *goths* were also given land on a renewable one-year lease for agriculture and livestock grazing. As a result, over the years, the right bank of the northern branch had a large number of Baloch *goths* along it with extensive orchards irrigated through wells in the Lyari bed. Most of the Baloch population, however, worked as port labour, gravediggers (they also looked after the cemeteries, as they still do) and in the tanneries and salt works. When Karachi expanded in the nineteenth century, they worked as building site labour and also acquired skills in stone masonry and carpentry. They rightfully claim that their ancestors built modern Karachi. In addition to the Baloch *goths* and their mosques, graveyards and Eidgahs, Hindu cremation sites, which are still in use, were also established on the right bank of the northern branch as early as the beginning of the nineteenth century.

After the blocking of the southern branch of the Lyari, the northern branch became the boundary of the city to the north. The area between it and the old town became the working class district which also housed small scale manufacturing and cemeteries. This area, after the Devolution Plan of 2001, is known as Lyari Town. Colonial Karachi developed to the south of the old town and contained the major wholesale markets of the city, port related warehousing and business houses, civic institutions and residential areas for the indigenous merchant classes. This was the situation at the time of partition.

Partition changed Karachi. From a city of 450,000 in 1947 it increased to a city of 1.137 million in 1951. This was because of an influx of migrants from India. There was also an exodus of Hindus and Sikhs as a result of which the Hindu population decreased from 51 per cent in 1941 to 2 per cent in 1951. Since the migrants were Urdu speaking, the Urdu speaking population increased from 6.3 to 50 per cent during the same period. Meanwhile, the Sindhi speaking population decreased from 61.2 to 8.6 per cent.[1] Most of the migrants settled in the properties vacated by the Hindus and Sikhs in the old town and its suburbs. They also occupied all available open spaces and public buildings in the city from where they were shifted to the lands adjacent to the Baloch *goths* on the right bank of the Lyari River. Thus, a number of informal *Mohajir* settlements developed adjacent to the Baloch *goths* and on land that the Baloch *goths* used to acquire for agricultural and grazing purposes through yearly leases from the government. In the fifties, formally planned settlements were built on the right bank of the river and the orchards and grazing lands disappeared. The graveyards, however, remained.

As Karachi's population expanded, more migrants settled along the Lyari River. The Mianwali migrants came in the 1950s along with their camels which provided transport for port related cargo. Eventually, they became truck owners and established their garages, workshops and warehouses adjacent to their settlements. In the 1960s, communities displaced as a result of the building of the Tarbela Dam also settled along the Lyari River. Their settlement is called Tarbela Colony. Pathans, Hazarawals and Afghans settled on the right bank at Sohrab Goth between 1980 and 1995. Almost all of them are involved in the transport trade. Sarais, Katchis and Bengalis are the latest arrivals. Most of them work as domestic servants in the neighbouring middle income settlements, in the garbage recycling business or as day wage labour in the neighbouring godowns and markets.

The wholesale markets and warehousing in the old town and its colonial extensions expanded rapidly in the 1970s and 1980s due to an increase in population and industrial activities in Karachi and in port activity. The main markets that expanded were the Dhan Mandi, chemical market and paper market. Metal related manufacturing and garbage recycling (most of it in the informal sector) also established itself in these areas and in what today constitutes Lyari Town. This expansion of industrial and wholesaling activity, along with its transport and warehousing related needs, has caused massive congestion and environmental degradation. Densities in some of the neighbourhoods are as high as eight thousand persons per hectare and air and noise pollution levels are well above the National Environmental Quality Standards.[2] This process of degradation has forced the wealthier residents to move to the newly planned areas of the city. As space for the development of warehousing and small scale informal industrial activity was limited, it spilled over into the Lyari Corridor and into the river bed itself. Much of the labour that worked in these establishments built shacks in the river bed by bribing the police and continued to live in the shacks by paying *bhatta* to police touts and musclemen.

The operators of the wholesale markets and informal manufacturing have constantly petitioned the government agencies for shifting them to areas that are easily accessible by rail and/or road transport and where badly needed space for their planned growth is possible. Residents of these areas have also asked for the shifting of these functions as this would improve environmental conditions and reduce congestion.

The Baloch *goths* have ownership papers going back to the early British period. In the case of Ilyas Goth, the ownership papers date to the Talpur period. These *goths* did not feel insecure and as such they have invested in a big way in building their homes and acquiring infrastructure. This investment was made possible because of migration to Muscat in the 1970s. Makranis were given preference by the Muscat government because of its long association with the Makran Coast. A sizeable proportion of the population of these *goths* is now employed in running businesses and in government jobs. They have developed urban middle class values and aspirations. Successive governments have also supported the Lyari *goths* in acquiring water, electricity, sanitation, schools, health centres, telephones and gas lines. Most of the non-Baloch settlements that are above the flood line have also been declared as *katchi abadi* by the municipal authorities over the last two decades. Almost all of them have built their homes and acquired physical and social sector infrastructure. In addition, the *goths* and the *katchi abadi* have formed community organizations and got them registered. Through these organizations, they, like all other Karachi communities, have promoted their claims with government agencies and politicians and guarded their gains.

The political affiliations of the Lyari Corridor settlements vary. The Baloch settlements invariably vote for the Pakistan Peoples Party. However, they contain a sizeable number of left wing activists who have supported Baloch nationalist parties and have close links through the Baloch Ittehad Foundation (BIF) with other Baloch communities and political groupings throughout Pakistan. The Mohajir settlements by and large vote for the Muttahida Quami Movement (MQM) (formally the Mohajir Quami Movement). The Mianwali Colony has links both with the Jamiat-ul-Islam and the Jamiat-i-Ulema-i-Pakistan. The Pakhtoon communities support the Awami National Party and a minority among them are active members of the Jamiat-i-Ulema-i-Islam. The groups living in the river bed or in the non-notified *katchi abadi* are not effectively organized politically or socially.

THE LYARI EXPRESSWAY PROJECT

The northern and southern bypasses were proposed by the Karachi Development Plan 1975–85. They were to be built from the Port to the Super Highway and the National Highway respectively, and as a result, all port related traffic would be able to bypass the city. The Plan considered these bypasses to be important both in economic and environmental terms. The Southern Bypass could not be built because of opposition from the DHA (then the Defence Housing Society) through which a part of its alignment passed. The DHA was concerned about the environmental pollution that the bypass would cause to some of its neighbourhoods. It was also politically powerful enough to get its point of view accepted. The Northern Bypass was not built either. This was because of a state of administrative and political anarchy in the post-1977 period of Karachi's history that made decision making difficult and development projects a non-priority.

In 1978, heavy rains caused flooding in Karachi. In the Lyari Corridor a number of houses along and in the riverbed were washed away. About 200 persons lost their lives. As a result, WAPDA prepared a Flood Protection Plan for the Lyari river belt. Monuments were established marking the flood levels on both banks. The proposal included creating embankments and channelizing the river. The plan was also not implemented.

In 1986, a group of public-spirited citizens proposed the Lyari Expressway as an alternative to the Northern Bypass. This Lyari Expressway proposal consisted of building a road from the Port along the Lyari River to the Super Highway, which is Karachi's main link with the rest of Pakistan. A government study found the construction of the Lyari Expressway unfeasible along the banks as over 100,000 people (at that time) living along the river would have to be evicted as a result of its construction. However, the idea of the Expressway appealed to the politicians and planners and so in 1989 the KDA involved the Canadian International Development Authority (CIDA) in the Lyari Expressway project. CIDA proposed an elevated corridor (on columns) in the middle of the river as the most feasible option as it would not displace any Lyari Corridor communities. The cost of the elevated expressway was put at six million rupees. However, in 1993, rains again flooded the lower lying Lyari Corridor settlements. As a result, planners proposed the building of the Lyari Expressway along both banks as a solution for flood protection and also for generating funds through a toll for cost recovery. The skyway project, however, remained unaffected.

The URC, a Karachi NGO involved in research and advocacy, objected to both the proposals. The URC's objection was that the expressway was not an alternative to the Northern Bypass; it would cause immense noise and air pollution for the most densely populated of Karachi's settlements; the elevated expessway option would be aesthetically ugly and the bank roads would displace poor communities. In addition, the expressway project would not open up land for relocation of the inner city markets, warehousing and informal manufacturing units which the Northern Bypass would. The URC expressed its point of view through a number of forums and newspaper articles. However, there was little or no response from politicians and government planners on the concerns raised by the URC.

The URC then held meetings along the Lyari Corridor and explained the Lyari Expressway project to the communities. Separate meetings were held for women and men. As a result, the Lyari Nadi Welfare Association (LNWA), consisting of forty-two community organizations, was formed. Meanwhile, the URC also developed alternative plans for redirecting port traffic from the Port to the Super Highway and costed them. These plans, along with photographs, maps and estimates, were given to the LNWA and they in turn contacted their MNAs and MPAs and the Chief Minister of Sindh. As a result, the project was delayed. All this information and documentation was also sent to CIDA and the Canadian Embassy. A visit of a Canadian journalist, John Stackhouse, was also arranged to the Expressway site. CIDA finally backed out and the skyway proposal was shelved.

Finally, in 1994, the KMC during the second Benazir Bhutto government decided to build the Expressway on either side of the river on a Build-Operate-Transfer basis as an alternative to the Northern Bypass. The cost of the Expressway was 720 million rupees. It was to pass under twelve existing bridges on the river. Eight thousand shacks and small business enterprises at the lower end of the river were removed for its construction. No compensation was given to the affectees and since almost all of them were encroachers, they were politically weak and not able to put up a resistance. The project was further modified after the involvement of the Frontier Works Organization (FWO). As a result, the underpasses were abandoned for bridges over the existing bridges and the cost increased to 3,200 million rupees. This change also meant a considerable increase in the number of affectees. An Abu Dhabi Consortium was contacted to build the Expressway on a Build-Operate-Own basis. However, the demolitions along the Lyari River led to opposition of the project by citizens, NGOs and the more consolidated and comparatively politically powerful Lyari communities, due to which a number of politicians became concerned. This opposition led to public hearings in 1996 which were arranged by the senior minister of the Sindh government. As a result of the public hearings, it was decided to build the Northern Bypass and abandon the building of the Lyari Expressway.

Subsequently, in 2001, the Karachi Port Trust (KPT) after considerable consultation with interest groups, finalized the proposal for the building of the Northern Bypass as a six-lane highway of sixty-eight kilometres length. It was to join the Super Highway well beyond Karachi's municipal limits so as to minimize congestion on Karachi's main exit point to the north-east. However, in June 2001, the government of General Pervez Musharraf decided to build both the Northern Bypass and the Lyari Expressway within the Northern Bypass budget and on the basis of the FWO Plan and in violation of the decisions taken as a result of the 1996 public hearings. To subsidize the Lyari Expressway the Northern Bypass alignment was changed to reduce its length. It now joins the Super Highway just beyond Sohrab Goth and its six lanes have been reduced to four. Previously, the proposed expressway project was a Sindh government and KMC undertaking. This too was changed and the National Highway Authority (NHA), a federal government institution, was entrusted with its construction.

The NHA's Expressway Proposal 2001 is a 16.5 kilometres long three lane road along both banks of the Lyari River. The expressway consists of sixteen overpasses and its construction cost has been estimated at 5.1 billion rupees and the cost of evictee resettlement is 2.1 billion rupees. Completion time for the project was set as three years. Evictee resettlement consists of providing a plot of 80 square yards in the peri-urban areas of Karachi for each demolished housing unit plus 50,000 rupees in cash. The government has justified the project by saying that it will ensure easy traffic flow within the city and will also remove people from the flood zone to safer locations.

CITIZENS AND COMMUNITY CONCERNS

When the project was announced in the press, the LNWA and various other community organizations approached their political representatives and local government functionaries. They asked for details of the project, especially of houses that were to be affected and for plans showing the Expressway alignment. They demanded consultations on the project. None of this information was made available to them. In addition, they were told that there was no way that the project could be changed or altered and that this was a project completely controlled by the federal government. The district *nazim* and a number of town *nazims* (the Expressway passes through six Karachi towns) came out strongly in support of the Expressway and emphasized that its construction would remove people living in miserable conditions to better locations. However, as opposition to the Project increased the *nazims* of all the six towns the Expressway passes through, have expressed concerns at the inadequacy of the resettlement plan and four of them have also expressed a preference for the earlier 1994 plan.

A number of NGOs and academics related to urban planning got together with the Lyari community organizations and drew up a list of concerns. These were sent to the president, the city *nazim* and all other relevant agencies and government departments through the URC. No reply to these concerns was given by any individual or agency. The six major concerns are summarized below.

1. City Level Planning Issues

The Expressway project is not a part of a larger city planning exercise. There are cheaper and easier methods of easing traffic flow in Karachi that have been proposed repeatedly by the KDA's Traffic Engineering Bureau (TEB), Karachi academics and professionals. More than half of the affectees of the Expressway are not living in the riverbed or in areas prone to flooding. They are simply being relocated because their homes and businesses are in the Expressway alignment. For rehabilitating those who are living in the riverbed or the flood zone, an Expressway is not required. In addition, the building of the Expressway does not solve the major environmental problems of the city or of the areas it passes through. These problems can only be solved by the relocation of the major wholesale markets and congested informal industrial activity and warehousing in the inner city. On the other hand, the curtailing of the Northern Bypass will result in a lesser area being opened for Karachi's future development and will increase congestion at Karachi's main exit point. Also, the building of the Expressway and the demolition of settlements along it would introduce landuse changes along the corridor for which no planning has been done and for which no infrastructure exists.

2. Environmental Issues

If the Expressway is going to be used for heavy port related traffic, it will cause severe environmental pollution and hence further degradation along the already densely polluted Lyari Corridor. This degradation will lead to downmarket landuse changes and the expansion of industrial, storage and transport related activities which are inappropriate and should be shifted from the inner city. On the other hand, if the

Expressway is to be used only for intra-city traffic, a different sort of landuse change will occur. In this case, there will be a sharp increase in land values and will lead to the eviction of the remaining old settlements along the corridor. The residents of the trans-Lyari area are aware and afraid of this. In addition, the Expressway is designed as a roller coaster along the river banks. Its height varies from eight feet to twenty-seven feet above the banks. As such it will consist of two walls on either side of the river (dividing further an already divided city) with twelve gates (where the existing bridges are) linking it. Therefore, in social and aesthetic terms it is also undesirable.

3. Destruction of Homes and Businesses

According to government estimates, 13,531 housing units, 1,222 commercial and manufacturing units and 58 mosques, churches, graveyards and temples will be demolished. However, according to the URC and community surveys, the number of housing units being demolished is 25,400 and the number of commercial and manufacturing units being destroyed is around 8,000. As a result of these demolitions, the schooling of 26,000 students will be discontinued and about 40,000 wage earners will lose their jobs.[3] Almost all these persons work in the commercial and manufacturing units that are being demolished. At a modest estimate, residents and local government have invested five billion Rupees in building homes, schools, social sector facilities and in acquiring legal infrastructure connections (water, electricity, telephone, gas). Less than half of the affectees of the Expressway live within the flood plain as identified by the WAPDA Study of 1978 and as such there is no justification for shifting them.[4]

4. The Expressway Violates State Laws and Government Commitments

The government of Pakistan is a signatory to the Global Plan of Action of UN Habitat-II, 1996. The plan is against forced evictions and demolitions. Section 12 of the Pakistan Environmental Act 1997 binds any proponent of a project to submit an environmental impact assessment when a project is likely to cause an adverse environmental effect and on the basis of this seek approval (or modification of the Plan) from the relevant federal authority. This has not being done in the case of the Lyari Expressway. Again, land can only be acquired from leased settlements and notified *katchi abadi* through the Land Acquisition Act and its well laid out procedures. These procedures have not been followed.

5. The Resettlement Plan is Flawed

The Resettlement Plan is not an integral part of the Project. The alignment of the Expressway has been determined not by on-site surveys but through satellite imagery. As such, the affected houses have also been determined through satellite imagery. When actual demarcation of the alignment takes place (as it does in bits and pieces), major differences between on-site and satellite imagery details surface. In addition, the number of households in different buildings, many of them multi-storied and housing a number of families cannot be determined. Similarly, the difference between residential, commercial and industrial buildings cannot be determined either through the satellite survey. The Resettlement Plan also does not differentiate between old villages, leased settlements and informal occupation of land for residential purposes.[5] The commercial and manufacturing units that provide direct employment to about 40,000 wage earners are being demolished without compensation or support for relocation. Under law it is obligatory for the concerned authority to publish a notification of the affected people but no listing was available when the project was initiated and even now such a list does not exist. As survey for listing is carried out in bits and pieces, and areas for demolition are periodically determined, immense mental stress is caused to the affected families as they do not know whether they will be shifted or not. These periodical listings are carried out with the involvement of councillors, *nazims* and government officials but without consultation with community organizations and groups. Hence, they lack transparency and have promoted large scale corruption in the allotment of plots and in the compensation process. To make matters worse these listings are made available only three or four days prior to demolition. In addition, 50,000 rupees as compensation is not enough to build a home. Surveys show that this sum is consumed in transportation to the distant relocation site and/or in hiring a place to survive between demolition and considering the construction of a house. Surveys also show that the majority of people who have been given allotments have not built their homes and while retaining their plots, they have hired accommodation nearer to their traditional places of work.[6] The relocation sites will take well over twenty years to develop the social and physical infrastructure that had been acquired in most of the affected Lyari Corridor settlements. Surveys show that as a result of relocation, there has been an increase in unemployment (especially of women); discontinuation of schooling for children; exorbitant cost and time increases in commuting to and from work; unaffordable costs of house construction; an end to community support systems which had been built over the years; and a sense of insecurity especially among women and children when men go away for work.[7]

6. Absence of Consultation

The Lyari Expressway project should have been presented at the conceptual stage for consultation with the affected communities, concerned professionals, relevant academic institutions, NGOs and other civil society organizations. All attempts made by interest groups in initiating a meaningful dialogue with the NHA or with the district and provincial establishments have failed although many promises to initiate these dialogues have been made by the City Government. Such consultations are all the more important since Karachi has a long list of failed development projects which have damaged the city. Professionals, NGOs and concerned citizens had correctly pointed out the shortcomings of these projects, and offered viable alternatives when their details were published in the press.[8] During periods of military rule, such concerns were largely ignored. In addition, the Lyari Expressway Project has not been approved, or even discussed, by the national and provincial assemblies or by the City Council.

ALTERNATIVES TO THE LYARI EXPRESSWAY DESIGN

The URC and its supporters through forums and publications have proposed that instead of building the Lyari Expressway the river should be dredged and channelized according to the recommendations of the 1978 WAPDA Study and embankments should be built on either side. A proper resettlement plan for people living below the flood line of the Lyari River should be prepared through consultations with the affected communities and their nominated experts. The old settlements and notified *katchi abadi*, and a large number of shacks, would remain unaffected if the WAPDA Study findings were followed. The recycling and garbage sorting yards in the old city and the Lyari Corridor (and the labour working for them) should be shifted to solid waste landfill sites through negotiations with the owners and the labour working in them. Such negotiations have already been undertaken by the now defunct Governor's Task Force for the Improvement of Municipal Services. If the sorting yards and the garbage recycling industry moves along with its labour, very few homes and businesses will be left the Lyari flood line. Wholesaling, manufacturing and related activities should also be transferred to the Northern Bypass and all land acquired in the process and through the channelization of the river should be used for badly needed amenities for the trans-Lyari settlements and for resettlement of the affectees. The URC also emphasized that to reduce traffic congestion, priority should be given to the revival of the Karachi Circular Railway, building of inter-city and intra-city transport terminals, the development and implementation of a traffic plan for the city, and the development of a landuse plan including the establishment of an organization to oversee its implementation.

An alternative was also developed by Professor Shoaib Ismail who is the principal of Planning, Engineering and Services, a highly respected consulting firm. His design is based on the WAPDA Study of 1978 and reduces the number of affected families to less than one-quarter of those being affected by the NHA proposal. It saves approximately two billion rupees on account of compensation alone and one billion rupees on account of changes in construction technology. In addition, Professor Ismail's alternative makes the Expressway pass under the existing bridges and as such does not construct 'separation walls' along the river. Professor Ismail's alternative was also sent to the president and to all other concerned agencies but no response from any individual or agency was received.

In spite of the differences between the two alternatives, the two sides agreed on the following: one, that before deciding on a future plan for the Expressway, consultations between government representatives, NGOs, CBOs of Lyari settlements, relevant academic and other stakeholders must be held and a consensus reached between them; two, that the 1978 WAPDA Flood Control Study should be made the basis of all future planning; three, that all settlements and commercial and industrial units in the flood zone should be removed; and four, that a proper relocation plan following Pakistan laws and their procedures should be developed for the affectees and for the commercial and manufacturing units.

COMMUNITY OPPOSITION TO THE EXPRESSWAY

Lyari communities have voiced their opposition to the Expressway in a very organized manner and without violence in spite of the fact that their homes have been bulldozed and/or are marked for demolition. This organized opposition has been supported throughout by two NGOs: the Action Committee for Civic Problems (ACCP) and the URC. Initially, Lyari community turned to the LNWA leadership for initiating a dialogue with the government agencies. When the dialogue did not materialize, they pressurized the LNWA leadership to arrange demonstrations against the project. At this stage, some of the LNWA leadership disappeared from the scene and others became active supporters of the project. According to rumours, the LNWA leadership had been bought over by the government agencies.[9] Consequently, local activists emerged in different localities. The ACCP created a link between activists of different communities and settlements. It held, and still holds, regular meetings in the settlements under threat. Its members mobilize the communities to hold combined meetings in different settlements on a rotation basis. It assists communities in their legal battles and has helped to establish contact between politicians and the communities. It holds press conferences in which the activists participate. It is because of the linkages that it has created that black flags and banners were hoisted all along the river when General Musharraf inaugurated the Expressway in an unscheduled ceremony late at night on 27 April 2002.

The URC initiated the Expressway debate and has been involved in monitoring developments and commenting on them in the media and through public forums since 1990. It has provided documents on national and international laws on housing rights and *katchi abadi* to the lawyers representing the affected communities in courts of law. These documents have also been provided to the community activists. It has arranged tours of journalists, NGO activists and concerned citizens to the affected communities. As a result, articles and films against the Expressway project have appeared in the press and on the electronic media. It has sent letters to the President of Pakistan with copies to all other relevant government agencies regarding its concerns over the Expressway. It has published pamphlets on the project (both in Urdu and in English) and distributed them along with copies of documentary films made by different satellite channels on the subject. It has initiated a letter writing campaign on the subject and sent its concerns to NGOs, UN agencies and civil society organizations all over the world. As a result, on 17 July 2002, the UN took serious notice of the violations of human rights in the Lyari Corridor. In its letter to the President, it criticized the project. Meanwhile, over a thousand international human and housing rights organizations from all over the world sent letters expressing their concern to the President of Pakistan. In February 2003, the ACHR sent a Fact Finding Mission which visited the Expressway site and reported major housing rights violations. The Mission was received by the Karachi *nazim*. It also met with the Sindh chief secretary, the Sindh minister for housing and planning and the NHA general manager. The Mission was assured that the government would do everything possible for improving the resettlement process and would see to it that physical infrastructure and social facilities are provided at the relocation sites. As a result of this visit of the Mission, attempts to provide social and physical infrastructure to the relocation sites have been made.

As a result of this coming together, the communities collected three million rupees for litigation purposes. They filed cases against illegal demolitions and attended court proceedings in large numbers. The court stayed the demolitions of leased settlements and finally gave a verdict on 14 October 2003. This verdict will be discussed later in the paper. The communities have also held 'people's assemblies' in which more than three hundred men, women and children (in each assembly) from various settlements of the Lyari Corridor have gathered to protest against the project. These demonstrations have been held at the Karachi Press Club and at various settlements. Whenever teams for surveys and demarcations of the Expressway alignment have visited the settlements, there have been protests against them led by women and children.

Through the ACCP's support eight All Party Conferences (APC) have been held. At the APCs representatives of political parties have been invited to discuss issues related to the Expressway project and to the demolitions and evictions that are taking place. Representatives of all the political parties voiced their concerns and their opposition to the Expressway project. However, none of the political parties who were represented in the Sindh Assembly were willing to take this issue to the Assembly floor, in spite of the fact that settlements that were their vote bank were being affected. They were interested merely in changing the alignment so as to save the settlements that had voted for them. The strongest opposition to the Expressway came from parties that were not represented in the Sindh Assembly. The Pakistan Peoples Party could not oppose the Expressway because it was initiated in 1994 by them. They simply wanted the original design to be implemented. They expressed concerns over the flawed resettlement plan. The MQM leadership also expressed concern but has not been able (or does not wish to) to do more than that. The Jamat-e-Islami now runs the city government and as such its leaders cannot be expected to oppose the Expressway although a number of them have expressed their concerns in private.

As a result of the inability of the political parties to take a stand on the issue, the various settlements have sought help from their ethnic based or trade organizations. For example, the Baloch population approached the BIF, which is an all Sindh-Balochistan organization. The BIF has promised full support to the Baloch settlements and has begun a process of contacting its influential members and Baloch political leaders. The Mianwali settlements have sought help and intervention from Mianwali politicians who are members of the National Assembly. There are rumours in the settlements that as a result of these interventions, changes in the Expressway design have taken place to save Baloch, Mianwali and certain Mohajir settlements. However, in the absence of consultations and information sharing on the part of the government agencies, the veracity of these rumours cannot be ascertained. With the fear of bulldozing, communities have also become interested in their history. This is especially true of the Baloch, some of whose members have started collecting stories about their migration to Karachi from their elders. These stories have been repeated at the people's assemblies and demonstrations.

Many attempts at initiating a dialogue with the government agencies have been made. In March 2002, under pressure of demonstrations and press articles, the Karachi *nazim* promised that the city government would provide all details, feasibility studies, estimates and environmental assessments regarding the project to the community leaders. He also promised that a list of affected families will be published and that a committee of experts will be formed to review the projects. However, none of the above happened although demolitions were stopped and a nine-member expert committee was formed to review the project. The committee could not meet since, after its formation, the government agency experts were not available.

There is constant contact and dialogue however, between the communities and the Lyari Expressway Resettlement Project Director and his staff. The Director is very clear regarding his role. He is not willing to discuss the pros and cons of the project. His job is simply to resettle affected families after bulldozing their settlements or negotiating an agreement to move. The NHA, which is incharge of executing the project, is unapproachable. It's staff puts up the markings for the alignment and initiates construction. Thus, the construction of the Expressway is the job of the federal government and the job of the provincial and the city government is to acquire vacant land along the Expressway alignment and hand it over to the NHA. Resettlement is funded by the federal government but is the responsibility of the provincial and city government.

The stay granted by the High Court against the demolition of leased settlements has prevented their demolition. The Sindh High Court in its verdict of 14 October 2003 has stated that the Lyari Expressway is a project of national importance and therefore properties can be acquired for it. It has also stated that appropriate compensation should be provided to the affectees in accordance with law. However, the relevant law has not been quoted or identified. Furthermore, the judgement states that only such land should be acquired as is absolutely necessary for the construction of the Expressway. Since the judgement no bulldozing of leased properties has taken place.

The court had not granted a stay to bulldozing of unleased properties. As a result, people have been forced to accept compensation and move. Most have shifted to rented accommodation in the city while sending a member of their families to take possession of the plot that has been offered to them in the resettlement sites. This process has divided the movement against the Lyari Expressway between leased and unleased communities and in the process, the movement has weakened. How the government will deal with the leased settlements, remains to be seen. Paying compensation to them at market rates makes the entire project unfeasible in economic terms. Newspaper reports suggest that government has initiated a dialogue with the Kuwait fund for financing the Expressway and resettlement costs. Again, no details are available or accessible. Meanwhile, a public interest litigation against the Expressway has been filed in December 2003 in the Sindh High Court. It has not yet come up for hearing. The petitioners are political parties and/or their representatives along with a number of important Karachi based NGOs.[10]

The opponents of the Expressway (or of its present design) fail to understand why the government has refused to negotiate or consult with them or with the affectees and why serious concerns and alternatives presented by Karachi citizens, academics and politicians have been ignored. They also fail to understand why the details of the alignment cannot be made public. News items in the press have stated that 1.8 million square yards of land will be vacated for development as a result of the Expressway construction. Newspaper articles have also made similar comments. The Lyari Corridor community activists are also sure that this is the case and that the secrecy that surrounds the Project is because 'their' land is being handed over to developers. They argue that this is the reason that much more land is being acquired for the Expressway than would be required if the WAPDA Flood Protection Plan parameters are followed.

CONCLUSIONS

A number of lessons and conclusions can be derived from the Lyari Expressway project and the opposition to it. First that conventionally trained planners and migrant politicians do not give importance to the traditional rights of local communities to their land, history and culture. Nor do community related social and economic considerations figure in the design of projects which are seen as fulfilling a certain limited function such as facilitating traffic or 'beautifying' an area. Second, that movements become more effective when poor communities, academics, researchers and NGOs who can provide organizational and managerial guidance, come together. It is only then that the media and the middle classes support the interests of poor communities and overcome their deeply ingrained prejudices against them. Third, that manipulated and weak provincial and city governments who depend on the centre for their survival, cannot protect the interests of their constituents. In the absence of such protection, their constituents have no option but to seek support of their ethnic and/or trade related organizations. This fragments society and weakens the political and judicial process. Four, that city planning is no longer a priority in this age of globalization and cutbacks on public spending. Planning has been replaced by projects supported by external funding, mostly in the form of loans or through the BOT or Build-Operate-Own processes. In the absence of planning, land values determine landuse and project feasibilities and not social and environmental considerations. Five, the dependence of district governments and town councils on federal government funds makes them ineffective in challenging or disagreeing with programmes and projects that adversely affect their constituencies. And six, there is no de-facto and de-jure consensus making or consultative process which can resolve differences and conflicts and make planning pro-poor and environmentally friendly. In the absence of such a process, the more powerful interest manages to impose its decisions on other interest groups.

Paper read at the 'Comparing Urban Landscapes Workshop', LUMS, Lahore, 10–12 April 2004.

NOTES

1. Government of Pakistan; Population Census Reports.
2. Mirza Arshad Ali Beg, Status Paper on Urbanization of Sindh, prepared for the IUCN, 2004.
3. URC and community joint estimates quoted in newspaper articles and URC reports.
4. Ibid.
5. The following list of settlements contain about 85 per cent of the affectees: (1) Old villages: Hasan Aulia, Ilyas Goth, Angara Goth, Gauharabad, Jahanabad (2) Regularized *katchi abadi* and planned areas: Mianwali Colony, Liaquatabad, PIB Colony, Gharib Nawaz Colony, Muslimabad, Farooqabad (3) Notified *abadis* marked for regularization: Haji Murad Goth, Muslimabad, Madina Colony (4) Squatter colonies in the riverbed: Peoples Colony, Mohammadi Lane, Iqbal Colony.
6. URC monitoring surveys, July 2003. URC: Livelihood Substitution, Surveys carried out for an ongoing joint URC/WEDC research, February 2004. Ashish Toseef, Fatimah Rashid, Saima Ismail, The Rationale Behind Government Takings: A case study of the Lyari Expressway, LUMS unpublished report, 2003.
7. Ibid.
8. These projects include: (i) The Metrovilles of the KDA, 1975; (ii) The Lines Area Redevelopment Project, 1983 onwards; (iii) The ADB funded Greater Karachi Sewage Plan; (iv) ADB funded Baldia Sewage Project 1996; (v) The Karachi Mass Transit Project Corridor 1; and (vi) The Gulshan Flyovers.
9. Author's discussions with activists and the coordinator of the ACCP.
10. The petitioners are: (i) Taj Haider, Central Information Secretary of the Pakistan Peoples Party in his personal capacity; (ii) National Party; (iii) Pakistan Muslim League (N); (iv) Awami National Party; (v) National Workers Party; (vi) Jiye Sindh Mahaz; (vii) Human Rights Commission of Pakistan; (viii) URC; (ix) Aurat Foundation; (x) ACCP; (xi) Orangi Pilot Project-Research and Training Institute.

Glossary

aba	outer garment worn by women
abadi	settlement
abiana	agricultural water tax
adda	stand (as in bus stand)
afra-tafri	anarchy
ak	*Calotropis procera*
amriki samraj murdabad	death to American Imperialists
annas	$^1/_{16}$ of a rupee
anjuman	organization
arthis	middleman
ashaish	community land
awami	populist
azad	free
baigar	forced labour
bajra	millet
bajray ki roti	millet bread
bajjri	gravel
Bakra Id	Muslim festival
balisht	measurement unit, span, from the tip of the thumb to the tip of the little finger when the fingers are spread open
bunyu	a member of the Hindu trader caste
bara	elder
barani	rain-fed
batai	share-cropping
baypari	businessman
bhatta	illegal gratification
bhai	brother
beldar	labourer (one who uses a spade)
beri	*Zizyphus mauritiana*
beyricho	the minstral-cum-black smith caste in the Northern Areas of Pakistan
bhoosa	straw
booh	*Aerva tomentosa*
boog	cargo (literally weight)
bisee	informal collective savings scheme
biradri	clan
bunder	port

chaloo	some one who is 'with it'
chamar	tanner
charpai	cot
chawkidar	caretaker
choola	stove
dallal	middleman
dallali	brokerage fee
dargah	mausoleum of a Muslim saint
daroga	caretaker
dayhari	day wage
deeni	religious
diwali	a Hindu festival
dom	minstrel
dowhs	traditional ocean-going sailboards
dua	prayer
dupatta	scarf
farman	government order
gara	mud mortar
ghabarbunds	sub surface dams to prevent water run off in streams
ghee	clarified butter
ghoondaism	hooliganism
girti hoi diwaroon ko ek dhaka aur do	the walls that are falling, give them one more push
gora sahib	white man
gorpath	mats made by men (as opposed to by women) in the Makran district of Balochistan
goths	villages
gowar	fodder
gowcher	community pasture land
gunia	term used in the building trade for a right angle and/or for a tool that establishes a right angle
gup-shup	chatting—, chit-chat
Hadood	Islamic law
halaat	conditions
halli	the bark of the Taal (Birch) tree
halwa	a dessert with the consistency of a very thick pudding
puri	deep fried bread
haq-e-shifa	right of pre-emption
haris	peasants/serfs
janab, hazoor, sain, sahib, mai-bap	traditional ways of addressing a person of high social status
hijab	covering of the hair by Muslim women

imambara	religious hall for gathering of the Shia sect of Muslims
izzat	honour
jagirdar	big landowner
jaal	net
jawar	barley
jhor	depression filled with stagnant waste water
jirga	clan or community committee that decides on community related issues in the NWFP
jogis	a clan for performers
kalma	verbal expression of Muslim faith
kammis	term used for the artisanal castes in the Punjab. Literally meaning 'low caste'
kanal	measurement of land (600 square meter)
karez	an underground system of water channelization
katcha	temporary
katchi abadi	informal settlement
katcho	riverine flood plains in Sindh
khaddi	handloom
khalasis	boat-hands
khatta	a form of blanket made of camel and goat hair in Tharparkar
kharboza kharboza ko dekh kay rang pakarta hai	A melon changes colour by being in proximity to another melon (Urdu proverb)
Khejri	*Prosopis cineraria*
khip	*Leptadenia*
khoka	smack kiosk, usually selling beetle-leaf and/or cigarettes
kuts	fortified settlements
kumhars	potters
kurta	long shirt worn by both men and women in Pakistan
lai	tamarisk
lana	a form of grass in the flood plains of the Indus delta region
langas	community of performers/village musicians in Sindh
langar khanas	rest places/places where food is given as charity
lassi	traditional cold drink made of yogurt
lepai	application of mud mortar to adobe buildings
maddrasah	seminary
malakhro	wrestling competitions
mandi	wholesale market
mandirs	Hindu temples
manzil	destination

marla	measurement of land (25 square metres)
matkas	earthen-wear jars for storing water
maltori	stone breaker
maulvis	Muslim cleric
mazdoor	labourer
mazdoori	wages for manual labour
mazlum	oppressed
melas	festivals or carnivals
milads	a Muslim religious festival
mistri	mason/skilled worker
mohajir	refugee
mohalla	neighbourhood
motabirs	notables of an area
muashara	society
mukato	cash contract
mukhtarkar	mid level revenue official
murraba	a measure of land (25 acres)
mushairas	poetry recitals, competitions
muzaira	peasants
naib	deputy
nakhuda	captain of a ship or vessel
namaz	Muslim prayer
numbardar	government appointed village revenue collector
nazim	mayor
Nazim-e-Sala'at	person who wakes up persons for the morning prayer
niazmandi	to seek the honour of a meeting
nulla	natural drain
painti	the side of a cot where the feet are placed
paras	neighbourhood
parchoon	grocery
patels	village headmen
peechay	back, before
pir	Sufi saint
pir khanas	homes/hang-outs of the pir
phog	*Calligonum*
pucca	permanent
punchayat	council of five community members
patti	commission or share
patwari	collector and keeper of revenue records
purdah	the Muslim code of segregation of women
qana'at	contentment; ability to do without luxuries
quom	clan/tribe/nation
raaz	secret
rah	path, road

rajaki	unpaid labour. Term used in the Northern Areas
roti	bread
saim nalis	drainage channels in irrigation systems
sanads	degree, academic certificates
sardars	tribal chiefs
sardari	tribal
seths	well-to-do businessmen
shamlaat	community land in rural areas
shagardi	apprenticeship
shalwar-qameez	baggy trousers—long shirt
sharf hasil hona	to receive the honour of
sipahis	soldiers
sirhana	side of the cot where the head is placed
sohand	a variety of grass in the Indus delta region
sulimani chai	tea without milk
Sunnah	traditions of the Prophet (PBUH)
tabaydari	subservience
tagrid	mats made by women (as opposed to by men) in the Makran district of Balochistan
taal	timber mart
taluka	a unit of administration in Sindh
tandoor	traditional oven to make bread
tanzeems	organizations
tarais	a natural depression which fills with rainwater
tehmat	a sheet wound round the lower part of the body
tehsil	sub-district
tehsildar	revenue official in charge of a tehsil
thaik-thak hai	okay (slang)
thakur	an upper caste Hindu, normally a large land owner
thalla	manufacturing yard
thana	police station
tik-tika, chaloo pan	being with it (slang)
tikri	a form of fishing net
till	sesame
timmar	mangrove
urs	birthday of Muslim saint
ushr	an Islamic tax on land
ustad	teacher
vanaspati ghee	brand name vegetable cooking oil
wadera	landlord, elder of the village/clan
wara bandi	system of distribution of irrigation water
yak sala	yearly
zakat	a mandatory charitable donation in Islam
zalim	oppressor

zamana	the times (in which we live)
zamindar	landowner
zari	golden work on cloth
ziarat	visit to a shrine for pilgrimage

Index